Praise for *Why Not?*

"This book is filled with great ideas. The best one of all is that innovative solutions are waiting to be discovered and that it is both easy and fun to find them. The information overload, cynicism, and entrenched interests of modern life have created an almost impenetrable thicket of obstacles to creative change; this wonderfully energizing book sweeps all that away, shows us a way to make things better, and dares us to try."

—NELL MINOW, editor and founder, The Corporate Library, and author of *Movie Mom's Guide to Family Movies*

"This is a call to inventiveness and entrepreneurship for and by individuals . . . an empowering message delivered with humor and passion."

—JUAN ENRIQUEZ, director, Life Sciences Project, Harvard Business School, and author of *As the Future Catches You*

"In twenty years and countless adventures in growing our business, our only progress and for that matter our only interesting breakthroughs have resulted from someone asking 'why not?' Nalebuff and Ayres have crafted an inspiring, imaginative, informative, and best of all, fun treatise that will arouse the entrepreneur in all of us. You will fly through this book, and you will never look at a problem the same way again."

—GARY HIRSHBERG, president and CEO, Stonyfield Farm Yogurt, Inc.

"This is an extraordinary, thought-provoking, and enlightening book—it is must-reading for any entrepreneur or business person. In the turbulent and unforgiving economic climate we're living in, *Why Not?* is one of the few books that I'd buy in hardback and pay retail."

—HERB COHEN, author of *Negotiate This!*

"You finished the market research. You understand the competition. Your company's situation is clear. But it's not clear what to do. Conventional actions will produce conventional results, but you have high aspirations. The creativity inspired by *Why Not?* can help uncover a strategy that the other guys won't expect."

—BILL BARNETT, director, McKinsey & Co.

"*Why Not?* is full of clever, stimulating ideas. Even better, it provides principles to help you generate your own brainstorms. Read it yourself, and buy it for your employees."

—HAL VARIAN, University of California at Berkeley,
and coauthor, *Information Rules*

"A perfect blend of sound theory and real world examples. Nalebuff and Ayres lead the reader down a path of what's possible and away from looking through the same old lenses. By flipping ideas on their heads and gaining fresh perspectives to enhance the development process, they provide an invaluable tool for business today."

—PAUL WARME, manager, Global Marketing, U.S. Borax

"*Why Not?* is a terrific read. It is chockablock not with mere heuristics, but authentically interesting innovations. Many are wise; all are worth thinking about. And their ideas grow out of a disciplined effort to force creative thinking."

—REED HUNDT, former chairman, Federal Communications Commission

"A lot of fun, and full of imaginative ideas and surprising approaches. Highly recommended."

—CASS SUNSTEIN, University of Chicago Law School,
and author of *Republic.com*

"*Why Not?* is a frontal assault on today's corporate battle cry of 'You can't, because . . .' It is infused with a spirit of unconventional creativity and playfulness that lights a fire under your backside and in your cranium. You'll solve problems more effectively by embracing asymmetric thinking and looking beyond the obvious."

—LENNY STERN, CEO, SS+K

Why Not ?

Why Not?

How to Use

Everyday Ingenuity

to Solve Problems

Big and Small

Barry Nalebuff
and Ian Ayres

Harvard Business School Press
Boston, Massachusetts

07 06 05 04 03   5 4 3 2 1

Library of Congress Cataloging-in-Publication Data
Nalebuff, Barry, 1958–
    Why not? : how to use everyday ingenuity to solve problems big and small / Barry Nalebuff and Ian Ayres.
        p. cm.
    Includes bibliographical references and index.
    ISBN 1-59139-153-9 (alk. paper)
    1. Problem solving. I. Ayres, Ian. II. Title.
HD30.29.N35 2003
153.4'3--dc21

                                                                    2003010767

To Helen and Jennifer,

who politely suggested that we

put our modest proposals into a book—

and then lock that book away in a drawer.

We followed half their advice.

CONTENTS

Why *Why Not?*

Discovery consists of seeing what everyone else has
seen and thinking what nobody has thought.

—Albert von Szent-Györgyi

On July 30, 2002, Deborah Woods, a dental hygienist in Syracuse, New York, became the first person to buy protection against a market decline in the value of her home. Would you like to be next?

Our point isn't to sell you home equity insurance. Lord knows there will be plenty of people who will do that. We want to get you thinking. Provoke you a little. You can buy insurance against fire, theft, and even a lost cell phone. So how come there was no way to buy insurance that protects the equity in what is typically your single biggest asset—your home? We estimate that home equity insurance could generate annual premiums of $10 billion. Why didn't this product already exist?

There was no good reason. A few of us professors, with lots of help from Neighborhood Reinvestment, Freddie Mac, and even Congress, took the protection of home equity from an idea to a reality in about a year.

Let's try another. Have you ever used a 900 number? Neither have we, but we all know what they are. It's often a bit of a shady business with fortune tellers and sex lines. Yet, underneath it all, there's an interesting idea: a pay-per-minute phone call.

What if we turn this idea around to create a reverse 900 number? Instead of paying per minute to make a call, you would get paid per minute for taking a call. Think how this could change telemarketing. If telemarketers want to call you, make them use a reverse 900 number. That way, you would get paid for listening to their pitch. While they are trying to sell you a product, you can be selling them your time.

Telemarketing is a $500 billion industry. What is the potential business opportunity for the reverse 900 number? Would Gallup pollsters be happy to call from a reverse 900 number to increase their dismal response rate?

Now consider a related problem: e-mail spam. In 2001, 10 trillion e-mails were exchanged. So it wasn't just your in box that was overflowing. Can you see how the idea of a compensated call could also eliminate nuisance e-mail?

The two of us spend much of our professional lives making suggestions. Businesses and governments seek our advice. But the truth is, even without being asked, we still find ourselves dreaming up better ways to do things. We have a passion for clever ideas. It's in our blood. We can't stop ourselves from generating these ideas in almost all aspects of our lives.

We see ourselves as the "anti-Dilbert." While Scott Adams's cartoons are funny, they are also profoundly cynical. We, however, are optimists, perhaps even idealists. We like the line of Calum Fisher, a contributor to halfbakery.com: "Optimism can make you look stupid, but cynicism always makes you look cynical."

We don't mind being a bit unconventional. We took it as a good sign when we discovered that we share an unusual habit. While we're in the office, we intentionally leave our keys in the office door.

Leaving the key in the door, it turns out, is a pretty foolproof way to avoid locking yourself out of the office. It also helps you avoid wasting time looking for keys. We've even started a small trend. The only small problem is that every now and then someone interrupts us to hand us the keys they've so thoughtfully rescued from the door.

Why is this relevant? Because leaving the key in the door is the kind of idea that leads to the European hotel innovation of having a receptacle for the room key card right next to the door. Putting the key in the holder turns on the lights in the room. More important, taking the key out of the holder turns off all the lights. Thus, hotel guests don't lose their keys and the hotel doesn't waste electricity.

There is real pleasure in encountering a simple but elegant idea for the first time—mulling over the pros and cons. We remember getting excited when we first heard about Andrew Tobias's idea of pay-at-the-pump insurance as a way to solve the endemic problem of uninsured motorists. (It's hard to drive without gasoline.)

But even more pleasurable than reading about other people's ideas is to solve problems yourself—to experience, firsthand, the joy of figuring out how to make things work better. This book will teach you simple methods for generating your own ingenious solutions.

Some people have the notion that coming up with concrete solutions for real-world problems is somehow reserved for the experts—that the techniques for innovation are beyond the capacity of the typical person. Baloney. Innovation is a skill that can be taught. And what's more, the potential for innovation is all around us. The problem is that the sense of innovation as everyday ingenuity often gets lost in our high-tech world. That is a problem we aim to fix with this book.

We'll share what we've discovered and what we've learned from others. Our combination of law and business backgrounds gives us valuable tools for both generating and testing ideas. We employ insights from economics, game theory, contracts, and an appreciation for the law of unintended consequences. These tools are especially important when it comes to poking holes in ideas.

Most innovation books are backward looking. With the benefit of hindsight, it is easy to see the great solutions of the past. Gee, weren't Post-it notes a great idea? While we can analyze and second-guess past business decisions, it is difficult to simulate the experience of innovating.

We'd like to put you in Charles Schwab's shoes back in 1973 and let you rediscover the idea of discount brokerage. The problem is that now you can't pretend not to know about discount brokerage, and hence it is almost impossible to recreate the discovery process.

Likewise, if we just looked to success stories of the past, you'd never really know if our approach would have helped come up with the idea in the first place. The good news is that there is a ready-made lab for experimenting. We use the world as it is for our case study.

It's harder to look forward—to see solutions no one is doing. But forcing ourselves to tackle as-yet unsolved problems is a sure-fire way to show you how our tools can be used to generate solutions that are, well, actually new.

This book will look both backward and forward (and sideways at current solutions in other countries). We'll examine problems solved in the past, look at problems bubbling up in the present, and make some bold and probably wrong predictions about solutions that will emerge in the future.

Of course, we won't always be able to prove that the ideas are good ones. But we're willing to take that risk and let you—and time—be the judge. We don't expect to bat a thousand.

More important than the ideas themselves is how we go about generating and evaluating them. We want to let you in on the ground floor to see how several why-not ideas were discovered. Indeed, our case studies are constructed so that you can beat us to the punch.

A common approach to developing problem-solving and lateral thinking skills is to work on made-up problems and brainteasers. We enjoy solving brainteasers as much as the next person (okay, probably more). We even include a few in chapter 7. But it is even more gratifying to come up with a solution to a problem in which something of real consequence turns on the answer. Simply put, we think it is more fun, more challenging, and more rewarding (including financially rewarding) to solve practical problems than made-up ones. Why not imagine what you would do differently if given the power to change things at GM, the IRS, a health plan, or the phone company?

Why Not? is about problem solving with a purpose. In some cases, the results will lead to improvements in social norms and law. Other times, the ideas will be the seed of a new business.

Of course, you don't have to start a new business to profit from knowing how to innovate. Constantly looking for new and better ways of doing something is both a skill to develop and a way of life. When you start thinking this way, it soon becomes second nature. Indeed, it pays to be known as the ideas person in your organization.

Even when there is no personal monetary benefit, you can join the thousands of others in the open-source movement who solve problems in their spare time and give away the ideas. This "just share it" mind-set is not just for computer programmers. Multitudes share their insights on Amazon.com by reviewing books, and mavens compile lists of favorite books and movies on every topic imaginable. Online communities such as About.com or Epinions.com offer literally millions of product reviews and culture guides contributed by people with passion and often great expertise.

Imagine how good you would feel if you found a way to make it easier for people to contribute to charity, reduce teenage driving accidents, refinance mortgages, or eliminate spam. There is a great satisfaction in having come up with an idea that really works.

We aspire for this book to change the way people think about their own ability to affect the world. Our goal is to make it natural—even expected—for everyone to challenge the status quo and ask, Why not do it this way instead?

The Way Things Never Were

Some men see things as they are and say, "Why?"
I dream of things that never were and say, "Why not?"

—Robert F. Kennedy, after George Bernard Shaw

A Wake-up Call

The phone jolts you from a deep sleep at 2:00 A.M. Not only does it wake you up, but the high-pitched squeal in your ear tells you that it's a fax machine that has dialed your phone by mistake. And you can bet that the fax will automatically redial your number every five minutes. What can you do?

Think of all the ways that you could solve this problem. No, that's not a rhetorical question—we really want you to think of some solutions. We know it's not the world's most pressing problem, but we've just started. Let's see how much we can do without any formal training.

Start with simple solutions that don't require any new products or services. Write them down. Then figure out what is wrong with these answers and how you might overcome these problems.

When you've done that, then see if you can figure out a way to solve the problem before it happens again. How could you prevent future wrong numbers from waking you up at night? Take some time to think these questions through before you read on.

Simple solutions might be to turn down the ringer all the way, unplug the phone, or put a pillow over it. But none of these options is very satisfactory. They block everyone from calling you—even important callers. And you end up short a pillow.

If you have both caller ID and call block, you could identify the offending number and then program your phone to block the call. But you'd have to be pretty awake to do this. It would be much easier if this two-step process were automated and you could just press *69 to block the last number from calling.

If you have a home fax machine, you could plug it into your regular phone line, get the offending fax, and be done with it. Or, if you have a service called delayed call forwarding, then an even better option exists. With delayed call forwarding, only calls left unanswered are forwarded. You could forward calls to your office fax number and then let the phone ring one more time and go back to sleep.

These are all reasonable proposals, but the best solution is one that prevents the problem from arising in the first place. You need to intercept the call before it wakes you up the first time.

This sounds like a role for an answering machine. But once again, while this measure stops the call from disturbing you, you still need to find a way to let the emergency call through.

There *is* a way that an answering machine—or better yet, voice mail—could do this. The caller would get a prerecorded message and have to type in a code to get through.

But what if the person doesn't know the code? If the goal is to prevent wrong numbers, faxes, and friends who call too late, then no code is even necessary. We don't have to be fancy. They'd call and get the message:

> *Hello, you've reached the Trumps. We're home but don't
> wish to be disturbed right now. If this is an emergency, you
> can hit 0 and our phone will ring. But it had better be good.*

Many office voice mail systems already do this (press 0 and you'll be connected to an attendant).

The final step would be to automate the timing. If alarm clocks and heating systems can be programmed to turn on and off at regular hours, why not voice mail? You would set the phone to automatically roll into voice mail at 10:30 P.M. and out of voice mail at 7:30 A.M.[1] The result wouldn't be perfect, but it would prevent all but the most determined wrong numbers from waking you up.

In the end, it all seems so logical. Perhaps the only mystery is why the phone companies don't offer this service today.

The core goal of this book is to teach you simpler ways for finding these kinds of solutions. Here, we stumbled our way to one of them. We did it by putting together bits and pieces of solutions that were already out there. What is most important, we didn't have to start from scratch and we didn't have to rely on any new technology. In chapter 3, we'll return to this late-night call problem and resolve it using our problems-in-search-of-solutions methodology.

Innovations That Are Just Waiting to Happen

The why-not attitude lets you see potential improvements that are just waiting to happen. And once this mind-set is activated, it's hard to turn it off. You start seeing potential solutions everywhere. We start by tackling smaller problems in familiar settings:

Why not have firms call you back rather than have you wait on hold?

Why not sell generic first-class postage stamps that remain valid when rates go up?

Why not have a fixed-rate mortgage that automatically refinances when interest rates fall?

Don't stop there. You can use the same techniques that this book cultivates to make progress on larger and seemingly more intractable problems:

How can we get people to contribute more to charity?

How can we improve corporate governance?

How can we make driving safer?

How can we reduce the costs of strikes?

You may like some of our ideas. We certainly hope you will. But that's not the main purpose of this book. What we really want is to get you hooked—hooked on a way of thinking that leads you to come up with solutions to problems, big and small.

We know you can do it, because the types of solutions we have in mind don't depend on high-tech breakthroughs. These are ideas that could be implemented today—or could have been implemented five years ago—if someone had only had the inspiration and gumption to do it.

> The whole of science is nothing more than
> a refinement of everyday thinking.
>
> —Albert Einstein

Why Not? taps into a new emphasis on a rather old-fashioned kind of American ingenuity. Think, for example, about the innovation of "right turn on red" or the secret ballot. (Okay, the secret ballot was Australian ingenuity.) Think about the innovation of one-way tolls or rolling luggage. Prewashed lettuce, the ultimate low-tech invention, has become a multibillion-dollar business. Frozen, pre-chopped onions save time and tears. You can now buy government bonds with interest rates indexed to inflation. There are plenty more great ideas like these just waiting to improve the quality of our lives.

Many of our why-nots are counterintuitive—or maybe we should say temporarily counterintuitive. Ideas that never before occurred to us often reveal and explain themselves with as little as a single question:

Why not open coffeehouses inside public libraries?

Why not have cell phone contracts that automatically switch you to the plan that's best for you?

Why not market DVDs that give parents the option to show the PG-13 airplane/TV version of an R-rated movie?

Until recently, the economy looked to technology as the engine for innovation. Many great ideas have been born there. But the

A Good Cover-up

Liquid paper was invented in 1951 by Bette Nesmith (mother of the Monkees' Mike Nesmith). Working as a secretary, she wondered why artists could paint over their mistakes, but typists couldn't. In her blender, she mixed up a batch of water-based paint to match the company stationery and brought it to work in a nail polish bottle. With the small brush, she could paint over and fix typos. Some twenty-eight years later, Gillette bought her company for $48 million.[2]

emphasis on high-tech, biotech, and the Internet has meant that ideas hatched from everyday ingenuity have often been overlooked.

History is littered with great inventions that are simple refinements of everyday thinking. It was Ben Franklin, not an actuary, who in 1752 founded America's first fire insurance company. He also invented the library step stool, the rocking chair, the lightning rod, bifocal glasses, the odometer (to measure postal routes), and the Franklin stove. He even proposed daylight savings time. All this innovation is in addition to his work on electricity (and his role in drafting both the Declaration of Independence and the U.S. Constitution).

Pacific islanders invented a new swimming stroke, the Australian crawl. The butterfly was invented in the 1950s as a way to win the breaststroke when someone realized that the forward portion of the stroke would be faster above water than below.[3]

Wayne Gretzky invented a new offense for ice hockey. He stood behind the opponent's goal and thereby forced all the defenders— including the goalie—to swivel their heads back and forth to keep an eye on him and his teammates. Blind spots were created upon which Gretzky quickly capitalized. He would shovel a quick pass to an open teammate in front of the net or, if an opponent skated behind the net to attack him, Gretzky would dart out the other side to score himself. Gretzky's innovation remains one of the hardest plays in hockey to defend against.

These sports examples are instructive because these revolutionary strategies could have been implemented literally decades earlier. The solution was there all along, waiting to be found.

Jonathan Swift's *Gulliver's Travels* is a handbook for innovation wrapped in a children's story. By highlighting peculiar Lilliputian customs, such as limiting the length of any law to the number of letters in the alphabet or treating fraud more severely than theft, Swift challenged his readers to consider new ways of doing things. It took the Adelphia, Enron, and WorldCom scandals of 2002 for us to see that the Lilliputians were ahead of the Securities and Exchange Commission when it came to the punishment of fraud.

Innovation is not something that needs to be left to the experts or rocket scientists. Innovations are not just top-down, but bottom-up and sideways. In fact, nonexperts sometimes have the advantage of not being constrained by the accepted wisdom. It's easier to think outside the box when you don't even know where or what the box is. Not knowing "that's just the way it is" or "that was tried once but failed" may help the nonexpert conjure new ideas that the expert would not have discovered.

This theme of empowerment is also connected to a theme of optimism. *Why Not?* is a sustained argument against complacency. Our examples give lie to the kind of fatalism that holds that nothing can be done about existing problems.

We aim to make it socially acceptable for people to speak up and add their own two cents about how things should work. The world should be one big suggestion box.

Later chapters will talk about specific tools for generating new ideas. But first let's jump into another exercise. You already solved the problem of a late night-phone call. Let's tackle something a little more challenging. This exercise leads toward an innovation but starts from the other end. That is, we look at some unusual solutions that people have employed and ask where else they could work.

Problem Solving on the Fly—Just Say No

The issue of capital punishment has long been controversial. Jewish law has what at first seems to be a backward position: If the jury's vote is unanimous, the accused cannot be put to death. According to the sage Maimonides:

*If in trying a capital case all the members of the Sanhedrin
forthwith vote for conviction, the accused is acquitted. Only
when some cast about for arguments in his favor and are
outvoted by those who are for conviction is the accused put
to death.*[4]

While most everything in the Talmud is subject to several inter-
pretations, the one we find most compelling is that this rule helped
ensure that a criminal defendant was accorded a certain due process. The required lack of unanimity was only *temporary*. According to Aaron Schreiber:

*[A]fter the deliberations of the court, and before any judg-
ment was reached, the judges were required to spend the
night together in pairs, searching for a possible defense for
the criminal defendant.*[5]

The sages were concerned that the defendant be given a proper
opportunity for acquittal. They wanted to make sure that someone played the Henry Fonda role in *Twelve Angry Men*. The non-
unanimity rule was a way of enforcing that someone on the jury
make the case for acquittal. If everyone rushes to convict, then
there is a question of whether both sides of the argument were
really heard.

Jewish law is very similar in spirit to the role of an *advocatus
diaboli,* or devil's advocate, in the Roman Catholic Church. For the
church, elevating someone to sainthood is a momentous decision.
For more than five hundred years, this canonization process has
followed a formal procedure in which one person (a postulator)
presents the case in favor and another (the promoter of the faith)
presents the case against. Prospero Lamertini (later Pope Benedict
XIV, 1740–1758) described the promoter's charge:

*It is [the promoter of the faith's duty] to critically examine the
life of, and the miracles attributed to, the individual up for
sainthood or blessedness. Because his presentation of facts
must include everything unfavorable to the candidate, the
promoter of the faith is popularly known as the devil's*

advocate. His duty requires him to prepare in writing all
possible arguments, even at times seemingly slight, against the
raising of any one to the honours of the altar.[6]

There's a common thread to these two momentous decisions. In both cases, procedures were created to ensure that a debate occurs— that both sides of the argument are made and that all the facts are on the table.

Where else might this approach apply? In universities, the life-or-death decision is tenure. Frankly, we suspect that requiring one person to present the case against would be a useful check in the process. It can be difficult to argue against a candidate who you can predict will be promoted. The difficulty is that you have to live with your colleagues. If a person were *required* to play this role, however, it would not be held against him or her. This is the idea of a loyal opposition. In the end, the naysayer might well vote in favor of the candidate, but the discussion will have been fuller for having heard all the arguments. One good way to ensure that the process is played honestly would be to take a particularly harsh view of any negative facts that were not presented by the committee report.

Improving tenure decisions would be nice, but there are bigger problems that the preceding approach might well solve. Think about where people make big decisions that are often based on too little informed discussion.

Does corporate governance come to mind? In the boardroom, there is great pressure to go along and get along. If you challenge the CEO and lose, you might even feel compelled to resign.

In the 2002 battle over the HP-Compaq merger, we saw plenty of debate. But the opposition by dissident board member David Packard illustrates the problem of disloyal opposition. The goal is not to have disputes spill out into the press and the courtroom. Rather, the idea is to require someone on the board to present the counterarguments: why we shouldn't make this merger; why this compensation package is too high or too low; why we shouldn't build a new plant.

Instead of having a board populated with yes-men (and yes-women), the Jewish and Catholic examples suggest that there may be room for "no-people" as well—people who are duty-bound to make the strongest argument against the proposal. Of course, one criticism is that if we have someone whose job it is to speak out against, then the rest of us can free ride. We can let the devil's advocate do the hard work for us when in fact everyone should come prepared to discuss both sides.

A good board already does all this. That is because the best CEOs look for a board that will challenge their assumptions and conclusions. But this type of boardroom debate is far too uncommon. People who dissent are often quickly cut out of the information loop. Thus it is critically important that the devil's advocate be someone who is truly a trusted party—a loyal opposition.

It turns out that companies located in countries with a civil-law tradition (as opposed to a common-law tradition) have something akin to the devil's advocate role in the office of the commissioner. This corporate position exists in Mexico, France, Italy, and Chile. The process doesn't work all that well, however, as the person is too low in stature to have the required powerful voice. In the United States, the idea of creating an independent lead director is a step in this direction, but not as big a step.

Stepping back, what's important about this exercise is that we generated a why-not proposal for governance through a reverse direction. We didn't start with the problem and say, "How do we solve it?" Had we done so, we might not have thought about the role of a devil's advocate.

Instead, we started with an unusual solution from Jewish and Catholic law that has stood the test of time and then found a new application. Typically, the underlying problem being addressed arises in more than just one context. Thus, after finding the solution, we figure out what type of problem it is really solving and then look for other arenas in which similar problems arise.

Preemptive Strike

Let us make a preemptive strike against what the nattering nabobs of negativism say: If that's such a good idea, why hasn't someone already done it?

This is a fair question. It is a test used by all venture capitalists. The mistake is to jump to the conclusion that if it hasn't been done already, there must be something wrong with the idea.

It is absurd to suggest that all the good ideas have already been thought of, and yet, this refrain keeps reemerging. The Spanish Royal Commission rejected Christopher Columbus's proposal to sail west with the view that "[s]o many centuries after the Creation, it is unlikely that anyone could find hitherto unknown lands of any value." Lord Kelvin predicted in 1900 that "[t]here is nothing new to be discovered in physics now. All that remains is more and more precise measurement." John Horgan's *End of Science* made a splash in 1997 and then sank into oblivion (right before the genomics revolution).

This "nothing new under the sun" theme is also captured in the old joke about two University of Chicago economists going for a walk. One sees a twenty-dollar bill lying on the ground and starts to bend over and pick it up, but the other stops her, saying, "It's a counterfeit. If it were real, someone would have picked it up already." Concluding that an idea must be flawed because it hasn't already been done is rather like presuming any money on the sidewalk must be a fake.

You might be saying to yourself, okay, there will, of course, always be some good ideas waiting to happen. But if the particular ideas that you're touting in this book are so good, Ayres and Nalebuff, why haven't you already done them?

This is certainly the kind of question we ask when a stockbroker touts a new stock. Do you drink your own Kool-Aid?

In our case the answer is yes, quite literally. Except it's Honest Tea. Inspired by a why-not idea, one of us (Barry) cofounded a company that makes barely sweetened bottled iced teas. In 2003, the company turned five, which is a respectable age measured in beverage industry dog-eat-dog years. With sales of $5 million, it's even profitable. (You can learn more about Honest Tea in chapter 8.)

We have also worked to make home-equity protection, three-year business schools, and automatically refinancing fixed-rate mortgages a reality. Unlike buying stocks, it is hard work to put ideas into practice. And no one can do everything.

More important, there are some things that we and you shouldn't do even if others can. *Many great ideas do not make great new businesses.* They're often better realized by existing firms.

e-Toys spent a great deal of money to demonstrate that toys can be sold over the Web. But it was the incumbents Toys 'R Us (through Amazon.com) and KBToys that showed how to make money. As an entrepreneur, you don't want to be overrun by big players that enter the game having used your start-up as market research.

Of course, sometimes, an established firm will be less capable of implementing a new idea. New creations can undermine the flagship product. Snapple might have a harder time marketing a less sweet, healthy iced tea, because to do so would risk pointing out that its best-selling teas taste like liquid candy.

Other times, there is no good reason why not. We will often push existing firms to explain why they have not put a simple idea into place. For example, why doesn't the telephone company offer nighttime call screening?

It is always important to ask the "money on the ground" question. If why-not ideas really have just been waiting to happen, why haven't they already happened? We will provide answers for many of our ideas along the way, and chapter 10 will flesh out our theory on reasonable answers for why a good idea might not already exist.

And, lest we forget, the technology for writing novels and composing music and painting watercolors has been with us for a long time. But we don't reject new art out of hand because if it were any good it would already have been created long ago.

The possibilities for creation have not been exhausted. Good ideas are not a thing of the past, and we hope this book is further proof of that.

Why not dream of things that never were?

Our Plan of Attack

The next chapter begins with a user's guide for developing new ideas. It's one thing to tell people, Be creative. It's quite another to give them a framework for coming up with new ideas. While much has been written about how to make organizations more creative, our goal is to help *individuals* be more creative. The trick is to give people guidance on where to look.

We're just about to let the genie out of the bottle—to describe specific tools that innovators implicitly or explicitly use. (Indeed, the first two exercises already introduced you to some of these methods.) With tools in hand, we then turn things around in a guide to thinking *inside* the box, what we call the art of principled problem solving. This technique will not only help you test whether a why-not idea is likely to fly, but will also help you discover more ideas, more quickly.

In the last section, Problem Solving with a Purpose, we showcase ideas for business, law, and everyday life. We'll present more in-depth coverage of these ideas, leading you through the process of innovation. We'll also invite you to solve real-world puzzles: how to reinvent mortgages, reduce the cost of strikes, eliminate hidden pricing, or fix the process for organ donations. We'll present the case for Honest Tea. Along the way, you'll find stories about the implementation and evolution of why-not ideas and the people behind them.

We conclude with a discussion on how to make your ideas real. We emphasize how to sell your ideas, especially how to go about changing the attitudes of others to help them become more receptive to a why-not perspective.

Good Ideas and How to Generate Them

The sources of invention [are] more interesting than the inventions themselves.

—Wilhelm Leibniz

Routinizing Ingenuity

There is a myth of genius surrounding innovation: This is a job for rocket scientists and creativity gurus.[1] While we don't dispute that Edison and Einstein were cut from a different cloth, if we focus on innovation outside the technology arena, it no longer looks like rocket science.

One of the more prolific modern-day inventors is Jay Walker, founder of Priceline and Walker Digital. Here are some of his ideas:

Instead of having the firm state a price to customers, let customers state a price to the firm.

Instead of giving 23 cents change at a fast-food restaurant, offer the customer a special deal on fries or a soda. "Sir, your total is $3.77. For your 23 cents change, we can supersize your fries from a medium to a large."

Instead of lotto tickets that expire after a single use, let people buy, for a premium, tickets that are valid until someone wins the entire jackpot.

We'd like you to be impressed, but not in awe. Walker is neither the genius he was labeled when his company was worth $36 billion nor the goat when Priceline's stock fell by 97 percent. After five years of losses, Priceline had its first period of profits. The fact that its market capitalization is no longer $36 billion doesn't mean it is a failure. Building a $900 million business from a single idea is an extraordinarily impressive accomplishment.[2]

How does one go about imagining the unimagined? While some people claim that the route to innovation is indescribable, we argue that there is often a simple, recurrent structure to thinking outside the box.

Most "original" ideas aren't completely original, but instead are the result of two basic methods for generating ideas: *problems in search of solutions* and *solutions in search of problems.*

People usually think of problem solving as a search for solutions. But in everything we do, we look for symmetries. (So will you after reading this book.) Thus, we also see that problem solving can be a search for problems once you've found a good solution. Both approaches have their advantages. If this seems odd, think of television game shows. *Who Wants to Be a Millionaire?* looks for the right answer, while *Jeopardy!* starts with the answer and looks for the right question.

In this chapter, we offer an introduction to these two approaches and four distinct problem-solving tools—which are motivated by four questions:

What would Croesus do?

Why don't you feel my pain?

Where else would it work?

Would flipping it work?

Each of these question tools is laid out in detail in its own chapter. But before we dive into the details, this chapter will give you a larger perspective.

We make no claim that these four tools are the only way to generate new ideas. Far from it. Innovations based on technological breakthroughs are still an important, independent source of progress. We're not even claiming that these four tools exhaust the why-not tool bag. But we do believe that learning how to use these four proactively is a great place to start and will pay dividends by helping you produce plenty of new ideas.

Finding and identifying the problem is often the crucial step. One of the best ways to identify problems is to pay attention to what bugs you and other people. Like the princess and her pea, innovators have to pay attention to hidden problems, things that get swept under the mattress. Instead of becoming inured to the annoyance and accepting the status quo, innovators need to cultivate their sensitivity to displeasure and even empathize with the displeasure that other people might have long ago suppressed. We are on the lookout for situations where satisfactory could become optimal. Conceding "that's just the way it is" is the death knell of progress.

> The reasonable man adapts himself to the world; the unreasonable one persists in trying to adapt the world to himself. Therefore, all progress depends on the unreasonable man.
>
> —George Bernard Shaw

Some problems are pretty obvious, such as the yes-man pathology in corporate governance. But others are more subtle. Others are so large but so familiar that even the proverbial princess no longer notices those grapefruit-sized lumps. Part of the power of the *Jeopardy!* or solutions-in-search-of-problems approach is that it allows you to start with a known quantity and search for problems that you didn't know you had.

Problems in Search of Solutions

Once a problem has been identified, how do you go about finding a solution? Watching your customers is a fine place to start. Rather than invent a new solution from scratch, we can sometimes take the imperfect, often Rube Goldberg solutions that people have already found and improve on them. But consumer watching has its limits both as a mode of discovering problems and of identifying their solutions. While the unexpected reaction of consumers often signals that something is wrong with a product, there are some annoyances for which customers cannot practicably take up arms to protect themselves. And the partial solutions that real-world consumers put to use may divert attention away from even better solutions. Real-world consumers have limited resources.

WWCD?

An alternative tool is to ask how an unconstrained consumer would solve the problem. We call this approach "What would Croesus do?" as a shorthand for imagining solutions where price is no object.

In his day, Howard Hughes had a Croesus-like flair for spending money to find solutions to problems. There is a story told about Hughes in Las Vegas. Imagine that it's 1966 and that you have a hankering to watch old Bogart films. What do you do? Unfortunately, the VCR has yet to be invented. Remember, you have lots of money.

What Howard Hughes did was to buy a local television station, KLAS. He used the station as his private VCR. Whenever he wanted,

Rich as Croesus?

Croesus (rhymes with Jesus) was the supremely rich king of Lydia (modern Turkey), reigning from 560 to 546 B.C. His wealth came from mining gold in the river Pactolus, where Midas was said to have bathed. Croesus was the first to mint coins of pure silver and gold. His lavish gifts and sacrifices made his name synonymous with wealth. Even today we say "rich as Croesus."

he'd call up the station's general manager and simply tell him what movie to put on that night. We understand that KLAS played a lot of *Casablanca* and *Dr. Strangelove*.

In this spirit, "What would Croesus do?" begins by imagining a customized and very expensive solution. We don't begin with a view that the solution has to be practical. Instead we ask, Are there any solutions at all?

Thinking this way is a tool to get you to be a bit bolder and more outrageous than you might otherwise be. In fact, these impractical solutions don't even have to exist, except in your mind. In that way, you are lulled into finding solutions that you imagine might well exist—that should exist.

Of course, the purpose of asking WWCD is not to produce an immediate solution. Imagining what Croesus would do is just a first step.

In the real world, price *is* an object. The fact is that we are all creatures with limited resources—even, at some point, King Croesus, Howard Hughes, and Bill Gates. But imagining how you might solve a problem if you had almost unlimited resources often suggests ways that, ultimately, would benefit us all. And by automating or standardizing one of these expensive solutions, an innovator might produce 99 percent of the benefit for 1 percent of the cost.

Being Put on Hold.   Unconstrained consumers tend to get exactly what they want. They don't have to settle for just any bowl of candy; they can have their personal assistant pick out just the yellow M&Ms.* Sometimes WWCD becomes a manifesto for personal choice. Of course, we can't all afford personal assistants. But markets can be reorganized to facilitate choice. Instead of automation, what is sometimes needed is standardization that makes it easier to get what you want. Not as good as a personal assistant, but a fraction of the cost.

---

*When we wrote this, we were just kidding. Only later did we discover that this service actually exists. Mars will sell you a customized collection of M&Ms in whatever colors you want. See Colorworks Web page, http://colorworks.com.

Let's start with an easy problem—the annoying Muzak that is meant to distract you while you wait on hold. Why not be given the ability to choose different genres by pushing a number on the keypad? Pushing 1 will get you rock; 2 will get you classical; 3 will get you jazz; 4 will get you news; and 5 will get you silence.[3] And phones are not the only service that would benefit from this option.

Although offering a choice of music on hold is an improvement, WWCD suggests a way to attack the deeper problem. We doubt that Donald Trump or Bill Gates spends much time waiting on hold. What do these magnates do instead? They have an assistant wait on hold and then buzz them when the call goes through.

Is there any way the rest of us could emulate this strategy?

Well, yes. Instead of waiting on hold to speak with an airline customer representative, why not have the airline call you back (just like Gates's assistant) when the rep is ready to talk to you?

Arranging for the airline to call you back would be no harder than hanging on hold. With caller ID, you wouldn't even have to enter your number. The airline could simply play an announcement:

All agents are currently busy. Your call is very important to us. That's why we will be calling you back in approximately six minutes. If you'd like us to call back at another time, please enter that time now.

Waiting on hold is not only a pain for the caller, but also expensive for the receivers who have to pay per-minute charges for the time their toll-free customers are on hold. (The cynic in us might say that perhaps the reason they have you wait so long on hold is that they really want you to give up. If that's truly the case, then they could announce, "We'll call you back in two weeks.")

Since automatic callback is currently available when the line is busy, by asking where else it would work—translating automatic callback for busy signals to calls on hold—we might have come up with the idea. But we wouldn't get there by simply looking at what customers do.

Watching how constrained consumers come up with low-tech solutions and innovative applications is a valuable tool for routinizing ingenuity. But WWCD teaches us that imagining (or observing) how unconstrained consumers behave can lead us toward solutions that we might not have thought of if we had focused on the more constrained work-arounds.

With the benefit of hindsight, offering an automated callback seems pretty obvious. While it's hard now to imagine how we might have *not* come up with that idea, most of us have spent plenty of time on hold without hitting on this solution. Once you adopt a WWCD frame of mind and start looking at life through this lens, callback rather than hold almost jumps out at you.

Like a Virgin.   Managing money is a complicated problem. Typically, money is spread out into checking accounts, savings accounts, a money market account, perhaps even some municipal or treasury bonds. At the same time, off in a separate bucket, you may have a mortgage to worry about.

Let's say your checking account earns no interest and you're paying 6 percent on your mortgage. This doesn't make much sense. Why don't you just take all your cash and prepay your mortgage?

That way you would effectively earn an extra 6 percent on your money.

Unfortunately, this proposal seems totally impractical. You need to have some cash to pay your bills and cover emergencies. If you put all of your money into your mortgage, you couldn't get it back when you needed it.

Why not? Why can't you get your money back? If you can pre-pay your mortgage, why can't you *de*-prepay it? If you put some extra money in now and get ahead, why not take that money out later if you need it?

Actually, there is a way to do this. If you are a sophisticated banking customer, you can take out a home-equity line of credit, use that to prepay your mortgage, and then expand and contract the home equity line as you need it. Even this isn't a full solution, because we haven't found a line of credit service that lets you auto-matically write checks from your normal checking account that will be backed by the line of credit.

The general idea is that your money should be moved around to wherever it is most productive. What a modern Croesus would do, and what you'd like to do, is to arrange for all your cash to be "swept" into the highest paying account each night and then be made available again the next day. In short, the best person to move your money around isn't your adviser or even your personal CFO—it's the bank.

This may all seem like bankers' science fiction, but just such a product is available in the United Kingdom, thanks to the Virgin Group. Led by the flamboyant Richard Branson, Virgin's busi-nesses have evolved from the music industry to include everything from mobile phones to car sales, trains to airplanes, colas, bridal wear (Virgin Bride!), and mortgages. In the process, Virgin has become one of the three most respected brands in the U.K. (The other two are Marks and Spencer and Tesco, both retailers.)

In 1997, Virgin teamed up with AMP and Royal Bank of Scot-land to offer the Virgin One account. The Virgin One account rec-ognizes that the customer has a net state of indebtedness. A person with a $200,000 mortgage and $10,000 in a checking account really has a net debt of $190,000. Thus the Virgin One account charges the person interest only on this $190,000.

The Virgin One account is a model of simplicity. Your salary is directly deposited into your mortgage account. This and any other deposits you make reduce your outstanding balance. Meanwhile, your credit card and checking accounts are tied in the other way. Any checks you write or credit card charges you incur are taken out of this account, thereby increasing your outstanding mortgage.

Really rather nice, isn't it? Since you are unlikely to find a place to park your money that pays more than your mortgage rate, you no longer have to think about CDs, money market accounts, and the rest. Just put all your savings into your mortgage.

Virgin One was launched in late 1997 with a modest target of twenty thousand customers. The program beat that target, and by early 2001 had more than fifty thousand customers. That may not seem like many, but those fifty thousand accounts accounted for more than £4 billion in mortgages.

Mortgage Takes a Holiday

If you can take a vacation from work, why not take a vacation from paying your mortgage? There is no reason why you need to make mortgage payments all twelve months of the year. Christmas time often puts extra financial burdens on the family. You could make eleven payments a year, skipping December, and just extend the length of the mortgage. While skipping a payment means that you'll have to pay back more later, this is much cheaper than racking up credit card debt.

The feasibility of this option has been established in Australia, New Zealand, and the U.K., where it is a common feature of "flexible" mortgages. It is also has strong consumer appeal. As one happy customer explained: "I [asked] for a mortgage payment holiday to help pay for our actual holiday. We had an absolutely brilliant time with no bills to worry about when we came home. I'd never go back to a traditional mortgage now—they're completely old hat."[4]

The Virgin One account was sold to Royal Bank of Scotland, and this type of mortgage and its imitators have since become the most popular mortgage product in the U.K. So how much was the idea worth? Virgin and AMP's combined 50 percent share was bought out for £100 million (about $150 million). Not too shabby.

Although this all-in-one mortgage account is a great innovation, it isn't rocket science. The Bank of New South Wales in Australia first came up with the idea. It is a natural evolution of home equity lines—think of it as a mortgage with a home equity line built in. It is also an example of how a bank can automate money management for you. Banks already do this for their commercial customers, so it's clear that you don't have to invent the answer from scratch. Instead, you can take custom solutions that already exist, simplify them, and bring them to the mass market. This doesn't mean it's easy to do. Later, in chapter 10, we'll return to discuss some of the challenges involved in bringing the Virgin One product to market.

Why Aren't You Feeling My Pain?

In addition to watching what consumers do well, it is also useful to pay attention to what they do wrong. Among the many kinds of mistakes that people make, one class is of particular concern—self-interest sometimes leads people to do the wrong thing.

In theory, that's not supposed to happen in a free market. One of the most famous quotes in economics comes from Adam Smith in the *Wealth of Nations:*

> *It is not from the benevolence of the butcher, the brewer, or the baker that we expect our dinner, but from their regard to their own interest. . . . [H]e intends only his own gain, and he is in this . . . led by an invisible hand to promote an end which was no part of his intention.*

There is a view that if everyone were to follow his or her own self-interest, the outcome would be the best for society. While that is true in some cases, Smith's invisible hand has a limited span. The problem is that there are all sorts of actions that have consequences to others that don't get priced in the market. Economists call these *negative externalities.* For example, if you buy The Club to deter auto theft and all this action does is send the thief to the next car, then the price of The Club doesn't reflect its value to society (which is zero).

And it isn't just consumers who make mistakes. As we'll see in the example of video rental pricing (Blockbuster Blocks the Pain), sellers sometimes take actions that benefit themselves less than they hurt consumers.

Looking for inefficient behavior by buyers or sellers is a systematic way both to identify problems and to solve them. We can identify problems by looking for behaviors that create an external harm that is greater than the internal benefit. Or to put it more plainly, the trick is to look at some choice that buyers or sellers make whereby the decision maker's benefit from the choice is less than the costs that it imposes on others.

The general problem is one of misguided or missing incentives. But the good news is that there is a simple and powerful idea about how to improve defective incentives: internalization. The problem is that the buyer or seller doesn't take into account the external costs of his or her decision making. So the solution is to *internalize* those external effects. In other words, if the decision maker is made to "feel your pain," she will end up doing the right thing.

There's an old joke about two hikers walking through the woods. They come upon a hungry-looking bear. One of the hikers starts to put on his running shoes. The other hiker says, "You can't outrun a bear." To which the first hiker replies, "I don't need to. I only need to outrun you."

Of course, this joke is all about the negative externality that can be created when one person takes precautions to avoid being a victim. Sometimes the primary impact doesn't reduce crime but merely shifts it to someone else.

Why Lojack Scares Thieves (and The Club Doesn't).   Think about car alarms and burglar alarms. People have an incentive to buy too many of these crime-shifting activities because an individual doesn't feel the pain when the criminal or the bear goes down the street and victimizes someone else.

Not all victim precautions have this unfortunate side effect. Alarms that *silently* alert the police don't cause burglars to switch houses, because the intruders don't learn about the precaution until the police arrive to arrest them. This is in sharp contrast to putting bars on your windows, which potential thieves can observe before starting a job.

Silent house alarms and other types of hidden precautions can create a positive externality. If 20 percent of the houses in a city have silent alarms, thieves may be generally reluctant to break into any house—including unprotected ones—because they can't be sure which ones have a silent alarm.

This is not just a nice theory. One of us (Ian), with Steve Levitt of the University of Chicago, found that installing concealed Lojack car transmitters had a dramatic impact on reducing the overall amount of auto theft. Lojack transmits a signal that lets police track a stolen car, but because it is hidden, potential thieves can't distinguish the protected cars from the unprotected ones. Ayres and Levitt found that investing $400 in Lojack reduces *other people's* expected auto theft loss by more than $4,000.[5]

Lojack is particularly good at deterring professional car thieves. If only 3 percent of the cars in a city have Lojack, then a professional who boosts fifty cars a year suddenly has a 78 percent chance of encountering one. If the thief takes a hundred cars, the probability rises to 95 percent. A little bit of Lojack goes a long way toward discovering and deterring auto-theft rings. Lojack has busted up more than sixty chop shops in Los Angeles alone—thus helping not just the Lojack owner but the owners of all the other cars in the shop and all those that would be in the shop the next week.

So think for a moment what all this means for car owners' incentives to buy Lojack instead of The Club. The Club, like outrunning the other hiker, merely shifts crime to non-Club owners. Lojack helps other people; The Club hurts other people. The problem is that individual car owners have no economic incentives to take these opposite, spillover effects into account when choosing which device to purchase. People buy too many Clubs and not enough Lojacks.

Can you see how internalization could be used to solve this problem? Somehow we have to increase the price of The Club so that its buyers feel the pain of the deflected crime, and we have to reduce the price of Lojack so that its buyers share the benefits they provide to others. How could this be done?

One answer would be to turn to government. The government could impose a tax on crime-shifting precautions and subsidize hidden precautions like Lojack. Massachusetts does this by mandating that insurance companies give a 25 percent discount on theft insurance for cars that have Lojack. Not surprisingly, Boston has a higher proportion of cars with Lojack than any other city in the United States, and Ayres and Levitt showed that Lojack caused Boston auto theft to drop by about 50 percent.

But do we really need a government mandate? What private entity might help consumers internalize these two very different spillover effects?

Insurance companies are a natural answer because they directly feel the spillover effects. If an Allstate customer uses The Club, Allstate will most likely have to pay out less to that customer for auto theft. The customer's use of this device, however, increases the likely amount that Allstate will have to pay out to its other customers as the thief simply moves down the road. In contrast, if the customer buys a Lojack, Allstate saves money on the amount it has to pay out to all the rest of its customers. So instead of having Massachusetts mandate a subsidy of Lojack, why not just have insurers voluntarily set insurance prices that give the right incentives?

We've posed this question to several insurers, and their answers were disappointing at best. One explanation for their inaction is the lazy monopolist model. While the insurance companies have the claims data and plenty of actuaries to calculate the magnitude of the spillover effects, they profess absolutely no interest in learning about the ways in which one customer's actions affect another customer's losses.

But there is a subtler reason that insurance companies don't give the appropriate subsidies, and it, too, is an externality story.

The largest insurance company in any city controls only about 20 percent of the market. This means that most of the external effect of Lojack or The Club is going to fall on other insurance companies.

The same externality problem that distorts customer incentives plays out at the insurance level as well. An individual insurance company captures, at most, only 20 percent of the benefits of Lojack and thus does not have sufficient incentive to subsidize its use. Indeed, an insurance company may even want to raise its rivals' payouts. If Allstate got all its customers to buy Lojack, its rivals' payouts for auto theft would decline. Conversely, if Allstate got all its customers to buy crime-shifting devices, then the cost of auto theft would be concentrated on Allstate's rivals, driving up their cost of doing business.

That said, we'll stick with the lazy incumbent model. The spillover benefits of Lojack are so large that even if a firm captured only 20 percent of the benefits, that would be plenty. Recall that a $400 investment in Lojack leads to a $4,000 fall in car thefts; 20 percent of the gains is $800. A large insurance firm has plenty incentive to encourage Lojack usage all on its own.[6]

Blockbuster Blocks the Pain.   Not so long ago, Blockbuster's customer-relations strategy was "managed dissatisfaction." The stores were frequently out of the most recently released hit video. You often had to reserve the new release in advance and could rent it for only one night. But now, Blockbuster offers a guarantee that it will have the newly released video in stock and rentals are for two days.[7]

What happened?

Blockbuster found a way to solve a serious incentive problem and improved its business in the process. Let's start with the source of the incentive problem. The studio has a movie that has finished its theatrical release and TV pay-per-view tour and is ready to debut in the video rental stores. How should it set the price?

If the studio charges a low price, then Blockbuster will buy plenty of tapes. But it's Blockbuster, rather than the studio, that makes all the money.

Figuring that a hit video will be rented out some thirty to fifty times, studios used to charge Blockbuster around $65 for a new release. (A month or so after Blockbuster bought its supply at $65, the studios would then cut the price to $20 to promote retail sales.)

The high price made Blockbuster very cautious about which videos to buy and how many copies to hold. While empty shelves led to customer dissatisfaction, people often rented something else in place of the new release they wanted. It was better to have new releases be frequently out of stock than to buy extra copies at $65 a pop.

Incentive problems exist when the two players don't have the same objective—when the two parties don't feel each other's pain. The studios didn't feel the hurt when customers couldn't find their desired movie, and they didn't feel Blockbuster's pain when the movie sat on the shelf and didn't go out enough to earn back its price.

The studios simply wanted the video stores to stock up. Once the stores bought a movie, the studios didn't care how often the movie was either rented or out of stock. Meanwhile, the video stores were forced to play a tight inventory management game in order not to give away too much to the studios.

The result? Too few movies on the shelves, and unhappy customers. Predictions abounded that Blockbuster would be made obsolete by pay-per-view cable—and good riddance.

Before we flip over the cards and reveal how the studios and Blockbuster solved this problem, think about what it would take to get them to have a shared objective. Look again at the incentive problem. The studios wanted Blockbuster to take all the risk and pay its share of the rental profits all up front. The *Wall Street Journal* describes how the new CEO at Blockbuster (John Antioco) addressed the problem:

> *Mr. Antioco knew from his experience as a customer the frustrations of Blockbuster stores. . . . One of Mr. Antioco's first moves as CEO was to persuade studios to change their video-supply deals to make it easier for Blockbuster to stock*

*many copies of new-release movies. Blockbuster's revenue
skyrocketed so much immediately afterward that Mr.
Redstone, on seeing the figures in his New York office, joked
to an associate that his computer must have been broken.*[8]

What was the solution? The incentive problem was resolved when Blockbuster and the studios agreed on a revenue-sharing deal. Under this scheme, Blockbuster got to buy tapes at a much-discounted price. In exchange, the video chain gave up to 40 percent of the rental revenue back to the studio.

These deals also specified that Blockbuster had to take every movie the studio released on video, and the studios sometimes dictated the quantities. So, not only did the studios get potentially more money, they also got to push mediocre movies.

This practice was great for Blockbuster and the studios, but not for smaller stores. They used to be able to count on customers who didn't find (or even expect to find) the current hit at Blockbuster coming to them for their deeper and more idiosyncratic inventory.

The Film Is in the Mail

The Netflix business model is itself worthy of a why-not. Netflix is a mail-order version of a for-profit lending library—but for DVDs, not books. You pay Netflix $19.95 per month. For that fee, you can have three DVDs checked out at any time. When you're done with a movie, you mail it back to Netflix, and it will mail you the next film you want to see. The postage is on the company, and you never pay late fees (or what Blockbuster euphemistically calls "extended rental charges").

Three years into its rental exchange model, Netflix broke the million-member mark. While this is an intriguing mail-order business, the rental exchange idea might be even better for a bricks-and-mortar store. If an average customer rents five movies a month and round-trip postage and mailer costs are $2, that means 50 percent of the company's revenue is going to cover postage. Thus it shouldn't be too surprising that Blockbuster and Wal*Mart have both entered the rental exchange business.

Now, though, people simply turn to Blockbuster, and the independents are finding it tough to compete.[9]

It's worth noting that the revenue sharing was not extended to DVDs. The average purchase price was low enough, around $20, that Blockbuster decided to forgo the revenue sharing in favor of straight buy and rent. Perhaps this was because the other provisions of the deal ("You also have to buy one hundred copies of *The Adventures of Pluto Nash*") were too onerous. The studios do have a revenue-sharing arrangement with Netflix, the largest online DVD rental company, and revenue sharing is the standard practice with the movie cinemas.

The take-home lesson of Blockbuster is that there can be great payoffs to asking whether you're feeling other people's pain. Ignoring others' interests leads to inefficient decisions. The result can be worse for them and for you. The solution comes from designing incentives so that all parties more fully feel the impacts that their decisions have on each other.

At this point, we've had a chance to think about finding answers to unsolved problems. Now we turn things around and play *Jeopardy!* We start with some interesting answers and look to see what questions they solve.

Solutions in Search of Problems

> Judge a man by his questions
> rather than his answers.
>
> —Voltaire

Knowledge management is a process of codifying what an organization knows. If people have a problem, they can look at the firm's database to see what solutions others have employed. In this way, knowledge management is a tool to help people find solutions to their problems.

Try turning this around. You've come up with a great new solution. What other problems does it solve? Shouldn't there also be a database of questions that people want to have solved? Then if you have an answer to one problem, you can look through this database to see what other problems it might solve. Let's call this reverse exploration *ignorance management.**

Asking questions is a different skill from answering them. Some people are better at solving problems than at finding good questions to solve. We've been to many CEO conferences that begin by going around the table and asking participants to share their high-priority problems.

What is missing from most knowledge management databases is an opportunity for people to put these information demands into the mix. There is a supply of answers, but no way to present demand for information that isn't yet there.

It's natural for us to think of problem solving as a solution search, but we can also solve problems by undertaking a problem search—looking for problems to which we can apply particularly clever solutions. And as we become more proficient at this way of thinking, it is often useful to toggle back and forth between the two perspectives. Sometimes we might start with a particular problem and search for solutions, but then turn around and ask whether there are any existing solutions that with some adjustment might already solve this problem.

It is not enough to know that you want to use a solution search or a problem search (or both). The issue in each case is where and how to look. In the case of solution searches, we've discussed WWCD and improved incentives. For problem searches, we find that the tools of translation and symmetry are particularly effective.

Where Else Would It Work?

Sometimes it isn't helpful to start the problem-solving process by identifying a problem. Sometimes the solution has to come first. Only after we've discovered a better way do we realize in retrospect that there was a problem to be solved.

For example, no one starts by saying, "Kids really need a scooter that spins more easily." Instead, they might say, "The polycarbonate wheel has revolutionized roller skates and rolling lug-

---

*Okay, few people will want the title Chief Ignorance Officer.

gage. Are there any other products that might be improved?" Voilà! The Razor scooter. When we translate ideas that have worked in one context and modify them to bring them to another, we discover a solution to a heretofore unnoticed problem. Our devil's advocate exercise in chapter 1 was an example of translation—taking a solution from one context and seeing if it might work in another.

Translation often requires adaptation—not just brute arbitrage, but arbitrage with a twist. The translated solution needs to be well translated or blended to fit the context and institutions of the new setting.

Let's try another example. Frequent air travelers enjoy expedited check-in lines and preboarding at most airlines. Are there any other businesses that might offer a similar benefit?

In *Leading the Revolution,* Gary Hamel suggests that frequent grocery shoppers might be given expedited checkout. (The present practice of giving special treatment only to those who buy ten items or less seems particularly backward in this light.)

Or take Avis, which rents cars twenty-four-hours a day, starting virtually any time of the day (or night). What other products could be made available at any time? Anyone who's landed in Europe on an overnight flight can answer this question: hotel rooms. You arrive at 7:00 A.M. and want to shower and change, but it's six hours until check-in time.

Not that round-the-clock room check-in wouldn't be complicated. Coordinating room cleaning would be more challenging. And reservations would have to include a check-in time to ensure that a room would be available. But restaurants do this routinely, so why not hotels? Some airport hotels have begun offering this service. We think that some city center hotels should follow suit, perhaps designating one floor for this service.

In short, the translation tool takes existing solutions and searches for new applications.

What Goes Around Comes Around.   Tom Coleman and Bill Schlotter, two postal delivery men, were inspired on Halloween night 1987. They saw a kid carrying one of those bright, green-glowing cyalume light sticks. What else could these light sticks be used for?

Have you considered glowing candy? If you mount a lollipop on top of one of these sticks, the light would shine through the candy, creating a weird and fun effect. (Is glow-in-the-dark bubble gum next?) Coleman and Schlotter sold their Glow Pop to Cap Candy. Their next innovation was an even bigger hit.

Licking a lollipop is so much work. To make that job easier, they developed the Spin Pop, a motorized lollipop holder that spins the candy around to make it ever so much easier to lick. (You might say this is a WWCD approach to the lollipop.)

Spin Pop was a wild success, the first hit candy holder since the Pez dispenser.[10] Over the next six years, 60 million of these gadgets were sold. Yet, John Osher, who headed Cap Candy, felt that the Spin Pop had not even hit its full potential. After Hasbro acquired Cap Candy, Osher left to look for new problems that the simple spinner motor might lick.

This is where the real story begins. What other question does the Spin Pop answer? To give you a hint, think big. Think a half-billion dollars big.

To help get you thinking, the illustration shows you what the device looks like in the patent application, number 5,209,692.[11] To the right is the original version of the product.

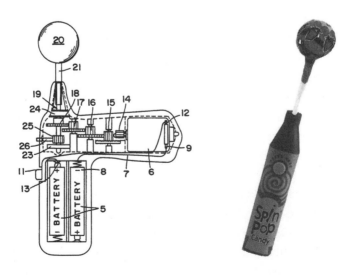

The entrepreneurial team led by John Osher had the answer. Now what was the question? *Business Week* described how the idea came about:

> *They can't remember who came up with the concept, but they know it came from their group walks through the aisles of their local Wal*Mart, where they went for inspiration. They saw that electric toothbrushes, from Sonicare to Interplak, cost more than $50 and for that reason held a fraction of the overall toothbrush market. They reasoned: Why not create a $5 electric brush using the Spin Pop technology?*[12]

The result was the Spinbrush, now the top-selling U.S. tooth-brush—and that includes the old-fashioned manual ones, too. In a little under four years, Osher and his team turned a $1.5 million investment into a $475 million payout when Procter & Gamble bought them out. Their success was based on finding the right problem that their existing answer had already solved.

The Airline Version of Movies.   A funny thing happened last summer when one of us (Ian) was flying to San Francisco. When the airline showed an edited version of *Shallow Hal,* Ian immediately thought of his son, Henry. For months, seven-year-old Henry had been pining to see the movie, first when it was in theaters and then when it came out on video. But Henry's prudish parents considered the movie a bit too crude for a seven-year-old.

It occurred to Ian that if he had bought Henry a ticket on this flight, he could finally have seen the airline version that had been, in the euphemistic phrase, "edited for content" so that the most problematic bits were cut. However, paying $350 for a round-trip ticket clearly was not a practical way to make Henry happy. Could someone translate the airline solution to the *Shallow Hal* problem to the ground?

There is a potentially big market for less explicit versions—and these versions are already being made for airlines and TV broad-cast. To our minds, the untapped demand for the less explicit air-line version suggests a business opportunity. And lo and behold, several entrepreneurs have started supplying this missing product.

Some of the entrepreneurs will sell you edited VHS versions of movies. For example, Edit My Movies (editmymovies.com) asks that you mail it a movie you already own. Then for twenty dollars per film and a four- to six-week wait, the company will send you a custom edit. CleanCut Cinema (cleancutcinemas.com) does the same thing, for twelve bucks. There's even an editing service, Cleanflicks.com, targeted to Mormons.

But these editing services have serious disadvantages. They're expensive, slow, and quite possibly illegal. The Hollywood studios have a right to control "derivative" products, and these edited versions may violate the copyright law.

An alternative approach is to facilitate the audiences' ability to edit the flick. And both Edit My Movies and CleanCut Cinema offer editing tools so that you can edit a VHS yourself. But what a hassle—that means you have to watch *Shallow Hal* twice so that you can watch it with your kid once! Ugh!

The most practical products facilitate different kinds of *automated* consumer editing. For example, TV Guardian (TVGuardian.com) screens the closed-captioned information for objectionable words and mutes the audio at appropriate moments. The product edits the actual closed-captioning, deleting objectionable words and substituting family-friendly content. This set-top box costs $130 (or $30 less if you're already a supporter of the Al Menconi Ministries). But this system, to be effective, has to be overly broad in its muting because closed-captioned information does not accurately pinpoint when an objectionable word is being spoken.

ClearPlay (clearplay.com) has developed the most sophisticated product on the market. The product takes advantage of the ability of DVDs to automatically skip ahead. ClearPlay members (for ten dollars per month) gain access to a library of ClearPlay Guides—instructions that tell the DVD software to skip the particular scenes or parts of scenes that contribute to a film's PG-13 or R rating. The library contains several hundred guides for current releases and older films.

Voilà! With ClearPlay, your kids can watch the airline version of *Shallow Hal,* and you don't have to book a cross-country flight. The only problems are that the ClearPlay Guides still might violate the copyright law (picky-picky), and it's still a bit expensive.

All these editing products are great translations of the airline movie. But there's an even better translation that has yet to happen.

Who is best suited to provide the ClearPlay product? It's not Delta Airlines, the Mormon Church, or, for that matter, ClearPlay. It's the Hollywood studios themselves. While we can understand why Hollywood did not offer expurgated VHS versions of its films, there is no reason why DVDs can't be programmed to offer the airline version if the viewer so desires.

DVDs today regularly offer different languages, and it would be child's play to program the DVD to omit parts of scenes or substitute particular words. Indeed, the DVD could offer a flexible filter that allowed parents to omit more or less material, depending on whether they were more put off by violence or sex (but just offering the airline version would solve 90 percent of the problem).

Hollywood would be doing itself a favor by expanding the market for its product. There would be no question of illegality. And consumers would get the ClearPlay service for a lower price.*

Would Flipping It Work?

The opposite of a correct statement is a false statement. The opposite of a profound truth may well be another profound truth.

—Niels Bohr

Sometimes flipping things around provides a powerful new solution. Even if it's not a better solution for the problem at hand, it may well offer a useful solution to a different problem. Think of symmetry as translation with a twist. It takes an existing solution in a given context and turns it around to get a new perspective.

Take pricing, for example. The standard way of doing business is to have the seller state the price. Airlines advertise their price, and you, the customer, can take it or leave it. But is there another

---

*By the way, we might also have reached the edited-DVD solution by asking WWCD. For example, Howard Hughes would pay for someone to edit the movie—this would have been particularly easy during the time that he owned RKO studios.

way of doing business? Jay Walker's Priceline.com made a big splash by turning the tables on pricing. Instead of having airlines offer prices that customers might accept, Walker set up a system in which the consumers offered prices that airlines might accept. This is a pure example of symmetry.

Let's try a few simple symmetry exercises. As you will see, the hardest aspect of the symmetry tool is having the courage to turn something around. The other way of doing something often seems so foolish that you censor yourself before you even start.

For example, recall our family-friendly version of DVDs that came from the airline or television translation. We could also have arrived at this idea using symmetry. One of the advantages of a DVD is that it typically comes with more material than was shown in the theater or on the video. There is the director's cut, often with extra scenes and more explicit violence or sex.

Let's try turning this around. Instead of providing more material, could the DVDs provide less? At first blush, this doesn't make any sense. Why would anyone want less? But instead of giving us the more explicit extra scenes of violence and sex, what about giving us an option to have these scenes cut a bit to make the movie more suitable for teens? And by providing this service, studios might even make the family-value hawks in Congress a bit happier.

Volunteering Not to Answer.   Everyone knows that when a teacher asks a question, students signal that they want to answer by raising their hands. What would it mean to flip this around?

Well, of course, it would mean that students who raised their hand *don't* want to answer. Just because you can flip something around doesn't mean that you would want to. In this case, it seems

Black Socks with Sandals

Hundreds of fashion magazines give advice on what to wear. In the U.K., Tinny Woodall and Susannah Constantine created a smashing BBC show and best-selling book with their essential guide, *What Not to Wear*.

pretty ridiculous to have students who don't want to answer raising their hands in the class.

But wait a minute. Changing the meaning of hand-raising could offer some distinct pedagogical advantages. Isn't it better to force the students who aren't prepared to go to the trouble and embarrassment of raising their hands? Maybe, maybe not. The point is that it's a closer horse race than you might think. As an experiment, Ian tried flipping the meaning of raising your hand and found that it improved the quality of class participation—particularly among shy students.

This is a classic solution in search of a problem. We start with an existing solution (raising your hand to answer a question), flip its meaning, and then ask whether it can work even better or work in a different context. In this case, it turns out that flipping the meaning of silence increases class participation. It's harder to be labeled uncool for just sitting there.

Although professors know all too well that raising your hand can be deemed uncool, the impetus for the idea was not initially to solve this problem. It was instead to simply do the thought experiment of flipping the default meaning of silence and to try to imagine what would happen.

You probably remember the old joke about the soldiers who are asked to step forward if they want to volunteer for a dangerous mission. But just like Ian's class, the joke's punch line uses symmetry to flip the meaning of inaction—because what happens is the soldiers who do not wish to volunteer take a step backward.

Video Rentals.   Let's keep flipping, but in a very different context. Is there any aspect of video rentals that could be flipped around? Well, having the customers rent to the stores doesn't make much sense.[13] What about the "onerous" task of rewinding? Everyone knows that polite renters should rewind their videotapes before they return them. And most rental stores try to enforce this norm with "Please Be Kind and Rewind" stickers and the threat of rewind charges.

But what would happen if we flipped around the norm and asked people to rewind at the beginning instead of the end of their rental? The downside is that renters would have to endure a bit of delayed gratification while waiting for the movie to rewind before watching. But the upside is that the task suddenly becomes *impossible to shirk*. You can't watch the movie unless you do your duty and rewind it. By simply flipping around the norm, video stores would avoid the hassle of enforcing the current norm. We guessed that somewhere a video store would have figured this out. Sure enough, Star Video in Berkeley has the initial-rewind policy in place.

Now, by the way, is a good time to put on your translation hats. Can you think of any other annoying tasks that might be better done *before* instead of *after*?

As teachers, we immediately think about the idea of cleaning the chalkboard. Although some professors insist on erasing their work at the end of class, others forget or shirk. But again, if we flipped the norm, there would be no way to shirk, because you couldn't teach *Hamlet* without erasing the prior class's accounting notes.

Interestingly, there is one arena in which this do-it-beforehand idea is firmly in place—the Laundromat. The Laundromats could, of course, ask their patrons to "please be kind and clean the screen after you use the dryer," but most lint screens say "please clean *before* each use"—not after. Again, the "before" norm eliminates the possibility of shirking.

These examples so far illustrate a common element of symmetry. In each case, we are changing the default—the meaning of silence or inaction. By default, we don't mean not paying your mortgage. We mean the preset condition that will prevail if you take no action, such as your word processor's default one-inch left-hand margin, which you must actively change if you want something else.

As we look around, we see many cases in which the default could go either way. Sometimes we will argue that one default option works much better than the other—and that the existing legal default gets it backward. Those of you who aren't lawyers may be surprised to learn that laws are not all about forcing choices for people. It isn't "you must do this and you can't do that." Rather, many laws are just about establishing what rules obtain if people fail to "opt out."

Trespassing in the Woods

Existing default: Allowed unless property is posted with "No Trespassing" sign

Opposite default: No trespassing unless explicitly permitted

Right Turn on Red

Existing default: Allowed except where posted "No Right Turn on Red"

Opposite default: Prohibited except where explicitly permitted   ·

Organ Donation

Existing default: Not permitted unless prior consent has been given

Opposite default: Permitted unless prior denial has been given

Contributions to a 401(k) Plan

Existing default: No contribution unless you opt in

Opposite default: Automatic contribution unless you opt out

One aspect of the symmetry tool is to learn to look for defaults in business (video rewind), law (trespassing), and everyday life ("regrets only"), and to ask whether flipping the default makes better sense.

It's More or Less Symmetrical. While experimenting with the default option is an example of symmetry, it is just one of many ways to employ this tool. Thinking about how to do things the other way around is a way to look for new business opportunities.

Consider, for example, one of the great innovations of the 1970s: the automated teller machine (ATM). Banks cooperate with each other through the ATM network to allow their customers to withdraw money from each other's banks. The result is a great cost saving for banks, as they need not duplicate all of each other's branches. Great idea, but to see what's missing, put on the symmetry hat.

What's missing is the deposit side of the ATM idea. Why can't a customer make a deposit to any bank from any other bank? In the U.K. and Australia, a person can go to a teller inside any bank and make a deposit to any other bank. But to our knowledge, no ATM system will allow cross-bank deposits. For example, a Citibank customer cannot make deposits to her account from a Chase machine.

To be symmetric about symmetry, we should also recognize that *less* symmetric solutions can dominate the symmetrical one. Thus,

"Why not?" symmetry

in some cases, the trick is to break the symmetry. The one-way toll is the classic example. It's better to pay in only one direction.

Right turn on red is another asymmetry. Left turn on red doesn't work as well, because you would be forced to cross traffic. Ah, but this suggests that left turn on red onto a one-way street would also be a good idea. Here again, California led the way.[14]

The Right Tool for the Right Job

The renowned economist Joseph Schumpeter long ago recognized that it was possible to automate the process of innovation. So stepping back, we have now introduced our four central idea-generating tools: WWCD, internalization, translation, and symmetry. But we're not satisfied with simply giving you a passing (and passive) acquaintance with these techniques. The next four chapters will push you to actively apply these ideas to new settings.

Now, you might be asking, are these the only tools out there for generating ideas? The answer is clearly no. There are rich theories of how scientific discoveries play out over time—incrementally adding to our knowledge through systematic and painstaking experimentation. But our why-not tools are geared toward discovering solutions that in a sense already exist but have just not been put into effect.

Edison famously said that genius is 99 percent perspiration and 1 percent inspiration. For a certain type of discovery, he is clearly right. But there is another mode of discovery in which inspiration and attitude are a much more dominant force. We're focused on finding the great ideas (like the one-way toll both) that are just waiting to happen. We do not claim that this is the exclusive set of techniques for routinizing ingenuity, and we are not trying to solve all problems. Some solutions may require painstaking experimentation, while others may require a *eureka!* inspiration. Our central claim is merely that mastering these four techniques by themselves will help you develop a mind-set that can generate new ideas to solve real-world problems.

Instead of asking whether we need to study more tools, how about asking whether we really need to use all four? (Symmetry, oh symmetry.) The answer is yes. You need to learn different tools because some solutions can best be found with particular tools.

The path to some ideas only follows by applying particular rules. The symmetry tool applied to auctions easily produces the Priceline idea (so easily that we wonder whether it was sufficiently nonobvious to deserve a patent). But it would be harder to use the WWCD tool or translation to see the possibility of a market driven by customer offers.

Keep in mind that you can sometimes generate the same why-not from multiple directions. For example, we could have come up with the Virgin One account either by asking WWCD or by looking to break symmetries. We told the story as a way of sweeping your money between savings and mortgage accounts so that the automation component was emphasized. But the idea can also come from the symmetry concept of de-prepaying your mortgage. At present, people can pay their mortgage more quickly than required. Turning this around, why can't they also take the option of paying it more slowly? A half step in this direction is to let them undo any prior speed-ups.

Of course, you can generate great ideas without consciously applying any of these tools. Sometimes innovators implicitly or intuitively apply the technique so that it seems as though the idea just comes to them. We hope to convince you that actively asking simple questions—like Would flipping it work? or What would Croesus do?—can make it easier to dream of things that never were.

You've now seen a basic introduction to our four questions. The next four chapters will provide more systematic training in how to use them. We'll walk you through step-by-step exercises on how to use each tool. We'll test you with puzzlers that force you to apply the tools yourself. And we'll reinforce what you've learned with short case studies of the tools in practice. By the time you're finished, asking these questions should be second nature to you.

Problems
in Search
of Solutions

3

What Would
Croesus Do?

Taking the Perspective of an
Unconstrained Consumer

An easy way to solve a problem is to have someone else solve it first. You just have to find that person.

Customers are a regular source of solutions. Businesses watch their customers to see how they use and misuse products. In particular, looking at the way customers misuse a product can suggest a new problem along with a solution.

For example, spray-on cooking oils, such as PAM, were designed to prevent food from sticking to a pan. Apparently some customers were also using the spray on the bottom of lawn mowers—to prevent the cut grass from sticking to the blades and bottom of the mower.[1] Thus we have a new problem (sticky lawn mower blades) along with a solution (spray-on oil). Improving the improvised solution is easy; the spray doesn't need to be virgin olive oil or even oil fit for human consumption.

The point of this approach is to have the customer provide you with both an unrecognized problem and an accompanying solution. The easiest way to solve a problem is to take someone's existing but ad hoc solution and regularize it. Why try to come up with an original idea when someone else has already done the hard work for you?

Although watching customers offers valuable, even invaluable, insights, it isn't the whole game. There are many solutions you'd miss if that's all you did. You might have watched the wrong customer. Or the typical customer might not find it worthwhile or even possible to solve the problem on his or her own.

Thus we want to suggest an approach to watching customers that is less expensive and more expansive: Watch what a *hypothetical* customer would do. Since the customer is imaginary, this approach brings the costs way down. To encourage expansive thinking, we give our hypothetical customer extremely large resources—if there is a solution to the problem, this person can find it. In short, we ask, What would Croesus do?

Getting Started

Croesus is our stand-in for an individual with nearly unlimited resources. Just to be clear, we don't suggest actually asking Bill Gates or some other superwealthy individual. We ask our imaginary Croesus. Our hypothetical Croesus is richer and smarter than the real one. By asking this question, we too become smarter and richer.

This process reminds us of a scene in *Heist,* an otherwise just okay movie. Gene Hackman is playing the mastermind thief who is always one step ahead of everyone else. When his girlfriend asks him how he is so clever, he replies, "I'm not that smart, I just think about what a person smarter than me would do."

That's the idea. The first step is to think about what a person with vast resources—connections, money, or time—would do to solve the problem.

When you come up with an answer, you're not done. You know that a solution exists—the problem with Croesus's answer is that it will be too expensive to be practical. Turning the Croesus solution into something practical still requires a good deal of effort. Is there a way to automate or standardize the custom solution? Who could play the role of a personal assistant? To make the Croesus solution practical, we look for what we could call the 99/1 rule. (Normally, it's an 80/20 rule, but with Croesus, the costs are so high that you aim for 99 percent of the benefits for 1 percent of the cost.)

The Unwanted Call Redux

Let's revisit the nighttime wrong-number problem using this approach. We asked a group of executives how Donald Trump would prevent being disturbed at night by a wrong number. The immediate answer was that he'd have someone to answer his phone twenty-four hours a day. If the call were a wrong number or a fax machine, his assistant, not he, would deal with the problem. This is the first step of WWCD—simply answering the question, What would Croesus do?

The second step is then to think of ways to make this solution more affordable. How could we standardize or automate the services of a personal assistant? Well, instead of having your own personal assistant on call to answer your phone, calls could be directed to an answering service. Most doctors use this approach, but it's still too expensive to be a general solution.

What we need to find is a truly inexpensive way to do that screening. Anything involving a third party is likely to be too expensive.

Could the screening be done by a machine? One option is to create a list of approved numbers that would be able to get through. While this solves most of the problem, it would be a good deal of work to compile a list of approved numbers. You would always worry that the list would be incomplete. And even if the person were on the approved list, you still might prefer that he or she not disturb you late in the evening.

An alternative to the approved list is the use of a code. Preferred callers could be given a code to input to get the phone to ring through. But making phone calls could get a bit complicated when every phone number also has a code.

Think for a moment about these two machine-screening approaches. The approved-number list creates a screen at the receiving end, whereas the code pushes the screen out to the caller. The caller has the advantage of being smarter than a machine. Make the code something obvious, like "0." If we just give the caller the right information, the person can use discretion. Thus we return to the message:

You've reached the Trumps. We're home but don't wish to be disturbed right now. If this is an emergency, you can hit "0" and our phone will ring. But it had better be good.

The first part of the message prevents wrong numbers. The second part allows the caller to self-screen.[2] Perhaps the irony of this solution is that, while it would be 99 percent effective for most of us, it wouldn't work very well work for the Trumps. (This solution would also work for cell phones, especially in New York City, where an ordinance prohibits cell phone calls during public performances except for emergencies.)

We've revisited the telephone example in some detail as it helps illustrate the WWCD solution process. Asking WWCD pushes you to think expansively. Oftentimes people just try to solve the specific problem at hand—the current wrong number—rather than the larger problem.

One reason why WWCD works is that, for many types of problems, it just isn't worth it for a single individual to solve the larger problem. The cost of one person's developing the solution is too great compared to the potential benefits. That's why you won't get the answer by watching customers, as it isn't in any one customer's interest to find an answer. But our imaginary King Croesus would.

Some solutions can't be found if you focus on how customers behave. That's because the solution may require changing someone else's behavior. Seeing that customers unplug their phones or turn the ringer down reveals the problem, but not the solution of getting *callers* to behave differently. Customers are only one part of the puzzle. WWCD encourages you to look at the whole picture.

As we will discuss later, there is another, perhaps psychological, benefit of the Croesus approach. Simply knowing that a solution exists is helpful in giving you confidence to explore alternatives. While it is easy to give up and say that it can't be done, putting yourself in the King Croesus position makes it easier to imagine that a solution can be found. Adapting, modifying, standardizing, and automating a WWCD answer is often easier than coming up with the solution from scratch.

What would Clint do?

WWCD Puzzler: Refinancing Your Mortgage

How many refinance solicitations did you receive when interest rates last dropped? Borrowers with a fixed-rate mortgage have to pay attention to the market and decide over and over whether refinancing is worthwhile. Inertia causes most people to wait too long. When they do refinance, they still must pay for title insurance, appraisals, and legal fees. Even without points, transaction costs for a $400,000 mortgage refinancing typically exceed $2,000:

Appraisal	$180
Flood certification	$28
Underwriting	$150
Tax/service fee	$86
Processing fee	$250
Title bringdown	$50
Attorney's fee	$650
Record and bringdown	$120
Title insurance	$753
Total	**$2,267**

Add to that the borrower's and the bank's wasted time.

If refinancing mortgages is a problem for you, imagine the problem it is for someone with hundreds of properties, say, Donald Trump. Our educated guess is that Trump hires someone to take care of it for him.

Whom could we hire to get most of the benefit at a much-reduced cost? We asked a similar question with the phone-call screening. We first look to see if the process can be automated. Here, the answer is yes, but who should be in charge of that automation? The bank issued you the mortgage. The advantage of the bank's taking care of all this is that it already has all the information needed to make the right decision. It can automate the decision for you and all its customers.

Does the automation need to be perfect? We doubt it. Thus, a bank that followed a simple rule of thumb would be good enough: Refinance if the rate falls by 1 percent.[3]

There you have it. *Why not have a fixed-rate mortgage that automatically refinances if interest rates fall?* With these downward-adjustable mortgages, you could stop worrying about refinancing.

A natural industry response to this proposal is "Intriguing idea, but we can't make money doing it!" Automatic refinancing sounds great for consumers, but not so great for a bank that might offer it. Because of the current transaction costs and consumer inertia, many borrowers fail to refinance when interest rates drop. Lenders would be hurt by an automatic refinancing option if the new mortgage cannibalizes the potential profits that can be earned from lazy consumers.

The idea is *not* to transfer money from lenders to borrowers. If something is better for consumers, then they will be willing to pay more for it. This payment could come in one of two ways. The borrower could pay extra points up front to reflect the expected future savings in interest. Or, better yet, the extra payments could be made at the time the mortgage rate gets adjusted. For example, the interest rate would be automatically readjusted whenever rates fall by 1 percent, and the consumer would be charged half of the typical transaction costs. That way the bank and the consumer split the savings (and wouldn't have to guess in advance what the right up-front fee is).

Even the concern that banks lose money when people refinance isn't quite right, or at least it doesn't work the way most people might think. Typically, banks sell their mortgages after issuing them, so they don't lose any money if the home owner refinances. But many banks continue to service the mortgages in their portfolio, earning a stream of some thirty dollars a month. If the customer refinances elsewhere, that income stream would disappear.

Who loses? Mortgage brokers, lawyers, title insurers, and appraisers. Essentially anyone who profits from churn does worse under this scheme. Consumers win, not by paying lower interest rates, but by getting the same average reduction that they otherwise would have gotten, without having to pay the third-party fees and by never having to think again about refinancing. The bank wins by preserving its relationship with the borrower, by having a more predictable book of business, and by having an innovative product on the market.

Jim Riley, CEO of City Line Mortgage, understands these issues perfectly and makes sure his customers never have an incentive to leave his bank. He has come close to automating the refinance process for his customers. For the cost of title insurance and half the usual escrow fee, he arranges everything. In two days, all the paperwork is complete and you have a new mortgage. If rates have fallen and you haven't refinanced, he's likely to call you to remind you. In effect, Jim has become his own mortgage broker, and he no longer loses customers.

The next step is to save Riley even more paperwork. There is no reason why title insurers and others need to collect their toll. As City Line grows and others copy it—Countrywide already has— someone will create the mortgage that simply adjusts downward without needing to be refinanced. We discuss how to implement this idea in chapter 10.

The Supplier as Your Personal Assistant

The idea of having the supplier figure out the best course of action for its customers—playing the personal assistant role for you— makes a good deal of sense in many circumstances.

Tired of choosing which cell phone calling plan is best for you? The choices are confusing (even for Ph.D. economists). A typical plan will advertise 300 prime-time minutes for $29.95 a month plus 1,000 minutes evenings and weekends. While it seems as though the cost is less than 10 cents a minute, it never works out that way. Minutes above 300 are charged at 35 cents each, and unused minutes are lost forever.[4] A quick simulation with a 30 percent month-by-month variation shows that the real cost is closer to 25 cents per minute—and that's if you pick just the right plan.

Why make the choice? Let someone else figure this out for you. In particular, let the cell phone company figure this out. At the end of the year, the company could look back at your calling pattern and pick the plan that would have been best for you.

Never happen? This is done today in Germany for electricity. Customers are *retroactively* put in the plan that would have been the cheapest, given their usage. This system also provides a reward for loyalty; if you leave before the end of the year, you aren't retroactively placed into the best plan.

In some circumstances, the supplier isn't in the best position to be your personal assistant. For example, which long-distance carrier should you pick? Here, you could give your phone business to a third party whose job it is to pick the best plan for you.

Going one step further, why pick the best plan on a monthly basis? Why not pick the best deal on a call-by-call basis? Some businesses do this today using what is called *least-cost routing*. Essentially, each phone call is put out to bid, and whoever will carry the call for the lowest price gets the business. Although one call might go over AT&T and another would be carried by Sprint, you would still get a single, aggregated bill.

Pursuing this approach has a further benefit for consumers. Today, when Sprint lowers its rates, it has to spend money to advertise. Sprint doesn't expect to get the entire market, even if it has the cheapest price. With least-cost routing in place, if Sprint has the lowest price, it gets all the calls without having to advertise. This arrangement gives Sprint (and its rivals) a great incentive to offer a lower price. Consumers clearly win. Even the long-distance carriers can do okay, as they can save a good deal of the costs associated with marketing and customer acquisition.

Home Equity Protection

For most Americans, stocks are not their largest investment—their home is. Owning a home is a lot riskier than you might think. Between 1985 and 2000, nearly 10 percent of American home owners lived in a region in which home prices declined during the time they lived there. Nearly two-thirds of the states suffered at least one five-year period between 1980 and 1999 during which typical home owners would have lost money on their house.[5]

The downside risk is compounded by the large leverage created by home mortgages. Individuals often purchase a house borrowing 95—even 97—percent of the purchase price.[6] When housing prices rise, this leads to a large accumulation of wealth. But when prices fall, even by small amounts, home owners lose all their equity.

Leverage is the key to making a lot of money—and to losing a lot of money. That's one reason that Donald Trump has at various times made so much money and then lost so much.

For a concrete example, imagine that you buy a $400,000 home with $20,000 down and a $380,000 mortgage. If the value of your home rises by 10 percent, you'll make $40,000 on a $20,000 investment. You've tripled your money! But if your house price *falls* by 10 percent, then you have a $380,000 mortgage on a $360,000 house. Not only have you lost your entire down payment, you're $20,000 in the hole. At this point, you probably can't afford to move. There's no money for a down payment on a new house, and now you need to come up with $20,000 to cover the losses on your current house. And that's all without taking account of real estate broker commissions.

The point of this example is not to scare you into renting for the rest of your life. And we certainly don't want to discourage home ownership by requiring larger down payments. Rather, our aim is to identify a problem to see if it can be solved. Much of U.S. housing policy has focused on helping Americans own their own home, but relatively little has focused on helping protect them against the risk that home ownership entails.

The American Dream is to keep the upside potential that comes with home ownership. Can we do that while protecting ourselves from the downside?

What would a Howard Hughes or Donald Trump do in this situation? Our guess is that he'd call Lloyds of London to get insurance protection against a fall in the value of his property. Perhaps Goldman Sachs would securitize future rents, thereby offering some downside protection.

It's not just Hughes or Trump who shy away from these risks. Even banks don't take them. If you want to take out a mortgage with a 90—or 95—percent loan-to-value ratio (a $360,000 mortgage on a $400,000 house), the bank will require you to take out private mortgage insurance (PMI). That way, if you default on your mortgage and the bank has to foreclose, the PMI provider is mostly on the hook for any losses.[7]

So, if banks aren't willing to take this risk, why should you?

If you are like most of our readers, you have protection against health care costs, a car accident, or the theft of your possessions. But your single largest asset is woefully undiversified, highly leveraged, and unprotected. Your house is protected against fire and theft but not against a declining real estate market. *Why not?*

At this point, you might be wondering if this is another one of those idealist why-nots. Perhaps it is, but home equity protection is also a reality. A group of idealist professors (including one of your authors) and city planners from Neighborhood Reinvestment took this concept from the why-not stage to reality.

In the preface, we described how Deborah Woods was the first person ever to purchase protection against a market decline in her home equity. Woods had grown up in Syracuse and wanted to move back. The prices were certainly appealing. In 2002, she found a four-bedroom house with a detached garage, a nice lawn, and a corner lot on a quiet street for an amount safely under $80,000. We are not making this up.

At that price, what could possibly have held her back? She was worried about losing money: "It was a very serious concern. Friends and family were encouraging me to purchase out of the city because of that reason. But I had such a liking to the area, had grown up there, that I just felt such an allegiance. That's where I wanted to purchase, and then it just kind of all fell into place."

Her fear was not unfounded. Over most of the 1990s, more than 35 percent of those selling their homes in Syracuse lost money. And this is without taking transaction costs into account.

In the early 1990s, Deborah's house could have sold for $100,000. What if her $80,000 home became a $60,000 home? She would be wiped out.

Deborah is not alone in this fear. Market research conducted by Eric Mower and Associates showed that the investment potential has become the number one consideration for home buyers, even outranking schools. Among low-income buyers, fear is the main factor leading people to rent rather than buy.

That's one of the reasons that supply and demand doesn't work quite right with the housing market. Normally, if prices fall, demand goes up. But with housing, if you see prices fall, you get worried that you might be about to catch a falling knife. So a decline in price can actually lead to a fall in demand and further price declines. The result is a vicious circle.

But insurance companies don't want to sell you insurance based on your home's value, because too much of the value is under your control. The house could fall in value because the economy went south (which is the protection we want to offer), but it could also fall because you didn't maintain the house. Or, you might not work so hard to get the full value of the house in the market if you knew that all losses would be covered. While some of these issues can be solved through appraisals and maintenance contracts, the administrative cost and likely lawsuits could make the product cumbersome and unaffordable.

Fortunately, there is an approach that avoids these problems. Instead of getting insurance on your specific house, you could get insurance based on the average value of other houses in your neighborhood.[8] Thus, if house prices fall by 10 percent in your zip code, you can make a claim on 10 percent of your purchase price. The advantage to this approach is that it is clean and simple. You have every incentive to make your home worth as much as possible. If you sell your home for an extra dollar, you get to keep that dollar.

Pei Lin Huang, the Prudential First Properties Realtor who sold the house to Woods, explained: "It doesn't protect you if you don't take care of your property, and, therefore, you sell it at a loss. . . . It is just to protect you and insulate you from market conditions which you have no control over."

The only problem with getting insurance based on the zip code index is that it may not give you perfect coverage. Your house could go down in value while other houses appreciate, and the result is that you get no insurance coverage. On the other hand, you could fix up your house and have it go up in value while the neighborhood declines and then make money on both ends.

Although index-based coverage is a potential problem in theory, we can turn to the data to figure out how big a problem this is in practice. Data from New England housing markets suggest that index-based coverage will cover between one-half and two-thirds of the losses.

There is the old line that perfection is the enemy of good. Solving half the problem in a cost-effective manner is a lot better than doing nothing about it and waiting for a silver bullet. And, to the extent that the coverage is incomplete, the cost of the insurance is also lower. Nor would we ever expect to hit 100 percent protection. Some people won't maintain their homes, and the lower-than-average selling price of their homes is their own fault.

Because home equity insurance helps stabilize housing prices, it can break the self-perpetuating cycle of lower prices and falling demand. Huang explained it this way: "I am very excited at this program . . . more so for the ripple effect it will have on home values in the area, and the incentive it gives home owners to fix their houses. The ultimate result will be sustained home values, if not appreciation."

What makes this protection different from almost all other types of insurance is that its very existence reduces the risk of what is being protected. The Home Equity Protection program will increase demand and in so doing reduce the chance of the insurer's having to make a payout.

Day one was Deborah's. Since then, the phone's been ringing at Equity Headquarters. A retired couple whose savings are all tied up in their house was about to move out of town, but with this protection plan, the couple is now content to stay put.

The price is quite affordable. A onetime 1.5 percent premium is enough to cover expected losses and even provide a modest return on capital. That's a *onetime* 1.5 percent payment. Even those who don't buy the coverage are less intimidated by the risk of falling real estate prices. Home owners can better quantify the risk when they see that the insurance only costs 1.5 percent, or $900 for the typical house in Syracuse.

For now, the protection is being sold by Equity Headquarters, a local nonprofit affiliate of Neighborhood Reinvestment.[9] The program in Syracuse got its start with support from Congressman James Walsh and seed capital from the Department of Housing and Urban Development (HUD). The economics of this protection work better with more diversification, both across localities and across time. The goal is to make it available nationwide.[10]

Who knows? When the product comes to New York City, perhaps Trump will be one of our customers.

CASE STUDY

iPing

Some of us have been known to forget what we are supposed to do on Monday morning. True to the reputation of an absent-minded professor, one of us actually forgot to give a final exam in a course!*

---

*Apparently, this had never happened before in Princeton's 250-year history. The dean decided that all the students were to be given an A on the missed exam. And that absent-minded professor is now teaching at Yale.

We'd bet that Bill Gates doesn't have that problem. It's not just his sharp mind for details. He has a personal assistant to remind him of his engagements. As with late-night call screening, the personal assistant is a bit too pricey for the rest of us. One solution is to automate the reminder. The Palm handheld does a pretty good job of that. But it isn't so easy to leave a detailed message. And not everyone has a Palm. Is there a person who could do the job for us at a reasonable price?

Again, we could imagine a service that, instead of answering calls, makes reminder calls. The phone is still the best place to get a reminder, but who should be making that call? Who else could be your personal assistant?

Why not be your own personal assistant? Have you ever sent yourself a voice mail? As a way of reminding ourselves, we have been known to send ourselves a voice mail on Friday and then listen to it come Monday morning—assuming we remember to check. Aye, there's the rub. If you forget to check your message on Monday morning, you're out of luck (believe us, we know).

Why not send the voice mail on Friday afternoon for *delivery* on Monday morning? The phone would be set to ring at 8:00 A.M. It could be your alarm clock. You'd pick up the phone to hear yourself say:

Hey, handsome! Get out of bed. You have a meeting with the dean at nine. Don't be late.

What we've proposed here is to translate the Palm's alarm reminder feature to the telephone. The phone makes it easy to leave a message. In fact, you could set up a yearly voice mail reminder for anniversaries, birthdays, and the like.

This product already exists for e-mail. Hallmark uses it as a way to help sell greeting cards. You arrange to send yourself reminder e-mails about birthdays, anniversaries, and other special occasions, and the reminder comes in time for you to still send a card that shows you care. But what about the voice mail version?[11]

People often respond to a why-not idea with "Well, if that's so smart, why hasn't it been done?" As we discussed in chapter 1, there are many responses to this question. One is that the idea *is* being done, often by an entrepreneur.

The story of Darryl Shepherd and iPing is a good example of the challenges and opportunities in bringing a why-not idea to the marketplace. Shepherd is the founder of iPing, a company that provides a telephone service similar to the delayed voice mail just proposed. For example, iPing offers you customized wake-up calls or phone-call reminders to take your medicine.

Shepherd got into this business through one of those hard-to-explain paths of fate. A former college basketball and track star with a degree in information science, he signed with the Atlanta Falcons, but an injury ended that career. His interest in music led him to try his hand as an artist and record producer. (You can hear his keyboard work on the soundtrack to Spike Lee's *Do the Right Thing*.) But the music business proved no less bruising than football, and he decided to go back to information science. Working first at Standard & Poor's and then Citibank, Shepherd was perfectly positioned to start out on his own when the Internet mania hit.

He raised a little more than a million dollars in an initial round led by Grand Central Holdings to start a phone service called Mr. Distance. The idea of this company was to provide advertiser-supported long-distance services. Subscribers would get to make free long-distance calls, but their calls would be interrupted every minute or so and the user would be required to listen to an ad before the call could continue. It's not a crazy idea. But the type of person willing to put up with the constant interruptions to avoid paying for long-distance calls might not represent the advertisers' ideal demographic—except for teenagers, who are the target audience for many companies and are cheap enough to want to use this service.

As the company was developing the software for this product, Shepherd was annoyed by the high fees he was paying to use a 900-number wake-up call service. It was charging him $2.50 a call. With a little bit of tinkering, he found a way to program a server to do this for himself. As so often happens, the investors were more interested in the wake-up call (Mr. Wake-Up) service than in Mr. Distance.

The wake-up call service started out as a bare-bones product, but over time, different features were added: horoscopes, headline news, and jokes. Then, the idea of a wake-up call was extended to a reminder call, simply a wake-up scheduled for another time of the day. Now the call would come with a message, such as "Have you taken your medicine?" What's more, you could record your own message to be played back to you at a later time, or you could send it via e-mail and have the company's text-to-voice service read it to you over the phone. Thus, on Friday you could leave yourself a message to be delivered on Monday morning reminding yourself of what you have to do.

You could use the voice mail reminder service to invite people to a party. A message that you recorded would be more personal than an e-mail, and the ability for people to RVSP right away by hitting "1" for yes and "2" for no would likely increase the response rate. Business meetings could also be scheduled this way.

At one point, 1 million customers had tried the service and 250,000 were regular users. The company had a $35 million valuation when Arden Capital led a $4 million investment round. However, there was an underlying problem. The service was free, and advertising revenue (there was a short ad on the call) was not enough to support the costs. The company was sold to eCal.com, a Web-based scheduling company that was planning to do an initial public offering (IPO). But the market was shut down before the company could go public. Forced to scale back, eCal.com sold this messaging business to Net2Phone, then a leading player in Internet telephony. But the business didn't really fit, and Net2Phone decided to put it back up for sale—at which point Shepherd bought it back and came full circle.

Since venture capital had dried up, he knew that this couldn't be a free service. The question was, how many customers would stay on if they had to pay? The basic service, $5.95 for thirty reminder calls per month, allowed the company to keep about 8 percent of its 250,000 regular users, and the business is building back up.

The success of iPing is a remarkable indictment of the phone companies. Shepherd's creation of these services by working around the phone companies' systems and the demonstrated demand for

"Take a Letter, Ma Bell"

Some automated services will read your e-mail to you over the phone. This is plenty handy, but what about the other way around? Why not speak into your phone and have voice-recognition technology deliver an e-mail transcription to your computer? You could use the phone as a dictation or memo device and even get a written transcript of any call (though not without notifying the other party). You could also have the option of getting voice mails transcribed—reading them is much quicker than listening, and there would be no need to replay the message to catch the phone number.

PC-based voice-recognition programs such as IBM's Via Voice and Dragon's Naturally Speaking already exist. Sure, laptops are handy, but phones are handier. And phone companies have access to the most sophisticated voice-recognition technology, as evidenced by their success using it with directory assistance. Imagine how much better it could be if you could train the phone system on your voice. You would dial in to the special number, enter your access code, and dictate away.[12] In seconds, an e-mail would be sent to you with a transcript and a parallel recording to clarify misunderstood words (clicking on a word would get you the relevant sound bite).

them says that the phone companies should have done this themselves years ago. For the phone companies, billing would also be much easier. It could go right on your phone bill and be charged at twenty cents per call.

Again, we see the distance between a good idea and a good business. In our mind, there is no doubt that delayed voice mail is a good idea. In fact, for the incumbent phone company, it would seem to be a no-brainer. If there were ever any doubt about that, the quarter million regular users of iPing would be pretty good proof. Remember, this is a business with almost no advertising and no established brand.

The consumer market is not necessarily the right first step. A company called Televox has developed a similar product that doctors use to remind patients of their upcoming appointments. In this case, a computer-generated message calls the patient's contact information, tells the person the appointment time, and asks the patient to hit "1" to confirm.

Even if iPing starts to succeed, what will make the business sustainable? Eventually, the phone companies will wake up. What happens then? This is a key question for which wishful thinking isn't enough.

One view is that the incumbents are too slow and too hidebound to ever keep up with Shepherd. While the phone companies have done a remarkable job so far of demonstrating just that, this is a dangerous assumption on which to support a business. That's what has us worried about the future of iPing. It is possible that a phone company will try to buy iPing rather than reproduce what it

Electronic Receptionists

Callwave and Pagoo are two promising examples for iPing to follow. These start-ups provide a WWCD solution to the busy signal. For voice calls, the call-waiting feature works well. But if you are online, then there's no way to switch back and forth between two calls.

What would a modern Croesus do? His assistant would discreetly pass him a message letting him know who was on the other line. There would be a callback number if he couldn't take the call right then.

That's what Callwave and Pagoo do, without the need for a receptionist. These companies recognized that work-at-home households with a single telephone line have a problem: When online, they don't know if someone is calling them. The household could get a second phone line at three hundred dollars or more per year, but that's expensive. Callwave and Pagoo allow people to solve the problem through a clever use of the call-forward-if-busy function. Instead of receiving a busy signal, the caller is diverted to Callwave or Pagoo, which records a voice mail. These companies, in turn, send along the voice mail message in an e-mail attachment, letting the person online know about the call. In their first two years, Callwave attracted more than 6 million customers and Pagoo had 700,000.[13]

Again, this is the kind of service that the phone companies should have provided all along. Why didn't they? One reason is that they didn't want to give up that second-phone-line revenue. Nothing slows incumbents down as much as having to give up existing revenue today to build an unproven business for tomorrow. Unfortunately for iPing, there's no conflict for the local phone company to add iPing's service to its existing voice mail.

has done. iPing could be bought for its existing relationship with customers, but a local phone company would be interested primarily in the customers in the local service area and, consequently, would not pay a large premium. The brand name could be worth something, as could patents to various services.

The question for this business is not so much whether it can succeed, but rather, if it does succeed, how will it prosper once there is entry by deep-pocketed incumbents that have existing relationships with their customers, access to better technology, and simpler billing? The only thing harder than creating a new business is keeping it going in the face of competition. We're rooting for Shepherd even if it is a long shot. But, hey, he's hit three-point shots in the past.

Freeing Your Imagination

Watching how consumers with limited resources come up with low-tech solutions and innovative applications is a valuable tool for routinizing ingenuity. But WWCD allows us to imagine how consumers with very few limits behave. And imagining can lead us toward solutions that we never would have thought of when focusing on the limits rather than on the possibilities.

4

Why Don't You
Feel My Pain?

Internalizing the External
Effects of Decision Making

Imagining what King Croesus would do is a way of finding out what a model consumer might do to solve a problem. The flip side of watching the model customer is to look for systematic mistakes that people make. By going after the root cause of these mistakes, we can prevent them. One general cause of mistakes is a misguided incentive system. Poor incentives lead people to make poor decisions.

Airline on-time performance offers a quick insight into what we mean. In 1987, the Department of Transportation's Office of Aviation Enforcement and Proceedings started publishing the on-time performance of each major U.S. airline.[1] As a result, some airlines made operational changes that greatly reduced delays. But others realized that one way to be on time is to add twenty extra minutes to the scheduled arrival time. That turned out to be the cheapest way to solve the problem and move up in the rankings.

If you want to give people an incentive to be on time, you can't let them define what counts as being on time. With hindsight, this is obvious. And the situation only gets worse when different airlines build in different levels of slack. (One airline builds in thirty minutes to look better than its rival, which built in only twenty.)

Hurry Up and Wait

Measuring airline on-time performance illustrates another incentive problem. The focus is all on when the plane arrives. What about when the luggage arrives? It doesn't help if you arrive on time and then wait an hour for your luggage to appear at the carousel.

In this case, the solution to the incentive problem is simple. Require all airlines to use the same flight-time formula in calculating what constitutes an on-time arrival.

Now you can see the problem. People do what they are incentivized to do. Give them the wrong incentives, and watch them do the wrong things. If airlines can make a one-hour flight seem on time by calling it a two-hour flight, they will. It's the cheapest way. If they are given incentives to land their plane on time, they probably won't expend enough effort to get the plane to the gate. And they won't care enough about how long it takes to collect the baggage. In this sense, companies (and people) are perhaps too much like computers. Computers tend to do what they are told, even if it makes little sense.

When you provide someone with an incentive scheme, the person often doggedly pursues that single-minded objective at the expense of many related and equally important objectives. But goals that aren't measured don't usually count. In compensation packages, the typical problem is that salespeople are rewarded for volume and not profit. Thus, they are too willing to sacrifice profit margins in order to maintain sales and market shares. It is not uncommon to find a firm trying to extract itself from a price war that it inadvertently started.

Even General Electric's legendary Jack Welch got caught up in this gaming incentive system. Perhaps his most famous dictum is to be either number one or number two in an industry—or to get out. This seems like a fine incentive. But clever managers figured out ways to define their industry so that they were *always* number one or number two. Honest Tea may be number one in organic bottled teas. It's even the number one bottled tea in the natural foods market. So what? That's not looking big enough. What about all beverages in natural foods? What about all beverages, period?

Welch managed to solve this problem by requiring his managers to define the market broadly enough so that the GE business did not have more than a 10 percent market share. You can still be number one or two and have less than a 10 percent market share if you make the market really big. Thus, Coke is number one in the soda business, but it has more than a 10 percent share. Coke's competition isn't just Pepsi. It competes against water, milk, coffee, wine, and beer. That's why Coke and Pepsi execs talk about share of the bladder (where they are both less than 10 percent). We don't know if Welch was right in his dictum, but we do know that without the requirement to expand the industry, it would have no effect at all.

Closer to home, grade inflation is caused by a poor incentive scheme given to faculty. Students will give their professors better evaluations if they receive higher grades. Their inflated transcripts will also give students a leg up on their peers at other schools. But when everyone does this, we end up with grade inflation and meaningless transcripts.

How might you change incentives to prevent grade inflation? Establishing quotas or a forced grade curve would certainly do the trick, but that heavy-handed approach penalizes students in classes with lots of other bright students. Later in this chapter, we suggest some other solutions. Think about it in the meantime.

Looking for misguided incentives is a great way both to identify problems and to solve them. The problem often arises because people ignore the costs and benefits that their decisions have on other people. We call this approach "Why don't you feel my pain?" The more technical term for these effects is *externalities*. Decision makers who ignore externalities are bound to make bad decisions. This first step identifies the problem.

It's easy pickings to find cases in which people systematically make the wrong decisions. That's because, in many circumstances, your actions will have an impact on others, but you don't have an incentive to feel their pain or gain. These external effects often cause decision makers to act inefficiently. We are not suggesting that people should do the right thing simply out of altruism. Rather, if you want others to do something differently, you can reward them for doing things more to your liking—or punish them for not doing so.

A major source of misplaced incentives comes from poorly designed pricing schemes. Prices are the market's invisible hand. Thus, when the hand points in the wrong direction, there should be no surprise that customers don't get it right. In our earlier discussions of Lojack versus The Club, the problem concerned poor pricing. The price that car owners paid when buying The Club did not include the cost of more thefts for non-Club users (and the price that car owners paid when buying Lojack did not include the benefit of reduced crime overall). So people bought too many Clubs and not enough Lojacks.

Once you've identified the problem, coming up with a solution isn't that hard.[2] Figure out what you would like the person to do differently, and then provide the rewards and punishments accordingly. If the problem is an *externalized* pain or pleasure, the solution is to *internalize* the external effect. Change the price that the decision maker sees so that it incorporates these external effects.

If, for example, you want fewer Clubs and more Lojacks, it's pretty obvious that you need to increase the price of Clubs relative to the price of Lojacks. The internalization tool tells you *how much* to change the prices.

HMO Life Insurance

Let's start with an easy target: the much-reviled health maintenance organization (HMO). With coverage being denied more and more, people have a legitimate concern that HMOs have poor incentives to pay for needed care. Once the HMO has received your premium, it doesn't internalize the cost to you if it denies some treatment and you happen to die.

We've identified the problem. Now how can we provide the right incentives?

Somehow, we want the HMO to feel your pain. The tort system is one very crude attempt at internalization. If coverage is denied and you die, the HMO might get socked with tort damages. But the tort standard is woefully imprecise, and the cost of litigation is often prohibitive. And besides that, you're dead.

Isn't there a better way to make HMOs feel your pain? Another possibility is more-detailed contractual promises: "If you develop stage four carcinoma, we promise to aggressively treat it with drug y and operation z." The problem is that such a contract would have to be massively long and constantly updated, and patients would have to go to medical school to understand it.

As Russell Korobkin, a law professor at University of California at Los Angeles, has pointed out, the difficulty of specifying ex-ante treatments makes it very difficult for HMOs to compete for customers based on higher-quality service. They can compete for two-nights' stay after labor and delivery, but they can't compete over more sustained cancer treatment. So the broadly worded contracts create an incentives problem.

Here's a hint. Another way of stating the problem is that you're worried that the HMO won't treat you as if your life is worth a million bucks.

The internalization answer now should reveal itself. We just need to charge the HMO a million bucks if you happen to die while a member of its plan.

Does this sound outlandish? Who could afford to pay a million dollars if you die? Well, a life insurance company could.

Put these ideas together: HMOs might offer life insurance as well as medical insurance. Bundling life insurance will make the HMO act as though your life is worth a million bucks, because, suddenly, that is exactly how much your life would be worth to it.

If You Die, It's Free

The Chinese have tried an even cruder method to improve doctors' incentives: The doctor gets paid only if the patient lives. But guess what this has done to doctors' incentives to treat the terminally ill.

There will always be someone selling life insurance. The incentives work far better when the life insurance seller actually has the ability to help you live longer. If nothing changed, we'd be just where we are today. But if the health insurance companies took their life insurance liabilities into account, they would have better incentives to keep you alive.

We don't want to push the idea too hard. Society might be uncomfortable with the idea that people who pay more get better health care. Indeed, juries might ultimately force the HMOs to provide the $5 million care to those who didn't pay the higher premium. Nevertheless, HMO life insurance provides a vivid example of how the internalization tool might improve decision making.

Here's a less radical internalization idea. HMOs currently have inadequate incentives to provide preventive medicine, because of client turnover. Every year, a substantial number of clients change HMOs. This means that part of the money an HMO spends today will redound to another HMO's benefit when the employee changes jobs and health care providers. The problem now is one of externalized benefits. How could the internalization tool naturally be used to solve this problem?

Economist and Nobel Prize winner Joe Stiglitz suggested that HMOs should be allowed to pass on to subsequent insurers an amortized portion of the cost of preventive treatments. Preventive medicine can reduce total health care costs by reducing the costs for subsequent care. We want HMOs to invest in preventive care when it is cost-effective. Allowing HMOs to be reimbursed for some of their cost will give them a better incentive to invest in the right kinds of preventive care.

Imagine, for example, that an HMO, through normal turnover, expects to lose half its patients to other plans each year. Then the HMO will get only fifty cents on the dollar for what it spends on preventive medicine. But if the next provider has to reimburse the (amortized) cost of the treatment, then the first HMO will have an incentive to invest in cost-effective care. It will reap the benefits on 50 percent of its clients and have to pay only 50 percent of the cost.

Puzzler: All-You-Can-Drive Insurance

Americans drive some 2.3 trillion miles per year. As you might expect, the number of automobile accidents rises with the number of miles driven. Yet the price of auto insurance hardly varies at all with mileage.[3] Not only is this unfair, but it also leads people to drive more than they would if they had to pay the full cost.

What if gasoline were sold the same way: the one-price, all-you-can-drive gas deal? That, of course, would be ludicrous; it would be massively unfair. It would create terrible incentives. It would make no sense. Yet that is how auto insurance is sold.

To fix the system, let's look more closely at the problem, starting with who loses. Low-mileage drivers obviously lose. Women drive, on average, about half as many miles as men. And, on average, they get into half as many accidents. So it would seem that the fixed-rate policy discriminates against women.

The policy also discriminates against the poor, who also tend to drive a below-average amount. It hurts Detroit, too. More people would choose to have second and third cars if the extra insurance weren't so expensive. You might not drive any more miles if you bought an additional car, but you would have more fun with a rag-top for weekends.

In addition to being unfair, the flat fee creates an incentive problem. Driving more leads to more congestion and more accidents, and the problem is twice as bad as it might first appear. There's the accident in which you run into a tree. Then there's the accident in which you hit another car (or in which another car hits you). Not only do you get into more single-car accidents by driving more miles, but you also get into more multicar collisions.

The internalization tool makes it easy to see the problem: a classic externality. A driver, in deciding whether to take an extra trip to the store, doesn't take into account how driving those extra miles increases the chance that someone else may die.

Can you see how the problems of too much driving can be solved? How can we get drivers to feel the pain of driving the extra miles?

The answer should be obvious. We need to charge drivers for insurance on a per-mile basis. Instead of the all-you-can-eat type of coverage, people who drive more should pay more.

A per-mile system does *not* mean higher average insurance rates. It *does* mean that the low-mileage folks would stop subsidizing the high-mileage drivers. Indeed, University of California at Berkeley economist Aaron Edlin calculates that if the per-mile fee reflected the incremental risk, driving would be cut back by about 7 percent, and there would be insurance savings of more than $8 billion per year. (The reduced driving would also cut back on congestion, leading to another $8 billion in annual savings.[4])

Patrick Butler has been working for some twenty years to bring per-mile insurance to the marketplace. With the support of the National Organization for Women, he has drafted model legislation to allow firms to offer per-mile insurance. That's right. Apparently, one reason that firms don't make this available is that insurance commissions make it almost impossible to bring this product to market. Some states, like Massachusetts, set a single price for all auto insurance and are loath to experiment with new pricing schemes. Other states allow per-mile rates only if the mileage is based on self-reported claims of the insured parties. In those states, insurance companies are not allowed to monitor the distance using global positioning system (GPS) technology or even odometer readings. Imagine the uproar if state law required all restaurants to charge a single, all-you-can-eat price (or only let restaurants price à la carte based on what customers claimed to have eaten).

On January 1, 2002, Texas became the first state to permit per-mile insurance. Butler tried to enact legislation requiring firms to make this option available, but he had to settle for just making it permissible.

There has been some progress in this arena. In Texas, Progressive Insurance ran a pilot program based on GPS technology. Customers saved 25 percent on their insurance.[5] Norwich Union, the largest auto insurer in the U.K., is testing GPS-based insurance with five thousand customers. The firm's market research shows that nine out of ten customers prefer that insurance rates reflect the usage of their car, and a majority favor the pay-as-you-go system that we have with utility bills.

Given the consumer demand and improved incentives, there is a question of why insurance firms didn't offer pay-as-you-go a long time ago. One obstacle was a technology to monitor miles. But there were also many clever solutions to this problem.

To have mileage-based insurance, the insurer needs to know how far the car has been driven. As far back as 1963, Nobel Prize–winning economist William Vickrey suggested that insurance be included in the purchase of tires. More miles mean more tire wear—and more insurance payments.

The suspicious among you will quickly ask, Doesn't that lead people to drive on bald tires? Anticipating this problem, Vickrey suggested that drivers get credit for the remaining tread when they turn in a tire. That way, they pay insurance only for the tread they use.

In Vickrey's time, turning back odometers was, perhaps, too easy. Otherwise, having the odometer checked regularly (along with emissions inspections) would allow insurance companies to measure mileage driven. With digital odometers, rolling back the miles is not so easy. (It is also illegal.)

Andrew Tobias has campaigned to integrate car insurance with gasoline.[6] As he points out, you can drive a car without insurance, but you can't drive it without gasoline. He suggested trying out a pilot plan in Hawaii and Puerto Rico, where few people would be tempted to drive out of state to get cheaper gas.

The California Department of Insurance estimates that 28 percent of California drivers are uninsured. While pay-at-the-pump insurance would prevent the large problem of uninsured drivers, it would pose two other problems. First, insurance costs would be related to fuel efficiency. Thus, sport utility vehicle (SUV) owners would pay more insurance per mile driven than Toyota Prius owners would. (Perhaps that's not such a problem.) It would also be impractical to provide experience rating. Thus, everyone would have to pay the same fee, at least on the compulsory component of insurance.

The new high-tech approach is the use of a GPS device to monitor distance driven. For example, all new GM cars come equipped with OnStar, which makes it possible to track not only the mileage driven but also where and when the car was driven. Highway mileage could be given a discount and nighttime driving could be charged a premium. Speeding could also lead to higher premiums.

Such a fine-tuned tracking system brings up privacy issues—and may explain why some insurance commissions prohibit GPS-based pricing. With GPS monitoring, your insurer would know everywhere you've been. As Leslie Kolleda of Progressive Insurance explains, "There are certainly people with privacy concerns. This policy is not for those people."[7]

All things considered, why hasn't this happened?

There's no single explanation. For a long time, the issue was how to monitor usage. While GPS can solve that problem, it introduces a new set of issues, primarily revolving around privacy. That's why, for now, we favor using the odometer. We agree with Patrick

Butler that if an odometer reader is good enough for car-leasing contracts, it's good enough for car insurance.[8]

State insurance regulations that prevent insurance companies from verifying mileage driven don't help. Another factor that might be slowing down adoption is that Progressive Insurance obtained a patent for its Autograph, pay-per-mile policy. It is hard to know how effective this patent will be in blocking competition, but it may be a cause for concern.

Perhaps the biggest stumbling block is that an incumbent firm acting alone doesn't have as great an incentive to switch as you might first think. Remember that moving to a per-mile basis would lead to higher rates for roughly half the customers.[9] As long as other firms are still offering fixed-rate policies, the insurer would risk losing half its customers. It could still offer fixed-rate contracts as an option, but it would have to raise the price and, again, risk losing these customers.

Few companies want to embark on a course that risks alienating half their clientele. While the insurance company might lose some money on these high-mileage customers, it doesn't want to lose their clients' life, fire, and other insurance business. So, as long as the low-mileage drivers are willing to keep subsidizing the high-mileage ones, the incumbents are happy not to rock the boat. The product makes the most sense to a company that is trying to grow and to attract more women customers.

CASE STUDY

Acme Rent-A-Car

Acme Rent-A-Car (yes, Acme) is an unassuming operation in a converted gas station on the outskirts of New Haven. In the fall of 2001, Acme had its fifteen minutes of fame. Its cars came with a special gadget, a GPS device that let the company detect how fast the car was traveling.[10] Acme charged its customers an additional $150 if they drove faster than eighty miles per hour for more than two minutes.

The state of Connecticut shut down this interesting experiment. You might think that the state would have been happy with this innovation since it deterred reckless driving. But, instead, the state charged Acme with engaging in "an unfair and deceptive trade practice." It wanted to stop Acme from discriminating against speeders.

The state said that Acme didn't adequately disclose its speeding-charge policy to its customers. There are some grounds for the state's position. Although the charge was described both in the rental agreement and on a prominent magnetic sign behind Acme's rental counter, these disclosures didn't define exactly how the charge worked. It wasn't clear whether someone who sped continuously between New Haven and New York would be liable for one $150 charge or a dozen.

One renter, the Reverend Curtis Cofield II, testified that he was shocked when he found that his bank card had been debited. But, then again, Acme may have been shocked to learn that he had been driving faster than eighty miles per hour.

If disclosure were the real issue, Acme could have satisfied the state by putting the disclosure in larger type on its contracts and requiring that customers initial the clause. This is not a market in which better-informed consumers would all reject the contract—Acme's $27.15 daily rate was (and still is) one of the lowest in town.

At the heart of the litigation was the state's contention that Acme could not profit from provisions it puts in its contract to protect itself against certain kinds of damage. A seller is allowed to charge more than the cost of its basic product or service, but it is not allowed to gain from its penalties. This prohibition against excessive penalties has ancient roots in the common law: Acme obviously couldn't demand "a pound of flesh" for speeding.

Perhaps the innovation would have been more palatable if it had been reframed as something closer to preexisting practice. Connecticut doesn't challenge charges of four dollars, even five, per gallon of gasoline when the rental agency refills the car or fifty cents per mile when the customer drives beyond a prespecified distance. The state would be hard-pressed to complain about charging consumers an extra fee for providing them the convenience of driving fast.

Instead of directly penalizing speeders, Acme could have achieved just about the same outcome if it had used a discount for not speeding versus a penalty for speeding. Recall that its daily rate was $27.15. Acme could have charged a daily rental rate of $177.15, with a $150 daily discount for any renter who didn't speed.[11]

With this plan, the state of Connecticut would have nothing to complain about. Disclosure wouldn't be an issue, as the customer would have been told about the potential $177.15 price. Rewarding people for not speeding does not sound like a profitable damage provision. But who knows what Connecticut would do?

Right Idea, Wrong Problem

Acme was a bad implementation of a good idea. A better way to bring this technology to market would be to look for a customer set that wants to drive slowly. This technology would seem quite attractive to parents of teenage children. As a matter of safety, a parent might want to know if the child is driving above the speed limit. If the teenager knows that the parent is monitoring his speed, he or she will have an extra incentive to obey the speed laws— and avoid being grounded. And since it's voluntary, there's no veto problem. (Teenagers without wheels don't get a choice.) A connected advantage is that parents might worry less, because they could locate the car and, thus, their child.[12]

As for making this technology more affordable, the trick would be to get insurance companies involved. Car insurance for teenagers is often prohibitively expensive. Agreeing to abide by the posted limits, with GPS monitoring for enforcement, could be the ticket to lower insurance costs. We return to this issue in chapter 8.

Prizes versus Punishments

There's more than one way to skin a cat—or in Acme's case, more than one way to penalize speeders. The larger point is that whether something is a prize or a penalty simply depends on your initial perspective. What provides incentives is the difference between the two.

You can give people either a penalty for dying or an incentive to live. You can create a penalty for working or an incentive to retire.[13] Sallie Mae rewarded student loan borrowers with a quarter-point reduction in their rate if they had a flawless repayment schedule. This gets the same result as starting with a quarter-point-lower rate and taking it away if the borrower is late. But, the penalty for one late payment might well lead people to complain. In contrast, it's harder for customers to protest when they don't get a reward because they didn't earn it.

The take-away from this is to ensure that there's a reward or punishment that motivates behavior you want to encourage. Whether you do this with honey or vinegar depends on the best way to sell the deal. We suggest that you're less likely to get com-

Why not give children presents at the beginning of the
year and then take them away if they're naughty?

plaints or be sued for offering a bonus for good behavior than a penalty for bad.

Nielsen Ratings for TV Ads?

An advertiser has only one objective: to sell a product. If the content of the ad is boring but the product sells, that's fine. Advertisers have no incentive to make their ads entertaining. (There is even the perceived wisdom that the Clio Award–winning ads don't sell the product.) And since twelve to fifteen minutes of each broadcasting hour are filled with commercials, this means that more than 20 percent of what you see has no incentive to be good.

A commercial that turns off viewers is expensive to the network. It loses viewers for the next show. Even more immediately, the network loses viewers for the next commercial.

Why not charge advertisers based on how many people switch channels during their ad?

Under this system, Nielsen or another television rating service would monitor viewing habits during commercial breaks. If a show hands the advertiser 10 million viewers, but the ad turns off 1 million, then the advertiser would have to pay a very high price. But if the ad entertains viewers and keeps them watching so that it hands off all 10 million (or more) to the next ad, then the price would be reduced.

If one network adopted this policy, it would have the best ads and do a better job of retaining viewers. Even if it were copied, the result would be fewer kitchen runs during commercials, less channel surfing, and more TV watching. It would also reduce the incentive to employ TiVo to fast forward through the ads.

You might have developed this idea with the symmetry tool. Advertising prices are already contingent on how successful the regular programming is in capturing viewers. If the NBA finals fail to generate a sufficiently large audience, NBC promises to rebate some of its advertising fee. So why not flip things around and penalize advertisers if they fail to deliver many viewers to the regularly scheduled program?

Grade Inflation Transcripts

Every now and then it seems only fair to turn the *Why Not?* spotlight onto our own profession. Since the early 1980s, we've seen an epidemic of grade inflation. To give you a sense of how bad things are, in 2002, the median grade at Harvard was an A–, and 91 percent of students graduated with "honors." (A few schools have managed to hold the line, most notably Reed College and Swarthmore College, whose unofficial motto is "Anywhere else, it would have been an A.")

As almost any professor will tell you, giving out lots of A's is a pretty good way to get big enrollments and high teaching evaluations. Fewer students end up complaining about their grades. It is also an easy solution in that you don't have to spend time figuring out who really did better than others. And, right or wrong, there is a feeling that students who do poorly reflect on your performance as a teacher. If they fail, you've failed.

The antidote to grade inflation must be grade deflation. But what incentives will make this happen?

If grades were a currency, we'd just eliminate the D and create a new grade above an A. But that would be hard to do. While there is no Federal Reserve to control the grade supply, a forced curve does the trick. At Harvard Business School (HBS), grades are 1, 2, or 3. Only 10 percent of the students in each course can earn a 1 (distinction), and another 10 percent must get a 3 (the lowest grade). That system requires a lot of discipline and works best in cases such as HBS, where the classes are large. In some extreme cases, peer pressure can work. After the *Boston Globe* reported that 91 percent of Harvard College's class of 2001 graduated with honors, the faculty was embarrassed into restricting the number of honors graduates to 60 percent of the class.[14]

In general, we prefer incentive systems to the command-and-control regulation of a forced curve. The idea would be to penalize the professor who gives out too many A's. One way to do this is to devalue those A's when too many are given out. The transcript could show not only the student's grade, but also the grade distribution of all the students in that course. Thus, an A is much more valuable when the class average is a B than when all other students also get an A. Some professors will still be lazy and give out all A's, but the ones who employ more discriminating standards won't penalize their students.

A report led by Harvard University's dean of undergraduate education, Susan Pedersen, made just such a proposal to the faculty. The Harvard faculty voted it down, citing a concern that some courses are full of great students and, thus, a professor wouldn't want to devalue an A in a class full of all A students.

That's a fair point. Getting an A in physics against a group of B students is naturally much easier than getting that A against a class of Phi Beta Kappa physics whizzes.

The solution to this problem requires taking one more step. This idea, which comes from Joe Stiglitz, is a translation of the power index used to rank sport teams. Rather than just calculate win-loss records, the power index takes into account the quality of the teams that you beat. Simply do the same things with students. To help the transcript reader get a sense of how strong the competition is, put the grade point average of the other students in that class alongside the grade distribution.

After hearing too many times that this grades-within-a-context idea is a pipe dream, we discovered that a few schools have gone most of the way there and one has knocked it out of the park. Dartmouth College reports the median grade for the class along with the individual student's grade, and Columbia University reports the percentage of students who received the individual's grade. Indiana University provides a veritable kitchen sink of information. After the individual's grade comes the entire distribution of grades in the course, the average grade in the class, the average GPA of all the students in the class, and the percentage of majors. Our sample transcript on the following page shows that it is surprisingly easy to read.

This student obviously did well in the Capital Punishment class. The A+ grade is in a course where 85 percent of the students are

INDIANA UNIVERSITY
Semester Grade Report (Duplicate)
First Semester 1997-98   NOT AN OFFICIAL TRANSCRIPT

Name: TEST SAMPLE, IU STUDENT   Date Issued: 02-17-2003
Student No.: 000-77-7772   Campus: Bloomington
Address: 1234 TERRET LANE   Context Effective Date: 01-28-1998
              BLOOMINGTON, IN 47401

Descriptive Title of Course / Instructor Avg. Student G.P.A.	Dept Class G.P.A	Course Majors	Hours	Grade	Section	Index	A+ A A-	B+ B B-	C+ C C-	D+ D D-	F P S	I/R NR NC	NY W WX
CAPITAL PUNISHMENT BATTLE A 3.01	CJUS 3.78	P493 85%	3.0	A+	1351	6/26	6 9 8	1 0 2	0 0 0	0 0 0	0 0 0	0 0 0	0 0 0
CRIME IN THE NEW AMERICAN CITY KVETKO A	CJUS	P680	3.0	A	1362	***/***	****Index and grade distribution are not available**** ****************due to small class size******************						
THE VIETNAM WAR FOHLEN A 2.85	HIST 2.36	A300 12%	3.0	B+	2664	56/321	3 10 14	29 84 29	23 56 18	6 20 5	24 5 0	2 0 0	0 39 10
AMERICAN SOCIAL WELFARE POLICY ARONSON S 3.06	POLS 3.61	Y326 41%	3.0	A	3405	24/56	0 24 22	3 2 0	2 0 2	0 1 0	0 0 0	0 0 0	0 4 3

criminal justice majors and their average GPA is 3.01. By comparison, if you saw only the grade, you would be less impressed by the B+ in the Vietnam War course. But that professor was a tough grader. Only 17 percent of the students earned a B+ or better (whereas 23 percent of the students were awarded an A+ in Capital Punishment.)

The ability to figure out if the student is taking difficult courses normally requires a good deal of inside information. This transcript is a great example of giving the reader enough information to judge what the grades really mean.

Beyond giving the transcript reader a more informed view of the grades, the "big picture" transcript gives the professor better incentives to grade honestly. Giving all the students in your class an A when other professors give the same students C's could be embarrassing. So the Indiana transcripts help to internalize some of the external effects (and let the reader of the transcript figure out what's being externalized, to boot).

Now, other schools just have to act.

Two Grades Are Better Than One

Harvey "C–" Mansfield, a professor at Harvard, became famous for giving out two sets of grades—the official (inflated) grade and a private grade the student really deserved.

Working Backward

Starting with a problem and searching for the solution seems the natural and logical way to go about problem solving. That's why we started with this approach. Now we're ready to turn to the flip side of problem solving. You can start with solutions and search for problems. In fact, when it comes to solving problems, problem searches are sometimes more effective than solution searches.

Starting with the solution can help you identify hidden problems or deal with a known problem that you didn't know how to solve. The idea of solutions swirling in the environment looking for problems can be found in the "garbage can" model in organizational behavior.[15] In this classic model, there are problems looking for solutions and solutions looking for problems. Sometimes they find each other. In the next chapters, we'll help speed up that process by directing the search.

When all is said and done, you'll want to be working backward and forward at the same time. You can come at a problem from both ends. You'll want to solve problems by looking for new solutions as well as redeploying existing ideas from other contexts.

Solutions
in Search
of Problems

Where Else Would It Work?

Looking for Idea Arbitrage

*It is proper in philosophy to consider the similar,
even in things far distant from each other.*

— Aristotle

The translation tool starts with a solution and searches for problems. You can start with one of your own solutions and try to find new contexts where the same idea will solve somebody else's problems. Or you can start with other people's solutions and see if they can help you solve your own problems.

You've already seen several examples of both kinds of translations. The translation of neoprene wheels from luggage to in-line skates to the Razor scooter or the Spin Pop to the Spinbrush were examples where innovators took their own solutions and applied them to other areas. It's easy to think of others famous problem searches—such as the successful hunt for additional uses of Post-it notes ("sign here") or Velcro (you name it). We've also suggested some translations that don't yet exist: The Catholic Church's devil's advocate might be translated into a corporate devil's advocate.

Before you begin the problem search, you need, of course, to have a solution and an appreciation of why that solution works. Where do you go to find a solution?

We suggest taking Wittgenstein's famous advice: "Don't think, look!" You should first look to see what people in other parts of the world are doing to solve the same kind of problem. In some ways, looking over your shoulder to see what your neighbor is doing is the simplest—almost trivial—and most straightforward kind of translation. Still, we are amazed at how many good ideas from one country fail to catch on in another.

Other times a solution won't be found in another culture but in another context. Of course, this search is harder than geographic translation, because there is no obvious place to look for the new problem to solve. The second half of this chapter offers some guidelines for making these connections—what we call the principled problem search. As always, we illustrate these translations using a wide range of applications, everything from fixing leaky toilets to increasing charitable giving to finding a job or mate.

Travelers' Tales

Looking at differences across borders is a natural way of identifying new solutions, because the differences tend to stick out. And once we identify them, it's natural to ask whose way of doing things is better. If one country does X and another does just the opposite, can they both really be right?

The fact that a why-not idea has actually been tried and worked somewhere else also helps shift the conversation. Naysayers can't confidently proclaim that the idea is doomed to failure. The conversation turns instead to assessing the relative merits of the two existing systems.

Several of these travelers' tales (some of which we've already discussed) point to better ways of doing things—both big and small—here at home:

Europe's hotel key holders ensure that you don't lose your key and the hotel doesn't waste electricity.

In Italy, the kitchen cabinet over the sink typically has a slatted bottom and thus serves as a combination drying rack and cabinet.

England's Virgin One account uses your checking account balance to reduce your mortgage payments.

Some of the geographic translations are found closer to home:

Lojack subsidies in Massachusetts encourage the use of crime-reducing (rather than crime-shifting) precautions.

Of course, there are geographic translations ready for export. As Woody Allen said, right turn on red was California's greatest cultural contribution. If you can believe it, Italy (and most of the rest of Europe) still doesn't allow right turn on red. But when it comes to flush toilets, safety belts, and speeding tickets, the United States may be just as bad as Italy.

Royal Flush

Toilets in England work differently. The water is fed from the reservoir tank to the bowl via a siphon. As a nonmechanical system, it is a model of simplicity and low cost. Most important, a siphon never leaks.

The U.S. system uses a rubber flap. While the flap is also simple and cheap, if the flap doesn't return to land precisely over the hole, water leaks.

How big is the problem? A study in Greensboro, North Carolina, estimated that the town loses between one and two million gallons of water per day through poorly maintained toilets. Even a few very leaky toilets can cause a lot of waste. One in twenty toilets leaks more than a hundred gallons a day. It adds up: In the United States, more than 95 percent of wasted water is due to leaky toilets.

Until January 1, 2001, not only did the Brits favor siphons over flaps, but flaps were actually illegal. Meanwhile, the European Union chose the French knob and plug, or flap, system as the standard for Europe. In this case, 40 million Frenchmen *can* be wrong.

We are particularly interested in cases where a practice that is required in one country is prohibited in another. Such paradoxes make us suspect that both countries can't be right. In the next example, it's not just wasted water but rather lives that are at stake, and we feel it is the United States that has it backward.

Seat Belt Extenders

Infants and toddlers under the age of two can ride airplanes for free on a ticketed adult's lap. Lap kids pose an important safety concern because, as Jeff Bridges poignantly proved to Rosie Ruiz in the movie *Fearless,* it is impossible for a parent to hold onto a child during a plane accident. But, oddly, the FAA (Federal Aviation Administration) *prohibits* lap restraints for children. Even worse, devices that could be used as child lap restraints are already standard equipment on every plane, but flight attendants in the United States are trained to prohibit their use.

Seat belt extenders are the solution. These devices are simply free-floating seat belt canvas with a male flat metal part on one end and a female buckle on the other. The only approved use for these extenders is to extend the seat belt for larger people who need a longer seat belt. But these extenders could also be used to buckle kids by creating an independent loop—connected like the second link of a chain to the parent's seat belt.

This is standard practice in other parts of the world, where the seat belt extender is called a baby belt. The baby belt, introduced by British Airways years ago, is now a *mandatory* feature on all British, French, and Australian flights.

So, what could make the FAA think that an unrestrained child is better than a baby-belted child? Unrestrained kids are not only at risk themselves; in an accident they become human projectiles that can injure others.

As the editor in chief of airlinesafety.com, Robert J. Boser, explains:

> *The reason [the FAA] wants you to hold the baby on your lap, without restraint, is because they are fearful that some parents will try to attach the infant pack to the parent instead of to the seat belt, or worse, to wrap the seat belt around both parent and infant—which would lead to severe injury to the baby, in the event of rapid deceleration.*

Boser recommends willful noncompliance:

*Those of us with common sense find it hard to understand
why the FAA regulation cannot simply require that the Flight
Attendants check for those kinds of situations, without
requiring the parent to remove the infant from a front pack
carrier that is strapped to the parent (not to the seat belt). My
advice is to . . . ignore their request and put your baby and
common sense ahead of the idiotic rules of the FAA. But
please, do so courteously. It isn't the Flight Attendants' fault.
They are required to advise you of that irrational regulation.*[1]

The baby belt isn't perfect. Crash dummy tests—like the kind
they do with cars—suggest that the baby belt exposes the child to
risk of injury both by hitting the forward row seatback and by the
forward flail of the adult.[2] But this imperfect device is a clear improvement over the unrestrained status quo in the United States,
and most of the world already knows it.

The FAA may be holding out for a better restraint, which
would require the child to sit in his or her own airline seat. But this
idea is likely to kill even more people. What the crash-dummy em-
piricists ignore is that the extra cost of buying an airline ticket for
the toddler may lead some families to take a much more dangerous
mode of transportation—the automobile. Researchers at the Universities of Georgia and Mississippi have estimated that an FAA
proposal to prohibit lap children would likely cause five more
deaths per year. When the full costs of separate seat restraints are
included, the simple baby belt embraced by the rest of the world
looks better and better.[3]

"Bust Me" Lights

In chapter 4, we told the tale of Acme Rent-A-Car's use of GPS
technology to charge speeders extra money. This innovation gives
some people the willies because it raises concerns that the technology will allow Big Brother to track our comings and goings.[4] Many
low-tech options do almost as well at catching speeders without
the same privacy issue. In several European toll roads, your toll
ticket is time-stamped so that if you drive from point A to point B

faster than the speed limit allows, then your toll ticket proves you've been speeding and you automatically get a ticket.

Taxicabs in Singapore (and in Japan, too) have an annoying pinging sound that goes off whenever the car is going above the speed limit. Thus, the speeder certainly cannot profess ignorance. But the pinging may not be annoying enough. As one traveler reported, "Rare is the cab ride we have taken that hasn't been steadily accompanied by the two-tone ding-dong of the speeding chime."[5]

Singapore also requires commercial vehicles to install on their roofs a yellow light that begins to flash if the vehicle goes faster than its assigned maximum speed. As a result, the police don't need radar guns to detect speeders.

We can imagine taking this one step further. Once the speeding light goes on, the light would stay on until turned off by the police. These "bust me" lights would take the exigency out of this type of crime fighting. Cops wouldn't need to catch the speeder in the act, and there would be no need for high-speed chases. The speeders could run, but they couldn't hide. The cops could wait until the speeders came to them and politely asked for a ticket. And there would be no privacy concern. The cops wouldn't learn where you were speeding, only that you were. We imagine there are some parents who wouldn't mind knowing if their darling teenagers were driving too fast.

Movie Theater Passes

We have season passes to health clubs and to ski resorts. Why not movies? The movie theater that does this would create a loyal following. It would also bring more people to the cinemas and thereby increase the take at the concession stand. (Most of the profits already come from the concession stands.[6])

Such passes already exist in France and the United Kingdom. In France, unlimited ticket plans are offered by UGC in Paris and rival chain Pathé in Nantes and Strasbourg.[7] In London, Virgin Cinema chain first offered a four-week pass for £15 or an eight-week pass for £25. After Virgin Cinema was sold to the French company UGC, the two short-term passes were replaced by an annual pass priced at £9.99 per month (£12.99 inside London). For just under £120 a year, you can see as many movies as you can stand.

Corporate Vanity Stamps

We allow corporations to put their logos on the postage meter imprint. Why not allow corporations to subsidize the cost of post-age stamps?[8] If McDonald's will pay, say, five cents for a picture of Ronald on a U.S. stamp, the consumer wins by saving a bit on postage. Maybe the back of the stamp could even be made to taste like french fries. Consumers, of course, would be free to pay full freight for a noncorporate stamp. Indeed, with microprinting, we might soon have vanity stamps—just like vanity license plates—with your child's or cat's picture.

Sounds crazy? What if we told you that vanity stamps already exist in Canada and Australia? In the land down under, your pic-ture goes next to the stamp, while our neighbors to the north put your picture in the middle of a border (as below). The price in OZ is about a 100 percent pre-mium (for example, one hundred 40-cent stamps for $87), while in Canada the price is $24.95 for one sheet of twenty-five do-mestic stamps.[9]

Should it really surprise us that the U.S. Postal Ser-vice is ripe for reinven-tion? How about selling a unitless first-class stamp so that, when postal rates increase, you don't have to go back to the post office to buy the right number of one-cent supplements? You might say this wouldn't work, because the post office would lose money if people bought loads of stamps in advance. But advance buying actually makes the post office extra money because an early stamp purchase is like an interest-free loan from consumers to the post office. With a rate increase, the post office could raise the price of these stamps, just as the MTA used to raise the price of subway tokens.

Still think it's crazy? Well, explain that to the U.K. and Australia, which have already been selling unitless stamps for years.[10]

Religious Translations

Religions are a great source of solutions that might be applied to nonreligious contexts. We've discussed ideas from Judaism and the Catholic Church. The Mormon Church has several innovations that might be emulated.

Mormons ask their members to maintain an "Armageddon bag," a collection of food and other necessities for an emergency. Here we have the ultimate Boy Scouts' "be prepared" ethic. The emergency bag is a quite reasonable idea for the general public and would reduce panic runs on the grocery store in times of crisis.

Every member of the Mormon Church is supported by two other people. Each person is also assigned a two-person support team to help look after two other members. This interlocking support network is nonhierarchical, and there's no choosing favorites (assignment is from above). Moving to a new city? No problem. Two friendly faces will be waiting to lend a hand. The interlocking buddy system might be usefully applied to schools or work.

Why Not Here?

These examples don't come close to exhausting the supply of interesting geographic and cultural translations. You'll often come up with a translation from one context to another and then find that it has been implemented in some other country. Whether or not this is the source of the translation, the geographic translation can give you confidence that the idea has merit as well as guidance on the specifics of what is to be done.

Principled Problem Search

We almost feel as though we are cheating by suggesting that geographic translations are a way for you to learn how to generate ideas. After all, we're really just suggesting that you take advantage of smart ideas that other people have already come up with. But

An Inventor's Wake-up Call

You really have to open your eyes to see existing solutions in a new light. Take the telephone keypad, for example. Can you think of some *new* applications?

David Pogue, Mac maven and gadget guru, has a startlingly simple proposal. "PUNCH-IT-UP ALARM CLOCK: The modern clock radio can play CDs, wake up two people at different times, and even beam the current time onto the ceiling. So why do we have to set the time using the same controls cavemen used in the Stone Age? You still have to hold down slow, imprecise buttons that on most models go only forward in time. . . . Haven't these companies ever heard of a phone-style number keypad? We should be able to set the alarm for 8:45 just by tapping the 8, 4, and 5 keys in sequence. You'd save two minutes a night, which you could use for any number of activities, like sleeping."[11]

just because it's easy doesn't mean it's not worth doing. When good ideas already exist, we're with Tom Lehrer: "Why do you think God made your eyes? Plagiarize!"

So what do you do when your Malaysian doppelgänger doesn't do you the favor of dropping a great solution right in your lap? It takes a bit more effort, but we can do more than just copy existing solutions. We can find new problems they might solve. Start with a bona fide solution that's working in one context and look for other contexts—possibly radically different contexts—where the solution might also be applied. This is the most far-reaching type of problem search because, unlike the case with travelers' tales, you don't seem to have any guidance on where to look.

So, how do you proceed?

We recommend that you start by writing down simple declarative sentences describing the solution that you think might be ripe for translation. The goal here is to identify those specific attributes of the solution that explain concretely why it solves the problem at hand.

A second step is to try to restate the description of the solution in more general terms. The effort here is to identify the essential attributes of both the problem and the solution that might be generalized to other settings. The core task is to identify the general class of problems for which this type of solution might be effective.

An analogy to linguistic translation is helpful. Just as a linguist must understand the essential meaning of the original text in order to produce a faithful translation into another language, an innovator trying to translate a solution from one setting to another must understand the underlying mechanism that makes the original application work. Translators are often called upon to translate works into radically different languages and cultural contexts. The 1960 movie *Never on Sunday,* whose title referred to a working girl with a heart of gold—she never accepted clients on the Sabbath—became *Never on Saturday* when it played in Israel.

Constitutional law poses even more daunting translation dilemmas: What would the founders have wanted the expression "the right to bear arms" to mean in a world with machine guns and nuclear weapons?[12]

In some cases, the translation will be straightforward across product lines. After the corner grocery store was mostly replaced by supermarkets, it was a simple translation to see that other corner-store businesses might support superstores. This has indeed proved true with books (Barnes & Noble), hardware (The Home Depot), pharmacies (Walgreens), office supplies (Staples), pet supplies (PET-CO), and even baby supplies (Babies 'R Us).

Formulaic translations can also lead to disaster. Selling pet food on the Internet might seem just like selling books, except that that ratio of shipping costs to value is much less favorable. Selling wine online works in terms of value to shipping, but state regulations make this business almost impossible. Selling cars online works, as the customer can still get a test drive from a regular dealer or a friend. Selling a used car online poses a much greater challenge because of the need to inspect the car.

Just as a literal translation of language often makes no sense without an understanding of the context, our translation tool requires an understanding of why the business works. We don't suggest you just take something from business A and country B and try it out in business C and country D. The goal is to translate what makes the idea work into a different context.

Video Rewinds Redux

So, let's go to work. Here's a practice example that begins with the simple solution of asking customers to rewind videotapes before they watch the movie instead of after. How would you go about searching for other problems to apply this solution to?

Let's begin by trying to describe both the solution and how it solves a concrete problem. Here's an initial go.

The problem: Video customers (through laziness or inadvertence) sometimes fail to rewind the video after a rental, which in turn annoys subsequent renters and causes video stores to expend resources to ensure better compliance.

The solution: Initial rewind solves the problem by forcing renters to perform their duty of rewinding the tape before they can use the product.

So far, so good. But now let's see if we can state the solution a bit more generally.

Generalized statement of the problem: People have a tendency to shirk or free-ride (through laziness or inadvertence) in their use of a product by failing to perform certain tasks that impose costs on others' ability to use the product.

Generalized statement of solution: Force people to perform the shirked task before they can use the product themselves.

The idea here is twofold. First, pushing ourselves to restate the problem in this more general fashion lets us see other problems that have similar characteristics. And restating the solution more generally suggests how the initial solution might be translated.

Let's take this a step at a time. First, do you recall any other problems that we've already discussed that present the same kind of shirking issue as the video rewind?

The lint screen on Laundromat dryers should come to mind. Many people forget to clean or can't be bothered with cleaning the screen. The idea of asking people to clean before use instead of after is a straightforward solution (although some sloths will use the dryer without cleaning and leave two loads' worth of lint for the next user—we can remember encountering virtual carpets of lint in commercial dryers).

Another version of a shirking problem was the problem of uninsured motorists (chapter 3). One out of five motorists in the great state of California enjoy the benefits of driving but don't have the wherewithal to compensate the people they injure in an accident. This is literally free-riding, as the uninsured ride around free from the cost of insurance while imposing higher uninsured-motorists premiums on the rest of us.

So how does video rewinding suggest a solution? Think of a way of forcing people to perform the shirked task before they can use the product. Regulations try to do this by requiring proof of insurance before you buy a car, but we all know that people often do not renew their insurance, and we're back to square one.

The more hardwired solution is pay-at-the-pump insurance. You can't drive without gas. So bundling insurance with gas makes sure that people buy insurance before they drive. Voilà!

But why stop there? Can you think of other shirked activities for which we might try our hands at translating this same solution?

The "motor voter" law is an analogous move against citizenship shirking. If you want to gain the privilege of driving, then you must fulfill your citizenship obligation and register to vote. But, again, as with organ donation, the current political compromise is to merely give people the *opportunity* at their motor vehicle registry to do the right thing.

Can you think of any other shirking problems? What about voting itself? Like Australians, we would require all citizens to vote (and back up the requirement with a mild sanction). Another approach would be to shut off people's television or telephone or credit card until they entered a code that was received at the voting booth.

Of course, there are lots of free-speech problems with this particular implementation of the idea, but the main purpose of this exercise is to illustrate how ideas can be translated to radically different contexts. Starting with the relatively trivial problem of rewind shirking, we are quickly led to uninsured motorists and somnolent voters.

Child Care at IKEA

Many IKEA stores provide baby-sitting for parents who come to shop. Where else might this idea be applied? A bunch of answers are probably jumping into your mind, but let's stick with the program and more formally state the problem and the solution. To speed things up, however, we'll jump straight to a generalized statement:

The problem: Parents with young kids have trouble making last-minute shopping excursions because they can't easily arrange for baby-sitters.

The solution: By providing drop-in baby-sitting, a retailer can sell products that would be difficult to sell if parents had to bring the kids along or set up baby-sitting in advance.

So, where else does the lack of baby-sitting impede parents from patronizing retailers? Disney long ago understood that lack of baby-sitting can impede parents from enjoying vacation services for adults. What did Disney do? Kids' clubs at Disney World allow moms and dads to enjoy massages or have that long-overdue, romantic dinner.

As academics, we know that the difficulty of setting up baby-sitting sometimes impedes professors from attending conferences. At long last, conferences are starting to provide the baby-sitting that often is crucial to mothers' participation.

Though the vacation and conference applications are good examples, they already exist—to varying degrees. Are there any contexts in which the lack of baby-sitting is a real impediment to consumerism but the service is not supplied by the retailer?

To our mind, one big answer is the local cineplex theater.[13] At the last minute, you and your spouse decide you want to go see the latest thriller. Forgetaboutit. You can take the kids to IKEA at the last minute, but not to an R-rated movie at Showcase Cinemas.

Why not let parents drop off their tots for a fee and go, beeper in hand, to that R-rated movie? The kids might watch videos in a day care (or night care) room (visible from the lobby through a large glass window). Or better yet, the theater could sell the kids a ticket and chaperone them to watch a G-rated movie on one of its other screens.

Again, the fact that this is a straightforward translation of an existing solution goes a long way toward silencing the naysayers, who say this just can't be done because of child-care regulations or safety concerns. If IKEA can do it, so can your local googolplex.

Translation Puzzler: The Extended Deadline

Our friends at the Internal Revenue Service allow taxpayers to deduct contributions to an individual retirement account (IRA) all the way until tax day. Most other deductions have to be made by December 31. But with an IRA, you can contribute as late as April 15 and still deduct it from the previous year's taxes.

What problem is the extended deadline trying to solve, and how exactly does it solve it? And what similar problems might be solved by extended deadlines?

We recommend that you pause here and force yourself to write down a statement of the problem and why the solution is a solution. Some of you will have the urge to shirk just about now (and the video rewind discussion makes us wish we could force you to turn in an effort before you could read ahead), but resist the temptation.

So here's a go at it. The deadline extension is designed to encourage people to save. If the IRA deduction deadline were the end of the year, this contribution to savings would have to compete with holiday spending. There would also be the problem of delayed gratification, as you would then have to wait four months to see the tax benefit.

Postponing the deadline until the filing day radically increases the salience of saving. Everyone looks for last-minute ways to cut taxes. But other than the IRA, there aren't any. Make the contribution today, and immediately see your taxes fall. The smaller tax check (or bigger refund) helps fund the IRA savings. Moreover, tax day, for many people, is a time of financial reckoning, when they take stock of their overall fiscal health. Thus, it becomes an excellent time for households to assess whether they are saving enough.

Now comes the moment of truth. Can you think of a similar kind of problem—where simply delaying the deduction deadline would help?

Well, what other things can you claim as a deduction on your taxes? And in particular, what other socially desirable activities can you claim as a deduction?

How about charity?

Notice all the parallels between charity and IRA contributions. Charitable contributions are deductible and are quintessentially discretionary. There are similar liquidity and disconnect problems with getting people to give at the end of the calendar year. It is harder for people to see the salience of donating when they don't reap the tax reward until four months later.

But, maybe most important, April 15 as a day of financial reckoning is an ideal time to reflect on whether we've given enough to charity. Thanks to Schedule A, tax day is often the first time that we add up how much we've given and see how it stacks up against what we've earned over the year.

Under the current deadline, by the time you can see how much you made and how much you gave in the past year, it's literally too late to be more generous. Simply extending the tax deductibility deadline of charitable donations to April 15, in line with the IRA contribution rule, would allow people to make more informed choices about their generosity.[14]

Most Americans are deeply confused about what is an appropriate amount to give to charity. We teach our kids to tip at least 15 percent in a restaurant. But, except for the few folks out there who tithe, we don't teach our kids how much they should give to charity.

By the same token, we generally know how much our parents tip, but very few of us know what percentage of income our parents give to charity.[15] In fact, most people don't even know what percentage of their own income they give to charity.

Ask yourself this question: Are your contributions above or below average? Most people can't answer. First, they don't know what percentage of their income they donate, and second, they don't know what the national average is.

Our informal survey of Yale undergraduates found that very few students had any idea what percentage of income their parents donated. The topic was never discussed. The national average is 2 percent, but there is a huge variation, and many people with above-average incomes give virtually nothing.

Delaying the deduction deadline could be part of a strategy to give people more information about how much they are giving and how much they should be giving—at a time when they can do something about it. If a simple lack of generosity is the explanation for a low level of charity giving, then there's no easy solution. Certainly, there are some Scrooges out there. But another cause of the problem—and one much easier to fix—is a lack of information and the corresponding lack of a social norm.

Here, the IRS might also translate a solution from the theory of social-norms marketing. In 1990, H. Wesley Perkins, a professor at Hobart and William Smith College, discovered that most students think that they drink less than the average—and thus increase their consumption to be more like others. When the true drinking data is publicized, and students discover that few of their peers have more than five drinks at a party, peer pressure to binge is greatly reduced. The results were so successful in reducing heavy drinking that this approach has been employed throughout the California state university system and beyond. Rather than telling students to "Just say no," it is more effective to say, "Just be like most everybody else."[16]

The IRS could apply the same approach to charity by simply reporting how much other people give. Instead of urging, "Just say yes!" to charity, it would likely be more effective saying, "Just be like the average."

By requiring everyone to calculate his or her charitable giving as a percentage of income, the IRS could powerfully and simply solve the self-ignorance problem. Suddenly, donation percentages, like tipping percentages, would be something that people know about themselves.

The 1040 instruction sheet could also report on an income-by-income level what the average contribution rate is. The IRS already has these data, and with enough digging, you can find them on the IRS Web site. Currently, the information is used by tax software—such as Turbo Tax—for the purpose of assessing audit risk. A much better use would be to allow individuals to perform a Scrooge (or moral conscience) audit on themselves.

Few people want to see themselves as above-average drinkers. Conversely, for charitable giving, few want to see themselves as below average. If people think that income is a good indication of ability to give, then they wouldn't want to fall too far below the average for their income group.

Of course, a comparison with the average percentage might induce some above-average givers to reduce their contributions. But, since the median contribution is far below the mean, the number of people who will feel pressure to donate more will greatly exceed the number who might be tempted to give less. And, generally, we predict a Lake Wobegon competition of people all trying to be above average.

Publishing information about social norms for charity dovetails with the IRA-inspired delayed deduction. When April 15 comes around, suddenly it's not too late to give more when households finally get around to toting up their charitable gifts. If you discover that you haven't given quite enough, you can still give more to *last year's* charities when you file.

As people look for ways to trim their tax liability, seeing the immediate tax savings from donations would similarly encourage people to give to charity. By letting people know more about their own giving and the giving of others, the IRS would help create a national norm of giving. And allowing people to deduct contributions up until they file would encourage Americans to be more generous. People who inadvertently find themselves below the norm would have an additional chance to step up to the plate.

Most people think of April 15 as tax day, but a few simple changes—built around the translations of the delayed IRA deduction and the just-be-like-others norm—could make us start thinking of the ides of April as "charity day," a moment in our lives when we reflect on whether we have been doing enough for the less fortunate.

Bookstore Coffeehouses

Here's a pretty straightforward translation. Barnes & Noble (and many other bookstores) have learned that people enjoy a cup of joe while browsing for books. Nowadays, it's hard to find a bookstore that doesn't have a Starbucks or some other espresso vendor. A perfect synergy.

Might some other places benefit from offering coffee? Increasing numbers of retailers—from hair salons and car dealerships to gas stations and minimarts—are providing high-end coffee. However, we're thinking of a translation closer to the Barnes & Noble implementation.

Hint: Where else can you browse for books?

The public library, of course. Why not have Starbucks at your local branch? It's a little bizarre that people prefer to hang out at a place where they have to pay for books, rather than one where they can borrow them for free. The lack of quality caffeine may be part of the reason.

Now, the constraints of architecture may provide part of an explanation why we don't see more library coffeehouses. The library building stock was not designed to accommodate coffee sales. But we've seen retailers fit coffee corners into all kinds of pre-existing spaces, and old library buildings have accommodated consumers in ways never initially contemplated.

Probably a deeper problem is a lingering attitude toward libraries. A librarian at the Brooklyn Public Library pointed out to us that the majority of libraries in the United States were founded when libraries were more like temples than service or entertainment centers. Andrew Carnegie would roll over in his grave if he thought someone could spill coffee or smear chocolate on a book!

But bookstores don't want their inventory trashed either, and they've proved that you can lubricate the consumer without unduly risking the stock. And, let's face it, it's better to get some sinners in the seats than to have an empty temple in which no one prays.

Still think this is a crazy idea? What if you learned that several of the largest U.S. cities have already started this experiment? Not surprisingly, West Coast libraries have taken the lead with espresso bars in at least some of the libraries in Los Angeles, San Francisco, and Seattle. A Starbucks is coming to the main branch of Portland's public library. But the phenomenon can also be found in Brooklyn and Detroit, where the library's main branches operate cafés. The new British Library in London has had a café since it opened in the 1990s.

Aficionados might worry that the government just can't brew a good cup of coffee. But public museums in many different cities have shown for years that it is possible to run quality restaurants (at least sufficient to our taste buds). And the existing library espresso bars are invariably run by outside vendors. There's no reason why the skinny vanilla latte at Portland's main branch should not be every bit as good as the one you can currently buy at Borders.

Libraries might also take a translation lesson from what has become the largest private lending library—that's right, Blockbuster. When a hit book comes out, the local library could buy extra copies with the idea of reselling them soon thereafter on the used-book market (say, Half.com or Amazon.com). Perhaps it could even work out an arrangement with publishers to lease extra copies of newly released titles. Here the translation comes from automakers. One of the advantages of the leasing structure is that the used cars come back to the dealers, which then have some control over the second-hand market. Book publishers might prefer to lease best-sellers to libraries and then regain control of the second-hand market.

We discussed the translation of coffee shops from Barnes & Noble to libraries. Perhaps an even more immediate translation is the idea that libraries might even sell some books. Now, before you gasp in horror, keep in mind that the new British Library has a bookstore, and many libraries offer used book sales, but only periodically (no pun intended). We wouldn't expect a library bookstore to compete with the chains. It might emphasize books on school reading lists or those requested by local reading groups. It might use the bookstore to promote acquisition—buy this book at a 50 percent discount and get a tax deduction if you agree to donate it to the library after you've read it. Oh, and you get to be the first one to take it out.

CASE STUDY

Black Box for Cars

Driving a car is one of the most dangerous things we do. In the United States, there are 24 million auto accidents each year and 2.3 million people injured. The number of auto fatalities is the equivalent of a 737 plane crash every day.

For the most part, we don't want to think about the danger from driving. We've become so dependent on cars that we decide it is one of those risks we have to accept as part of being a modern society.

That fatalistic attitude is wrong. Sweden has a Vision Zero Initiative—the stated goal is to reduce auto deaths to zero. If you think that's impossible, consider that the Swedes are already halfway there. Their accident rate per mile driven is the lowest in the world and is 30 percent below the U.S. rate. If the United States could achieve Sweden's current standard, this would save 12,500 lives per year.[17]

Flying is safer than driving. Applying the translation tool suggests that we might look to airline safety to find ways to make driving less dangerous. Everyone knows that the first thing people do after a crash is to look for the black box, more formally known as the event data recorder. Why not a black box for cars?*

At first impression, you might not think that a black box in cars would do much good. The potential gains may surprise you. First, the black box would allow police and carmakers to understand what actually happens in a car crash. The traditional way of estimating crash severity looks at factors such as skid marks and steel deformation. These inputs are fed into a computer model known as WINSMASH. But the results can be wildly inaccurate.

The National Highway Traffic Safety Administration (NHTSA) found this out when investigating a fatal accident that had occurred at an estimated 23 miles per hour. As it considered the possibility that the car involved, a 1998 Chevrolet Malibu, might have

---

*Speaking of black boxes, why are the boxes kept on the plane? It would seem that the data should be transmitted to the ground.

a design flaw, the GM representative let the investigators know that the car had stored all the data about the crash. The NHTSA's WINSMASH estimates were off base by 100 percent. The car was going approximately 50 miles per hour.[18]

Remember the Audi scare about sudden acceleration? With black boxes, we would know once and for all if the drivers had their foot on the brake or the accelerator. What about Ford Explorer roll-overs? We would know what the g-forces were at the time of an accident. Job one for fixing something is to understand what went wrong. Without these data, it is mostly guesswork.

It isn't hard to see that black boxes can make for safer cars. What is perhaps surprising is that they can also make for safer drivers. A lot safer. A NHTSA report describes some results from Europe, where trials are already taking place.

> After the Berlin police department employed data recorders in its patrol cars, accidents fell by 20 percent. Damage during rescue trips fell by 36 percent. The savings were about a thousand deutsche marks per car.
>
> Similar results were found in tests in Vienna, Netherlands, and Belgium. Crash rates fell by 28 percent.
>
> In Oldenburg, Germany, the Hatscher taxi company put these boxes into its fleet. Collision rates fell by 66 percent.[19]

If there were a drug that could save this many lives, people would be clamoring outside the Food and Drug Administration for its approval. If they knew that it was saving lives in Germany and yet wasn't available in the United States, they would smuggle it into the country. The event data recorder is a life-saving drug with no side effects.

How does it work? It turns out that just knowing the box is there changes behavior. If you get into an accident, you know the truth will out. Fear of getting caught may be a more powerful motivator than fear of getting killed.[20]

Ricardo Martinez is a doctor and former head of the NHTSA. He remembers his days working ambulances in North Carolina. The ambulance service had something called a *growler* installed in all the cars. If he accelerated too fast or took a corner too hard, the machine would start squawking. It he didn't slow down, it would start squawking louder and soon thereafter record a mark. When he got back to base, he'd have to explain the marks.

Sunstar Emergency Medical Services of Pinellas County, Florida, has put growlers in its fleet of ambulances. Operations supervisor Scott Springstead described the results:"[A] reduction of 20-to-1 in the severity of our crashes. Mirrors still get clipped and fenders get bent, but there have been no big accidents."[21]

American Medical Response has this feedback system in eight hundred vehicles. Ron Thackery, vice president for safety, risk management, and fleet administration, described the changes in behavior: "The entire group went from Level 1 to Level 5 in less than 90 days. It's almost like Pavlov's dog in terms of conditioned response. That immediate feedback and conditioning helps to improve the safety of the driving."[22]

Level 1 means the drivers get more than one violation per mile. Violations include speeding, hard braking, rapid acceleration, and hard cornering. By level 5, the violation count is down to one per eight miles. Many fleets consider level 6—one violation per sixteen miles—the minimum standard for safe driving.

At this point, you should be wondering why this product is limited to ambulances. Where else could this be employed?

Larry Selditz, president of Road Safety International, has taken the idea and translated it to the family car. As he points out, teenagers drive much better when their parents are sitting next to them. His black box device is always there watching the driver. When the kids come home, the parents can download driving information to review it.

The early results from the device's recordings have been eye-popping for parents. The box showed that Mallory Gompert—both smart and polite as she addresses a reporter—had a lead foot. She routinely cruised in the family's Ford Explorer at more than 80 mph, and she took turns dangerously fast. She had no idea, she says, that she was over the limit. Neither, of course, did her parents. "I used to dread it when my dad would come home with his PC and say, 'Let's see how your driving is,'" Mallory says. Now she likes the way the box reminds her to pay attention when she "spaces out." Because of her improved driving, she says, other parents ask her to drive their kids, and she hauls her siblings to practices and other places. "I was a soccer mom at age 16."[23]

Road Safety has a great product. Some people are worried about privacy. We're not. If our teenagers are concerned about privacy, they can get their own cars. Until then, we and they will both be better off looking over their shoulders.

Our question is, why have Ford and GM—even their Volvo and Saab brands—dropped the ball? They already have these data collection devices in their cars. The data exist thanks to the computers in a modern car. Antilock brakes are digital. Air-bag sensors record g-force. But the automakers haven't made it easy for us to access

"Relax, dear, that howling wolf sound is just
my new driver-monitoring device."

Keeping Your Eyes Open

The black box is one important safety idea. Other smart ideas are being implemented—just not enough and not fast enough. In 1975, the National Transportation Safety Board (NTSB) recommended center-mounted rear brake lights. It took ten years before these lights were required for cars and another eight years for light trucks. The center brake light prevents some 100,000 annual accidents, 60,000 injuries, and nearly $700 million in property damage. These property savings alone are three times as large as the cost of putting in the lights.[24]

States can learn from each other. In North Carolina, for example, teenage drivers can't be on the road after 9:00 P.M. Twenty states have adopted the graduated driver's license. But that leaves thirty states that haven't. The NTSB has been recommending the graduated driver's license since 1993. It upped the ante in 2002 with a call to require new drivers to take at most one passenger (under age twenty) unless accompanied by an adult. Seven states have adopted this rule; forty-three have not.[25]

With the exception of New Hampshire (whose citizens take their "Live Free or Die" license plate seriously), all states have seat belt laws. But only twelve states have adopted the NTSB's 1996 proposal to allow police officers to stop and ticket you for not wearing a belt. Those states have 15 percent higher safety belt usage. Meanwhile, only two-thirds of all drivers wear safety belts.

the data. In fact, for GM cars, almost nothing more needs to be done—except finding a way to download the information from the existing computer chips so that it can be used.

All the carmakers want the youth market. This is their chance to start the customer off on a lifetime relationship with their brand. For teenagers (and their parents), there are two large costs associated with having a new driver in the family. Insurance premiums go through the roof. Parents worry about the safety of their children.

If Ford took the lead and had the black box as an option in its cars, this could be a huge selling point. Insurance companies could offer significant discounts to families that agreed to employ the device.

Ford can work to make either its cars or other components of driving more affordable. The company can't do much about the price of gasoline (other than raising fuel efficiency). But if it can help cut insurance costs, this is just as good as cutting the price of its cars. Indeed, if the black box could save a thousand dollars in annual premiums, then over three years this would be a huge discount.

Carmakers have been too focused on bending metal—making cars—and not focused enough on getting passengers safely from one place to another. Safety is a business opportunity. How much more would you pay for a car that would cut in half the chance your child would have a car crash? Even better, what if you could get those safety enhancements and also save several thousand dollars on your insurance? The black box in cars is close to reality. With some public pressure, it will happen.

A Video Résumé?

Finally, for fun, let's take a look at two of life's more daunting activities—job hunting and dating—and try a double translation to see what each activity can learn from the other. In some ways, the two are birds of a feather. Both involve matchmaking. Both require one person to get to know the other. And in both situations, mistakes can be quite costly.

Two distinct solutions have emerged in these two contexts: the job résumé and video dating services. What would happen if we were to switch these two solutions around?

The dating résumé? Well, it certainly is fun to imagine. In the typical job résumé, the candidate provides a list of all previous jobs, what he or she learned from each experience, and references. Translating this idea, a dating applicant would list all previous relationships, what he or she learned from those experiences, and provide references. While we admit that the dating market may not be ready for this innovation, perhaps our married status puts us in too conservative a frame of mind. The TV show *Blind Date* (not that we watch it, but from those glances when changing channels) often begins with the two strangers providing just such an oral history. And we do note that speed dating—pioneered and even trademarked by Los Angeles rabbi Yaacov Deyo—has prospective dates interviewing each other for a strict seven-minute clock, much like a job fair.[26]

How about making the translation go the other way? What can job hunting learn from computer dating? Consider the video résumé. A big innovation in computer dating was the introduction of video clips. The parallel would be to include a link to a short QuickTime movie of the candidate as part of the standard résumé. For some job candidates, this would be a great service.*

As professors, we see that many of our foreign students, and even American students with hard-to-pronounce foreign names, are discriminated against in the job market.[27] Potential employers may be concerned about the candidate's English skills. A quick video clip would go a long way toward helping employers discover who is fluent and who isn't.

University admissions officers are in a position similar to that of employers. Although foreign students take the TOEFL (Test of English as a Foreign Language), it would be very comforting to hear students speak as a way of confirming their fluency, along with their reading and writing skills. (The TOEFL does include a spoken part in the exam.)

Another group of job candidates who would be receptive to this idea are those who are better looking than the rest of us. Unlike demonstrating English skills, using looks is much more likely to be problematic. Video clips make it easier for people to discriminate based on a candidate's attractiveness or accent or skin color.**

An audio clip would be enough to resolve the English skills question without facilitating discrimination. Right now, the situation is almost backward. Job seekers have begun to include a photograph on their résumés, which allows discrimination without offering an opportunity to demonstrate a mastery of English. It is quite unlikely that people will move from a photo to just an audio. With

---

*We even have a name for this service: CMECV.com (pronounced "See Me C.V.").

**Even if better looks lead to higher productivity, as may be the case with some sales jobs, this is rewarding discrimination by customers. Taller people earn more—and not just in the NBA.

digital camcorders and editing tools on the PC, it is really only a matter of time before we can expect video clips to become a standard part of the résumé.

To see how this technology might be best used, we also can translate from the real estate market. Many real estate Web sites, such as Realtor.com and others, offer home buyers a virtual tour of a property before they visit it. Although this seems an obvious use of technology, the idea of a virtual tour failed when it was first brought to market.

Jim Conner created Studio Realty in 1991 to market virtual house tours as a convenience for home shoppers.[28] His initial aim was to get the person to buy the house without actually kicking the tires, so to speak. He expected his technology would replace or at least diminish the role of the real estate agent. Real estate agents resisted his approach, the technology was a bit ahead of its time, and the business ultimately failed.

As things turned out, virtual house tours are now standard on the Web. Rather than replace real estate agents, the virtual tour enhances the agent's relationship with the buyer. The big problem in this business is sending people out to see a house that they don't like. Not only is this a huge waste of time, but it also puts into question whether the agent is trying to push a loser house onto the buyer (in order to collect a commission) or whether the agent simply made an honest mistake.

By sitting with the home buyer and taking the virtual tour together, the agent can do a much better job of understanding the buyer's preferences: Does the person like a ranch house, a colonial, a four square, and so on? In this setting, it may not even be important that the houses shown are actually on the market. Instead, this tour ends up being like the Briggs Personality Inventory, which helps reveal what sort of jobs a person would like. Similarly, video dating services may use the video clips of potential partners to uncover the person's preferences and thereby complement rather than substitute for the person's matchmaking skills.

Another benefit of the video clip is the ability to look at many prospects for a relatively low investment of time and money. For example, Conner was able to sell his listed properties in 59 days, compared to the market average of 120 days. Through his virtual tours, he was able to get many more people to "look" at the property. Driving out to view a home is costly for all parties involved, and being wrong is sufficiently costly that it makes people very risk-averse. In contrast, sitting in the real estate agent's office looking at houses on a monitor has a low cost. Thus, if the house isn't a right fit, the person can move on to the next one. But if the information piques the buyer's interest, the person might choose to go on a real tour.

The video clip on the résumé would work the same way. Many job seekers, especially those right out of college or graduate school, are applying to work in a different city. But a lot of firms aren't willing to fly someone out for an interview because the cost is too high given the uncertainty. The video clip lowers the risk and thereby allows more people to take the next step.

But don't expect career development offices to welcome this technology. Right now, they feel overwhelmed helping students write their résumés. The last thing they would want is to feel pressured to help kids script, act, and edit a short self-promo clip.

Would Flipping It Work?

Trying Things the Other Way Around

The photograph is a nighttime image of Natalie Jeremijenko's
Tree Logic at Mass MoCA, North Adams, Massachusetts.

By now, our obsession with symmetry is probably clear. You've already seen several applications of the idea. Priceline lets the buyer instead of the seller choose the price; Star Video has its customers rewind videos at the beginning of the rental instead of the end. Even the idea of solutions in search of problems is a flipping of the traditional problem-solving approach.

It turns out that there are potential symmetries all around us— ways of flipping things around that might be just as good or better—if we just look for them. Ian's students know to raise their hands if they *don't* want to be called on. Ann Landers asked her readers whether toilet paper should be dispensed from the top of the roll or from underneath. Thousands of readers wrote in to defend their position. More paper has been wasted on this topic than we care to discuss. Although we think the top is better, we'll leave this one to others to resolve—except to point out that Landers created a debate about symmetry.

Or consider the banana. Now, it might seem that everybody peels a banana pretty much the same way. You hold the banana in one hand and bend the stem with your other hand. Right? But what would it mean to turn this one around? Here we look to the advice of *Slate* columnist Steven Landsburg.[1]

He suggests that you can start at the nonstem end. Pinch the end a bit, and then pull. Peeling from the nonstem end is actually a bit easier and reduces the chance that those annoying, stringy fibers will stick to the banana. (If you have a banana handy, it's worth taking a pause and giving this a try.) Bananas also tend to ripen at the nonstem end first, so peeling a banana this other way often lets you avoid the bruised or unripe part. And you get a built-in handle.

You must be thinking, this is ridiculous. If this really were a better way of eating bananas, wouldn't we all be doing it? Is there any

Marriage Saver

Curtis Batts has an invention that lets the individual user choose which is better. His Tilt-a-Roll (featured on Jay Leno's *Tonight Show*) allows the user to swivel the roll so that the toilet tissue can feed from either above or below.[2]

evidence that might convince you otherwise? Trying it the other way for yourself is a pretty convincing experiment. And there are some banana-peeling "experts" out there who are pretty convincing on this subject. Monkeys peel bananas from the bottom up. Could it be that we humans have been getting it wrong all this time?

Who would have thought? This is an example where starting with the problem would definitely not have led us to the solution.

For the most part, people find an answer that works and don't get in the habit of looking for an even better solution. Or we think there is some natural way of doing things and stop looking for alternatives.

Did you ever store a ketchup bottle upside down? How long did it take for Hunt's and H. J. Heinz to figure out that they could turn the label upside down? According to Heinz's Casey Keller,

this change was no small matter: "We believe this is probably the biggest idea in ketchup since the invention of the plastic squeeze bottle."[3] In the old days, Heinz used Carly Simon's "Anticipation" as part of its marketing. The updated campaign is "No Anticipation." Ketchup is not the only product to take advantage of this insight: Toothpaste, shampoo, and even sour cream now all come this way.

What's the natural way of steering a car? Cars all steer from the front. Sure, we have front-wheel drive and rear-wheel drive and four-wheel drive, but this is the source of the power, not the steering. How would you go about imagining a car that steers from the back rather than the front? It isn't as strange as you might imagine. Forklifts steer from the back. Boats are steered from the back. So are airplanes.[4] (Trains don't have this problem.) To get a sense of how a car would work if steered from the rear, all you need to do is drive in reverse. We do this every time we back out of the driveway.

So, which is better—steering from the front or the rear? We don't know. We suspect that the best answer would involve some of each. This idea goes back at least as far as Buckminster Fuller's 1933 Dymaxion car. By turning the rear wheel, a driver could make this twenty-foot-long car do a U-turn inside its own length.[5] More recently, the Honda Prelude, Mazda 626, Dodge Stealth R/T, Mitsubishi 3000GT VR4, Nissan 300 ZX, and Suburu four-wheel-drive SVX all have this capability.

An interesting question is which way the rear wheels should turn. At slow speeds, turning the rear wheel in the opposite direction (like a fire truck) improves the turning radius. Indeed, the GM Sierra Denali pickup truck uses "Quadrasteer" to reduce the turning radius from 47.3 feet to 37.4. But at higher speeds, having the rear wheels turn in the same direction as the front improves handling through corners. The GM Quadrasteer system senses the car's speed and turns the rear wheels either with or against the front wheels accordingly.[6] We see that both answers work—to solve different problems.

The idea of flipping things around is one of the tools described in Edward de Bono's *Lateral Thinking:*

> *In the reversal method, one takes things as they are and then turns them round, inside out, upside down, back to front. Then one sees what happens. . . . There are usually several different ways in which one can reverse a given situation. There is no one correct way. Nor should there be any search for some true reversal. Any sort of reversal will do. . . . For instance, if the situation is, 'a policeman organizing traffic,' then the following reversals might be made:*
>
> > *The traffic organizes (controls) the policeman.*
> > *The policeman disorganizes the traffic.*
>
> *In lateral thinking one is not looking for the right answer but for a different arrangement of information which will provoke a different way of looking at the situation.*[7]

We share de Bono's enthusiasm for turning things upside down. But we want to do more than provoke—we really are looking for a right answer or at least a better one. If the flipped solution doesn't work in the original problem, is there a different problem for which it is a useful solution?

This is getting a bit ahead of ourselves. Before we can look for the problem to be solved, we first need to come up with the reversal. Thus we begin with a systematic approach to turning solutions around.

The Stress Test

Our goal is to move from a series of examples to develop a method for identifying a business practice that should be flipped. There are so many dimensions of even a relatively simple transaction that it can seem intimidating to know where to start.

We suggest that you force yourself to break the existing practice down into its component parts and write a description in simple, declarative sentences. More detail is better than less. Then, when you have the description, imagine what it would mean to turn around each or several of the components.

In *Co-opetition,* Barry and coauthor Adam Brandenburger played off the mirror symmetry between competing and cooperating.[8] There is extensive research on competitive strategy. What is the theory of cooperative strategy?

In turning things around, they noticed that the word *competitor* was missing its antonym. What is the opposite of a competitor? It isn't obvious. *Partner* is too general, as a customer or supplier could also be a partner. To turn the idea of a competitor around, it helps to start with a precise description of what a competitor is:

A competitor is a firm whose product or service makes your product less valuable to the customer.

The obvious switch to make here is to turn the word *less* into *more*. What type of firm makes your products *more* valuable? A firm whose goods and services complement yours. But no noun existed to describe this relationship. How about *complementor?* This is a word that you understand upon hearing it, and surprisingly, it didn't exist in any language. The lack of a term for this relationship strongly suggests that the strategic role of a comple- mentor was not well understood. Coining a word helped lead to a theory of competitive and cooperative business strategy. Indeed, the role of complementors is becoming recognized as a missing sixth force in the Porter five-force framework.[9]

The First Shall Be the Last

Here's an example of how to turn ideas around. We start with how Sotheby's would describe its auction business:

> *An item is put up for sale.*
>
> *The auctioneer proposes successively higher prices.*
>
> *The highest bidder wins.*

This list is just a beginning. But this rough start is more than enough to identify plenty of auction alternatives.

The next step is to take what we call a *stress test*. The idea here is to stress different words in a sentence. Robert De Niro, in *Taxi Driver,* taught us that the now-famous phrase "Are you talking to me?" can mean very different things depending on whether *you, talking,* or *me* is emphasized. Just stressing different words in the sentence forces you to destabilize your initial unconscious focus.

The final step is to try to systematically flip the individual words that you are stressing. "Are you *not talking* to me?" Like De Niro, you probably want to start with the nouns and the verbs, but adjectives *(good/bad)* and adverbs *(fast/slow)* are often flip-pable as well. Sometimes you will want to flip two words at once: "Am *I* talking to *you?*"

So, let's see how the stress test applies to our three auction sen- tences. Not every noun or verb leads to an interesting idea, but sev- eral do. Which words might you stress in the first sentence, and how might they be flipped?

> *An item is put up for sale.*

The main activity is always a good place to start:

An item is put up for purchase.

A potential buyer could put up an item that he or she seeks to purchase. Government procurement auctions do this all the time. The government wants to pave a road and puts a purchase order up for auction. In fact, a procurement auction is even called a reverse auction. Sellers compete to win the right to sell the services or product to the buyer, and the one offering the lowest price usually wins.

Let's turn our attention to the second sentence:

The auctioneer proposes successively higher prices.

Systematically force yourself to stress each of the words in the sentence (okay, you can omit "the"), and ask yourself which is the most flippable. Probably it's the word *higher*. Could Sotheby's have an auction in which the auctioneer proposed successively *lower* prices?

Well, sure. It could be a procurement auction, in which the low bidder wins. But let's assume that we haven't flipped the first sentence. We're looking for an auction in which something is for sale and yet the auctioneer proposed successively lower prices.

Do I hear $100? Do I hear $90? Do I hear $80?

How could this work? How could Sotheby's offer auction items for sale but still have the auctioneer propose successively lower prices? The auctioneer could start with a very high price and start lowering the price until a buyer is willing to bid. Instead of the item's being sold to the *last* bidder, it is sold to the *first* buyer to put in a bid. The symmetry tool led us to what is called a Dutch auction, which is the standard auction format used in Holland to sell flowers.

In the English auction, you can think of all the active participants as having their hands up. As the auctioneer keeps on raising the price, people drop out. The auction is over when only one hand is left up. In the Dutch auction, all the participants start with their hands down. As the auctioneer continues to lower the price, the bidders decide when they want to "drop in." The first person to raise his or her hand stops the bidding and wins the auction. Whereas the traditional English auction looks for the last person to back down, the Dutch auction looks for the first one to volunteer.

Symmetry Puzzler: Reverse 900 Numbers

The Sotheby's example shows how the symmetry tool can lead to other auction forms that we know are workable because they already exist in the world. Now let's roll up our sleeves and apply the tool to try to imagine a useful service that doesn't yet exist.

What would it mean to apply the idea of symmetry to the 900 service? What would a reverse 900 service look like? Let's start by applying the stress test methodology. First, try to describe the existing service in a single sentence:

> *By calling a 900 number, you trigger a payment that will be charged to your phone bill.*

What words in this sentence are prime candidates for alternative emphasis? Let's start with *charged*. How could it be flipped?

> *By calling a 900 number, you trigger a payment that will be* credited *to your phone bill.*

Under this flipped service, some businesses would pay you to call them. That's an interesting idea. Some casinos will pay you to visit them. Perhaps some businesses would be willing to pay you to listen to their pitch. In some sense, networks are paying you to watch their television ads by giving you the show that surrounds the ad. This idea makes even more sense if we now flip the action as well.

> *By* receiving a call from *a 900 number, you trigger a payment that will be* credited *to your phone bill.*

Voilà! We've just created the reverse 900 service. We have a new service. You would get paid to take a call. But who would pay you?

We have an answer that is looking for the right problem. Where might this solution prove valuable? We think this simple symmetry idea might radically redeem one of the great pariah practices of our time—telemarketing.

Telemarketers are almost universally despised. There are more than 200 billion reasons every year not to like them. (That's more than two calls per day, per household.[10]) Telemarketing came in fourth in *Time* magazine's list of the worst ideas of the twentieth century.

Twenty states have responded by prohibiting telemarketers from calling any number registered on the state's don't-call list. And the Federal Trade Commission has proposed creating a national don't-call registry.

The reverse 900 service is a better solution.[11] Instead of forcing the all-or-nothing choice of the don't-call solution, the reverse 900 idea gives households the opportunity to be compensated for listening to telemarketing calls. Under this scheme, you would get paid for each minute that you listen to a telemarketer's pitch. While the telemarketers are trying to sell you a product, you can sell them your time. You would still be able to register on the don't-call lists, but you would simultaneously authorize your local carrier to connect any calls that offer to pay your price per minute.

The local carrier, or some other authorized intermediary, could let you charge different prices for calls that come at different times of the day or that pitched different products. It could even only connect calls that were previously approved by Good Housekeeping or Jerry Falwell.

Many businesses would prosper. Companies with legitimate offers wouldn't be caught in the current din. Pollsters would get their surveys answered. Instead of hanging up, people would say, "Are you sure there aren't any more questions?" Just as phone companies profit from 800 and 900 calls, the authorized intermediaries would compete for household business so that they could charge a fee for reverse 900 calls, too.

This solution would also let us radically reduce regulation. For example, we don't prohibit prerecorded radio or TV ads, but several states prohibit prerecorded telephone ads. This regulation (along with the prohibition against solicitations to your cell phone and nighttime calling) makes sense if you aren't getting paid to listen. But it makes more sense to pay the listener minimum wage to listen to a recording of James Earl Jones than to pay a phone-bank caller minimum wage to speak to you. Instead of thinking of direct marketing as a pariah industry that needs to be caged or crippled, the simple compensation idea allows us to reconceive direct marketing as an attractive business opportunity for both firms *and* consumers.

As things stand, telemarketers are trying to take your time and attention without paying you for it. That's why their success rate is so low, which only leads them to call more often, which makes you like them less, and around it goes. This is a classic externality problem. Telemarketers call too often because they do not *internalize* the true cost of their calls. What do they care if they inconvenience or annoy fifty people to make one sale?

Thus, the internalization tool might have also led us to the same solution. If externalized costs are the problem, then internalizing these costs—making the telemarketer feel your pain—is the natural solution. With a reverse 900 service, you would receive fewer telemarketing calls, and the ones you did receive would likely be more interesting because the telemarketers would take more care to make sure they were offering you a product that you might actually want.[12]

But WWCD would *not* have helped us solve this one. A modern Croesus would screen the calls at his end. Here we need the screening to occur at the caller's end. So, while some ideas can be generated by multiple tools, you can't safely rely on any one tool to get the job done.

A New Meaning for Pay Phones

Using the phone as a way of getting paid suggests a radical remake of the phone's functionality. The phone is the best micropayment device that exists today. Phone companies have developed systems that are very well suited to tracking and billing penny-level transactions. Why not use the cell phone as the primary payment device? At the end of a meal, the restaurant would give you a number to call. You'd type the number, confirm the amount, input your code, and transfer the money from your account to the restaurant's. This concept is being test-marketed with vending machines—dial 888-THIRSTY for a soda. The phone company has taken too narrow a view of its business. It could well be the preferred financial payment option.

Before ending this symmetry puzzler, let's pull out the translation tool. Is there anywhere else besides telemarketing where the reverse 900 idea might be used?

If we step back and try to articulate the core idea behind the reverse 900 number, we see it as a way of compensating people for being annoyed. So the trick is to look for other annoyances that are currently uncompensated. There are big fish to be fried if we just focus on other types of marketing annoyance. TV and magazine ads are kind of a pain, but at least we're compensated by receiving the non-ad content of magazine articles and television programs. What's more, consumers opt for such ads by turning on their TV or by subscribing in the first place.

The slam-dunk translation of the reverse 900 idea concerns the analogous problems of spam e-mail and junk mail. Although we choose to subscribe to e-mail and postal services, we can't as easily "turn them off" when they annoy us, as we can with the TV. We don't consent to these intrusions into our privacy, and again, we aren't compensated.

But the predominant impulse for the blight of spam and junk mail is again the too-blunt instrument of the outright ban. It would be better to allow people to opt out of unsolicited mass mailings unless the sender compensates the recipient. Individuals would still have the option of a complete ban, but many consumers would rather receive some unsolicited mail in return for cash.

This compensation scheme is not hard to implement. Indeed, we could directly translate the reverse 900 idea to the Pitney Bowes machine—so that every time a junk mailer postmarked a letter to your address, your home telephone bill would be credited with your desired compensation.

E-mail is harder to manage through state or even federal regulation, because the Internet opens our in box to spam from the global village. But you (or your Internet service provider) could set up your in box to do this job for you.

The basic idea is that anyone who wants to send you an e-mail would have to attach a payment chit equaling the minimum amount that you set in order for the e-mail to go through.[13] This chit would not be an actual payment but would be a firm offer to pay that would only be activated (accepted) if the recipient clicked on the chit icon. The payment would use some sort of proxy payment service, such as Paypal.

You would have a list of people who could send you e-mail for free, and you could also decline the payment if the e-mail was from a person you wanted to hear from. Thus, all the e-mails that you want from friends and family—and, if you so choose, even unsolicited e-mails from strangers—could get through for free. But the service quickly screens out all the unwanted pitches for confidential Viagra, mortgage refinancing, and "Nigerian millionaire" business opportunities.

Under this solution, you would set up your in box to only accept e-mails that credibly offered to pay you, say, a nickel. But you would only actually accept the payments from spammers (or others who annoyed you). The real beauty of the Paypal chit is that it requires no lawsuits or government prosecution. Private filtering via the chit does the trick all by itself.

If you like this idea, you may be in luck. One start-up, Vanquish.com, has created the technology to create bonded e-mails. If the company can persuade AOL or Hotmail to adopt the policy of only accepting bonded e-mails, it will be "game over" for spammers.

CASE STUDY

'Tis Better to Receive Than to Make Cell Phone Calls

When you receive a call on your cell phone, who pays?

In the United States, the rule is that the receiving party pays.[14] (This is the reason that telemarketing was banned on cell phones.) The typical pricing plan for cell phones doesn't distinguish between minutes used to make a call and to receive a call. Nor is there any reason to do so from a cost perspective. Each uses the same amount of spectrum and switching capacity.

Yet the game is played quite differently in Europe and Asia, where it is typically free to receive a call on your cell phone. The only minutes that count are for outgoing calls.

Which system is better? Initially, the Europeans gloated, thinking their system was far superior. They attributed the much more rapid adoption of mobile phones to the free receiving pricing.

Finding Your Cell Mates

Why are cell phone numbers not listed? The lack of a directory makes it particularly difficult for people whose only phone is cellular. For those concerned about privacy or the cost of paying for unwanted calls, cell phone numbers, like home phone numbers, could be unlisted. Another problem is that there isn't just one provider, as with local numbers. But geographic translations may give us hope. In Denmark, TeleDenmark provides a cell phone directory, and not just for its own customers.

In the United States, the problem with "receiver pays" was that people were slow to give out their cell phone numbers. They didn't want to pay high prices to speak with just anyone. This understandable reticence delayed the adoption of cell phones and has led to other problems, such as the lack of a cell phone number directory.

At first blush, the European system seems right. If you want to speak to me, then you should pay. You can decide if it's worth it or not. As a receiver, I didn't choose to have you call me; therefore, I shouldn't have to pay.

While this caller-pays system worked well to help establish the system, today it has become a land mine. Per-minute fees are now much higher in Europe than in the United States. The reason is that people are shopping for only half their service—their calls out and not their calls in.

The problem is that most customers pay little attention to how much others will have to pay to call them—it's not their nickel. The phone companies take full advantage of this situation.

For example, in the U.K., if you have a T Mobile cell phone, then someone who calls you from a land line will have to pay as much as 23.14 pence per minute—that's almost 40 cents per minute.[15] Calling from a rival cell phone network can cost even more, 30 pence (50 cents) per minute.

In Italy, the situation is taken to an extreme. The charges levied on callers to cell phones are so high that the receivers can actually earn a rebate on those fees from their carrier. That is, you get paid for talking, but the money comes from those who call you.

This system was almost imported to the States. US West tried to institute a free-to-receive cell phone plan with high fees to callers. But land-line operators, whose customers would be the ones ending up subsidizing US West, refused to play along.

What is the best system in the end? Why not give people a choice? Why not give each cell phone two numbers? The first would be a caller-pays number that is given out publicly, while the second would be a receiver-pays number that you could give to your friends and family. And, in fact, you don't need two numbers to achieve this. There could be one number with a code at the end that switches the bill to receiver pays.

This example shows that the symmetry impulse should lead us to consider more than just the converse of the current solution (caller pays versus recipient pays). We can also decide whether a truly symmetric decision—in which both pay or either the caller or the recipient pays—is even better.

CASE STUDY

360-Degree Evaluations

Traditionally, bosses evaluate their subordinates. How would you flip this sentence around? The obvious answer is, Why not have subordinates evaluate their bosses? And, as we just learned, it doesn't have to be either-or. We can have the evaluation solution being truly more symmetric, with the top reviewing the bottom and the bottom reviewing the top (as well as the sides—coequals—reviewing each other).

Voilà! The idea of 360-degree evaluation is born. Everyone evaluates everyone else. The 360-degree evaluation has become a standard HR practice.*

Why not go one step further? Job applicants are typically asked to provide references from previous employers. The custom is for the boss to provide the recommendation. Why not also ask to see letters of reference from subordinates?[16]

---

*As professors, we are all too familiar with evaluating students' academic performance while they evaluate our teaching performance. Indeed, we are still waiting for grade inflation to hit teaching evaluations.

Opt-out Organ Donations

More than 80,000 Americans are on the waiting list for desperately needed organ transplants. And the list keeps getting longer, even though, on average, sixteen people die waiting each day. This shortage persists in spite of the large proportion (75 percent) of people who say that they would be willing to donate their organs. The problem is that they don't get around to making their preferences known.

How big is the problem? In 2001, there was a grand total of 6,081 organ donations in the United States.[17] That's it. The shockingly low number is a result of the default rule: Unless a person explicitly states that his or her organs are to be made available for donation, nothing can be done. Flipping the default could save thousands of lives.

The simplest and least controversial change would be a shift to mandated choice. Upon renewing a driver's license, each person would be required to state his or her preference.

In 1996, Sweden instituted a mandated choice law, in which all adults were required to choose between donating or not donating their organs. There was an immediate increase of 600,000 potential donors. A similar 1990 law in Denmark increased the donor registry by 150,000. Brazil is another country in this camp.

Next up on the list is weak presumed consent. In this approach, used by Finland, Greece, Italy, Norway, and Singapore, consent is presumed given, but next of kin may object and prevent organ donation.

Faulty Default

Flipping the default could also improve incentives to contribute to 401(k) savings plans. Some 85 percent of workers pick the default option, which is typically a contribution of only 2 or 3 percent, far below the $12,000 maximum. Why not set the default at the maximum? Even moving to forced choice leads to much higher savings rates, as people need to pause and make a thoughtful decision.[18]

Life and Taxes

While we are at it, why not give people a charitable contribution for donating blood? You get a deduction for giving old clothes to Goodwill. Giving blood is a lot more valuable. And, unlike paying cash, allowing a tax deduction won't encourage Bowery bums to give more blood.

The best-known success is Belgium, which passed its version of presumed consent in 1986. Only 2 percent of the population opts out, and the number of organs recovered has more than doubled.[19] There is no longer an organ-transplant waiting list!

Spain went even further in 1989 by passing a law that presumes consent unless the individual has expressly registered on a national computer his or her refusal to donate. Not surprisingly, Spain's donation rate rose from one of the lowest in the world to one of the highest, and the country now even exports donated organs.

This organ donation story is a powerful example of flipping the meaning of inaction or silence. J. Alfred Prufrock profoundly pondered, "How should I presume?" And you should, too. There is almost always another presumption to be considered.

CASE STUDY

Paying Not to See Ads

One of our Web site contributors (A. H. of Chicago) suggested flipping around who pays for television programming. It might be better to allow consumers to pay to avoid being annoyed by ads.

Can you guess how much the networks are being paid for you to watch an hour of TV? Five dollars? One dollar? It turns out to be only about 32 cents per hour for prime time.[20] The networks could collect this money from the viewers instead of the advertisers. Wouldn't you pay 32 cents per hour not to have any ads during prime time?

Let's put this 32 cents in perspective. A full-page color ad in *Forbes* costs about 9 cents per reader. To our mind, the hundred or so pages of ads that bring in some $9 per issue are a whole lot less intrusive than the twelve minutes of TV ads, which bring in 32 cents. We wouldn't pay an extra $9 to get an ad-free version of *Forbes*. This type of advertising is efficient. The problem with TV advertising is that our time is sold too cheaply.

The solution is simple: Allow people to buy ad-free shows at the time of their choice. Instead of fighting TiVo, networks should look for ways to allow people to pay 32 cents to download their favorite episode of *E.R.* or *Get Smart* to watch sans ads when they want. Cable systems are rolling out this technology, but the networks should be leading the charge.

Antisymmetry

Most things in life are symmetric. Adjustable mortgages adjust upward and downward. Phones receive and make calls. But some things are purposely asymmetrical—think of the one-way mirror. Sometimes it is useful to look for cases for which it would make sense to break what seems to be a natural symmetry.

Surely the most famous example of this is the one-way tollbooth, first introduced by San Francisco's Golden Gate Bridge on October 19, 1968 (and then by the George Washington Bridge in 1970).[21] Instead of paying one dollar each way, the motorist pays two dollars, but only in one direction. This reduces both traffic delays and the number of toll keepers by half.

Our earlier example of the automatically refinancing fixed-rate mortgage could also be described as an antisymmetry proposal. Instead of having the mortgage adjust both ways, we showed that it might be better for borrowers to have a mortgage that adjusted only one way, namely, down (and that lenders could capture value for this feature by charging additional fees for the loan).

While we are at it, how about a mortgage that refinances when the market rate of interest goes up? Does this make any sense? Yes and no. It sounds crazy at first because who in his right mind would want to change a 7 percent mortgage into an 8 percent mortgage?

But a borrower might actually make the trade if the lender would cut the outstanding principal so that the loan might be more easily prepaid. The bank recognizes that its loan at 7 percent is no longer worth its full face value. Hence it should be willing to give the borrower a financial incentive to pay off the loan early or raise the interest rate. Indeed, the lender could decrease the principal just enough to offset the increase in interest so that the borrower's monthly payments would be kept constant.

The Tools Are Now in Place

This chapter has shown how practical ideas emerge when you turn things upside down, or look at the flip side, or look at both sides, or even look at one side only. The use of symmetry is the last of the four idea-generating tools discussed in chapters 3 through 6.

Chapter 7 takes these ideas and shows how a principled or axiomatic approach to problem and solution searches can increase the efficiency of these tools even more. By this point, it shouldn't surprise you that just around the corner, you'll find a few more puzzles to solve and problems to discover.

Problem Solving with a Purpose

Principled
Problem Solving

A Guide to Thinking
Inside the Box

So far, we've given you a guide to thinking outside the box. You know by now that we are always on the lookout for symmetries, so you can guess what the next step is. How can we help guide you to thinking inside the box?

Thinking *inside* the box?

At first, this advice seems to contradict popular creativity mantras. "There are no wrong answers." "Consider all options." "Break the boundaries that prevent you from innovating."

Well, not all boundaries should be broken. Some boundaries are real and need to be respected. By understanding what the real constraints are, we can better identify the ones we artificially impose.

If you identify some constraints that any solution must obey, this can help channel your search into more productive directions. At some point, we have to take our possible solutions and figure out which are workable and which are not. Understanding what box they will ultimately have to fit into helps separate the wheat from the chaff. By imposing some constraints on our solution search, we can filter out unworkable ideas before they begin to take shape. Perhaps we can even *pre*filter our thinking so as to prevent these unworkable ideas from forming in the first place.

Take, for example, the Second Law of Thermodynamics (which states that entropy increases). We accept the constraints of this law and, as a result, save ourselves a good deal of time by not free-associating about how to build a perpetual-motion machine. Principled problem solving means that you take into account the principles that any solution must satisfy. The more of these principles you can identify, the closer you are to the solution. There may be fewer options to explore, but those are the right ones to focus on.

Principled problem solving, by clearing away the brush, can help you see the solution more easily. While we typically think of filters as constraints, we want to convince you that identifying the underlying attributes of any solution can be liberating and can actually help you generate ideas. So, this chapter is not just about filtering ideas; it is ultimately—and most important—an additional tool for generating ideas.

Principled Creativity

Gary Hamel enjoys shocking his audiences by asking about their corporate sperm counts. If you need ten million sperm to fertilize a single egg, then you're unlikely to come up with a winning idea unless you have lots of material to work with. He then does a brilliant job at helping his audience create an environment in which ideas are free-flowing.

The problem is what to do with all these ideas when you get them. It doesn't help to generate ideas unless you then evaluate them. But evaluating them is time-consuming and costly. In fact, the fear of being inundated is often what holds some companies back from asking their employees to contribute more.

You might say we prefer an in vitro approach. Without pushing this analogy too far, we'd like to find a way to help you prefilter your thinking. We want you to generate fewer—but better—ideas.[1] The trick is to impose the right filter.

Almost by definition, prefiltering reduces the need to follow dead ends. The surprise is that it can also spur you toward generating a good answer. Seeing a clearer picture of the underlying structure of the problem turns out to make it easier to find solutions.

But what are the right filters? This is where our principled problem-solving approach helps. Figure out what you *do* know about the solution, even if you don't know the whole answer. It's all too easy to get caught up in what you *don't* know instead of working from what you do know. Knowing 75 percent of the answer makes it easier to find the other 25 percent.

The first step is to identify all the attributes that will be a necessary part of any solution. These necessary attributes of a solution are the *principles* (mathematicians call them *axioms*) that will serve as problem-solving catalysts. This approach helps focus your search in that it prevents you from having to start from scratch every time you run into a roadblock.

A few brainteasers will illustrate how this works in practice. We're admittedly a bit nervous about giving you these puzzles to work on, because some of you might not like doing puzzles (and others of you might like doing them too much).

You've seen plenty of puzzles in creativity books. Can you see the young woman transform into the old lady? Which arrow is longer? How do you get the Ping-Pong ball out of the well? Our problem is not with the puzzles, but with the lack of a connection to solving real problems.

We think our puzzles have a point. The point is demonstrating a principled approach to solving them. They provide a controlled environment in which we can illustrate a prefiltering approach with broad applicability. These puzzles are only a means, not an end. After solving the puzzle, we then show how the same approach has relevance to real-world problems.

And we do hope you'll have some fun with them, too.

PRACTICE EXERCISE

The Four-Seed Puzzle

The task here is to plant four seeds so that each seed is equidistant from the other seeds.[2] Give it a try for a moment, any way you want. Then, we'll talk about using a structured approach to find a solution.

A common first stab is to draw a square and plant the seeds at each corner.

But the square is not a solution. The seeds at opposite diagonals are farther from each other than they are from the seeds in the vertical and horizontal directions.

So now you understand the problem. Think again for a moment before reading on.

Even if you don't know how to plant all the seeds, is there some part of the solution that you do know? Well, yes. You do know how to plant *three* seeds so that they are all equidistant—use an equilateral triangle.

Since all four seeds must be equidistant, so must any three of them. So one principle we know for sure is this:

(a) Three of the seeds must form an equilateral triangle.

Enunciating this simple principle lets us place three of the seeds immediately. The only question is where to put that fourth seed. We may not know the whole solution, but we are three-quarters of the way done.

Now, where does that fourth seed go?

It is common to see people place the fourth seed at the center of the triangle. Alas, that doesn't quite work. The problem with this location is that the seed in the center is closer to the other three than the other three are to each other.

Where else can we put it? Now we seem to be stuck.

At this point, there is a strong temptation to start from the beginning and give up on the triangle. *Resist that temptation.* The message of principled problem solving is to take something you know is right and build on it, even if that is not enough to answer the problem.

The problem is not with the location of those first three seeds. It can't be. If all four of the seeds are to be equidistant, then three of them must be equidistant—and three equidistant points always form a triangle.

This discipline of putting the three seeds down and focusing on just the fourth helps direct you to that one leap, that one small breakthrough to come up with the answer. In fact, given that the first three seeds are fixed in their locations, we can even extend our initial principle to say something about where the fourth seed must go. Not only must three of the seeds form an equilateral triangle, but we also know something else:

(b) Any three of the seeds must form an equilateral triangle.

Thus, the bottom two seeds and our fourth seed must form an equilateral triangle. So, then, where does the fourth seed go?

The constraint that isn't really there, but that we often impose with our mind, is the requirement that all the seeds lie on a single surface.

The previous solution of putting the fourth seed in the middle would have been right if we had simply elevated the fourth seed. But hold on a second—how do you plant a seed in midair? Although this can't be done, there's generally no problem with planting a seed on a hill or mound.

Putting on your symmetry hat, a second solution should now come to mind. What about planting the fourth seed in a hole?

Going to three dimensions requires a leap of imagination. But by forcing yourself to hold the first three points in the triangle, you were pushed to give up what turned out to be a false constraint, namely, limiting your answer to two dimensions.

This next puzzle uses principled problem solving to attack a more difficult problem. And this time, two dimensions are all you'll need.

PRACTICE EXERCISE

The Ten-Seed Problem

The task in this puzzle is to plant ten seeds in a way so that they form five distinct rows, each with exactly four seeds.[3] Again, please give it a try for a moment on your own, and then we'll talk about using a structured approach to find a solution.

At first glance, this task would seem impossible. We only have ten seeds, and it appears that we need twenty to accomplish the task. Of course, the same seed can appear in more than one row. In fact, a good guess is that each of the ten seeds needs to be used twice—because $10 \times 2 = 5 \times 4$—that is, ten seeds each used twice gives the same number of seeds as would be used in five rows of four.

What we know for sure is that in any solution, the following principles must apply:

(a) *At least one seed must appear in multiple rows.*

(b) *Each seed must be used twice* on average. *(If a seed is used only once, then some other seed needs to be used at least three times.)*

Laying out these principles is a first step to a partial solution.

Figuring out how to plant ten seeds leaves a lot of decisions to be made—ten, to be exact. That's too many to make at once. If we can somehow figure out where *some* of the seeds go, then we can make the problem more manageable. Is there anything else you can say about part of the solution?

Sure. Although it seems almost too obvious to say, you already know something else:

(c) There must be a row with four seeds in it.

This principle leads us to our first partial solution:

We've planted four seeds in no particular fashion other than their being in a row. So now we just have to figure out where the other six seeds go. In other words, we're almost halfway home.

The next point is to remember our first principle: At least one seed is in more than one row. So let's exploit this very basic principle and position three more seeds in line with one of the original seeds to create another row of four.

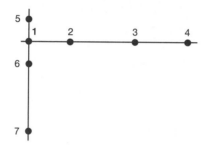

We've chosen to build the second row in line with seed number 1, which was at the end of our first row. Of course, we could put that seed at the end of both rows or in the interior of the 1234 row or at the end of the 5167 vertical row. And we could vary the angle at which the rows intersect. So, while the placement of these first seven seeds complies with what we know for sure, it also helps to keep in mind which parts of this proposed solution are not required (but were just chosen as an initial guess).

We still don't have much of a clue as to what the solution looks like, but we've managed to place seven of the ten seeds. Now, all we have to do is find places for the other three seeds. At this point, we'll leave it to you to plant those last three seeds. The partial solution we've proposed really does work. In the appendix, we fill in the steps.

We could have used another set of principles to solve this problem. The way we first tried to answer the puzzle was by planting seeds and then finding the rows. But try flipping it around. We could have first located five rows and then figured out where the ten seeds must lie.

Just as it was an obvious partial solution to start with a row of four seeds, we could also have started with five lines—any five lines. Even if we don't know anything about where the seeds will go, we know the solution will have five rows of seeds.

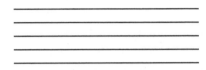

The five parallel rows shown above won't work. This configuration would require twenty seeds. That's because without any intersecting rows, we can't reuse any seeds. This violates our first principle. A little experimenting with rows should quickly lead you to the answer. (The appendix has the details.)

Applying Principled Problem Solving to Real-World Problems

Although puzzles like this can be fun—at least for some people—a more important question is whether these same tools work equally well for solving real-world problems. To our minds, many thinking-outside-the-box exercises don't help the game player solve real-world problems. But the seed exercises do have a real-world payoff: principled problem solving.

Identifying the basic principles or prerequisites of any solution allows problem solvers to limit their attention to the class of solutions that comply with the principles. Principled problem solving, therefore, constitutes a powerful way of filtering out solutions that are nonstarters. Thinking outside the box means breaking out of the false constraints that we artificially impose on problem solving. But it is equally useful to identify real constraints—the prerequisites for a solution—in order to narrow the list to a more manageable number.

Of course, principled problem solving can fail if we identify false principles—that is, if we impose artificial constraints on the problem. If a false principle causes us to reject real solutions out of hand, then we may never find an answer. This is why thinking out of the box has such appeal. But, with the seed problems, we've shown you that it is possible to deduce real constraints that allow you to improve the efficiency of your solution search. *Unprincipled* thinking outside the box often fails because it sentences the problem solver to consider any potential solution, no matter how farfetched.

Thinking outside the box and principled problem solving are, thus, the yin and the yang, the dialectic of efficient innovation. Think of these two approaches together as thinking inside the *real* box.

The tool here is to force yourself to enunciate and write down the necessary components of any solutions. Expressly enunciating the principles makes it *easier* to reject false constraints. That's why in the four-seed puzzle, the key step is getting to the point where you can see that placing the seeds on a plane is not a requirement of the solution. The usual problem with thinking inside the box is that you aren't even aware of the boxes that are constraining your thinking. Therefore, we suggest that you expressly describe the box, in part to test whether the boundaries are real or false constraints.

This principled approach can be a powerful complement to the idea-generating techniques that you have just been reading about. By now, you know that symmetry in all its manifest forms (creating symmetries, breaking asymmetries, flipping things around) can produce plenty of possibilities. But by itself, symmetry cannot tell which ideas are likely to work and which are not. That is where principled problem solving plays a role. It helps filter your ideas and focus your search.

Hard-core thinking-outside-the-box types might reject principled problem solving simply because they are afraid that this approach will jettison too many good ideas. If the principles are correct, that won't happen. Instead, you will jettison many bad ideas and direct your attention to the good ones.

The final and possibly biggest payoff is that you can use these principles as a springboard to *generate* solutions. That is just what we did with the equilateral triangle principle in the four-seed problem.

Before we turn to real-world examples, it is important to remember one last point. As you think about principled problem solving, symmetry demands that there should also be some guidelines for principled question asking.

And there are. Chapter 5 has already asked you to identify the underlying principles that make a solution work before translating them to a different context. For example, when we started with the idea of rewinding videotapes at the beginning of a rental, we pushed ourselves to see that a core principle of this idea is that it prevented a form of shirking before the consumer could use the product. Stating this principle in its more generalized form allowed us to go forward and see other settings in which a shirking problem might be usefully tied to some other use. Voilà! We have pay-at-the-pump insurance as a solution to uninsured motorist shirking and motor voter registration as a solution to voter shirking.

Indeed, a powerful way to identify new problems to solve is to focus on the artificial constraints that are limiting our vision. Once we have identified a false box that has kept us from seeing an answer in one context, we should systematically start looking for other contexts in which the same false box is distorting our thinking. One way to find other questions is to recognize that solutions are often found when we identify false or artificial constraints.

After we realized that libraries might not just be in the business of lending books, we were able to see the possibility that the public library could rent or sell books or even provide a tasty caffeine delivery system. After we realized that retail establishments such as IKEA and Disney could make drop-off child care work, we suddenly saw the possibility that movie theaters might be an even better application.

Whenever we have a way around one false constraint, we can seek other applications of our solution. We do this by looking for other situations in which this same kind of artificial constraint has been blocking people from seeing an answer.

Principled Problem Solving Puzzlers: Redesigning Mortgages

To bring the discussion down to where the rubber meets the road, let's now try to apply this same principled problem-solving approach to the redesign of a home mortgage. In its most general terms, a mortgage involves a bank (or other financial service provider) lending you some money that you promise to pay back. There are fixed-rate mortgages, floating-rate mortgages, and balloon mortgages. All these mortgages have one common denominator:

The present discounted value of your payments equals the amount that you've borrowed.

Take the case of a $100 mortgage and a 10 percent interest rate. You could pay $10 per year forever, or you could pay nothing the first year and then $121 in the second year and pay off the mortgage. There are a lot of different repayment methods that work, but the bottom line is that banks are not running a charity: They need to get back from you an amount of money that (in present-value terms) equals the value of what they give you. This is the first principle of any mortgage solution.

Constrained by Your Future Paycheck

With this principle in mind, let's look at adjustable-rate mortgages. People with a fixed salary and limited liquidity have a real problem borrowing with an adjustable-rate mortgage. They fear that rates will rise and so will their monthly payment. If the payment rises too much, they may no longer be able to afford the mortgage.

The problem is that since most borrowers rely on their salary to make mortgage payments, they cannot take the risk that their monthly payments will go up. Yet, from the lender's perspective, when rates rise, they need to get more money in order to restore the value of the loan. Is there some way to give borrowers the benefits of lower rates on adjustable-rate mortgages without exposing them to fluctuations in their monthly payment?

We have a principle and what initially looks like a conflicting objective. The core principle is that the bank must get the present value of its money back. The conflicting objective is that payments can't rise with interest rates. If we treat the objective of nonfluctuating payments as a constraint (and for some borrowers, it really is), then we force ourselves to ask whether it is possible to design an adjustable-rate mortgage that satisfies both constraints. In this example, the value of principled problem solving is that it focuses on potential solutions that are consistent with both the constant present value and the constant monthly payment prerequisites.

Focusing on these constraints can lead us toward a solution. If we want to keep the monthly payment constant when the interest rate rises, then some other term of the loan has to give in order to satisfy the present-value constraint. That is, something else besides the monthly payment will have to adjust with the market interest rate.

Pause and think for a minute. If the monthly payment is going be fixed, what other aspect of the loan might adjust with the market rate of interest? (Hint: If you're familiar with Excel functions, think about the different determinants of the @PMT function.)

Why not adjust the *number* of payments while holding the amount of each payment constant? We're not suggesting that the borrower make more frequent payments. Asking the borrower to pay twice a month could still make the mortgage unaffordable. A better solution suggests extending the life of the mortgage. A fifteen-year mortgage would adjust to become a sixteen- or eighteen-year mortgage as a result of a rise in the interest rate.

We might have come up with this solution purely by applying the symmetry tool. Think about applying the stress test to the following description:

> *An adjustable-rate mortgage is one with a fixed* term *where the* monthly payment *adjusts with the market interest rate.*

While switching the *non*italicized words would have produced a solution, it wouldn't have told you whether the solution would have worked. Principled problem solving contains in it a way of testing whether ideas will work, but, more important, it sometimes can suggest a more direct route to finding the solution by focusing on the real underlying constraints—in this case, to create an adjustable mortgage with fixed monthly payments.

There are some real constraints on the adjustable-term mortgage. Extending the life of the mortgage runs into diminishing returns. Once the mortgage reaches the point at which it would take forever to pay off, the term cannot be extended any further. This constraint need not be a problem. Many adjustable mortgages already have caps on the maximum possible interest adjustment. Similarly, the term adjustment might be limited to thirty years.

We now have a solution. But would there be any demand for this product? In the United Kingdom, these "adjustable-term" mortgages already exist and have been very popular.[4]

Constrained by Your Present Paycheck

For most people, the size of the house they can buy is limited by the size of their current paycheck. What you can buy is based on what you can borrow, and the amount you can borrow is determined by a bank formula based on your income. Banks will typically let people spend only 28 percent of their monthly income on housing, and people often want to borrow more than what the bank is willing to lend them.

This is not just people having eyes bigger than their stomachs. Housing prices have risen faster than incomes in most metropolitan cities. The problem is how to make housing more affordable.

Let's attack this problem by looking more closely at what the person can afford to borrow.[5] Ten years into a fixed-rate mortgage, it is usually much easier to make the monthly payments than it is in the first year. If you can make it through the first year, then you'll be fine. Mortgage payments are hardest in year one, because income goes up over time while the mortgage payments stay fixed.

So, the problem is this: People know that after their incomes rise they will be able to pay back a larger loan. But with traditional mortgages, banks don't want to lend more money, because that would necessitate taking too much of the borrower's current income. How could we redesign a mortgage that would let people tap into the higher expected future incomes to buy more expensive houses today—without breaking the borrowers' current budgets?

Time to apply principled problem solving. What are the real constraints? Step one: Gather together the constraints and put them into words. Stop, and try to force yourself to write them down.

We count three real constraints that any answer must satisfy:

First, as before, the bank needs to receive back from the borrower cash payments that are equivalent (in present-value terms) to what has been lent.

Second, borrowers can't be asked to pay back more at any date than their income allows.

Third, the market determines the price of the house. We just can't wish houses to be cheaper.

Explicitly enunciating these principles lets us see the freedom of play in designing loans. This is what happened with our first principled problem solving puzzler: Just fixing the monthly payment led us to focus on other dimensions of the loan that could accommodate rate adjustments. Thus the second step in using principled problem solving to generate new solutions is to focus on what's left over once the principles and constraints have been satisfied.

Where is there still some freedom to maneuver?

While lenders are going to demand that the present value of the principal be repaid, the first principle allows a fair amount of flexibility over *when* the money is paid. The real constraint on most borrowers is that they don't have enough income to make large payments at the beginning of the mortgage. But this constraint is most pressing at the beginning of the mortgage. We expect borrowers' incomes will rise over time.

Why not construct a loan that lets payments increase over time? In short, ask home owners to pay back less today and more tomorrow, when they can better afford it.

How much people can pay later will depend on their future income. Salaries go up for two reasons. One is promotions. The other is that wages keep up with inflation. You can understand why lenders don't want to bet on promotions, but why not offer inflation-adjusted mortgages? Instead of requiring borrowers to pay a fixed nominal amount each month, create a mortgage with which borrowers promise to pay back a constant *real* amount. If mortgage payments were indexed to inflation, then the real burden on the home owner would be much better spread out over time.

It is quite surprising how much even a small amount of indexing could do. Take the case of a low-inflation economy—say that inflation is 2 percent and that long-term interest rates are 6 percent. If the home owner were to take out a conventional mortgage, the monthly payments would be based on a 6 percent interest rate. But if the mortgage payments were indexed to inflation, then the mortgage could be based on the much lower real interest rate (the interest rate net of inflation). That means that the constant dollar payments would be based on a 4 percent mortgage. In the first year, payments would be about two-thirds as large. Or, to put it another way, a person could borrow nearly 50 percent more and still have the same first-year monthly payment.

An increase of 50 percent would make a big difference in the amount of housing people could afford. Even if the adjustment

That's Why Not

While we think inflation-adjusted mortgages are a great idea, we know at least one reason why you don't see them offered in New York. Such mortgages would be illegal. Inflation-adjusted mortgages can run afoul of predatory lending laws because they can create what is called *negative amortization*. That is, instead of paying off a little of the principal every month (and building up a small amount of equity), the home owner would temporarily go a little more into debt in the first years of the mortgage. This direction would ultimately be reversed as the monthly payments increased over time with inflation.

Negative amortization isn't as bad as it sounds. Although the debt is initially larger in nominal terms, inflation-adjusted mortgages guarantee that every month the real indebtedness (as measured in constant dollars) would be reduced. And remember that the value of houses also rises with inflation. As long as housing values increase at the same rate of inflation, the borrower is guaranteed to increase his or her equity in the house each month. A blanket prohibition makes little sense.

were only half of inflation, a person could still borrow an extra 25 percent. That, too, would also make a big difference.

So far, we've looked at the case of a low-inflation economy. Consider how things would be different if inflation were running at an annual 20 percent. Now the difference would be between borrowing at a nominal rate of 24 percent and at a real rate of 4 percent with payments rising 20 percent per year.

Without inflation adjustment, you could only borrow one-fifth as much, and housing would become simply unaffordable. To buy a $200,000 home at 24 percent interest rates would require a monthly mortgage payment of $4,000! You would have to earn around $200,000 a year to afford the mortgage payments on a $200,000 house. If, instead, you used an inflation-adjusted mortgage, then your payments would be about $800 a month—a mortgage that could be carried on a $55,000 income.[6]

It will come as no surprise, then, that in any economy that has had serious inflation—Brazil and Israel are examples—all mort-

Inflation-Protected Savings

When we see a good idea, we like to turn it around and look for translations. If inflation-adjusted borrowing is a good idea, what about inflation-adjusted investing? Why not a bond for which the interest paid goes up or down with inflation? This idea dates back at least to the 1970s and Milton Friedman. It has been implemented in Australia, Canada, New Zealand, the United Kingdom, Sweden, and, most recently, the United States.[7] Indexed treasury bonds became a reality in 1997 in large part because of the efforts of then Deputy Treasury Secretary Larry Summers.

In theory, the government saves money by not having to pay a risk premium.[8] Investors like the idea of protecting their returns from inflation. This suggests a translation to fill out the picture: inflation-adjusted municipal bonds. People are taxed on their nominal rather than their real return. Thus, what is missing is the ability to get an *after-tax* rate of return that is inflation-protected. State governments should follow suit and issue inflation-indexed municipal bonds.[9] This product would guarantee a real return so that retirees' purchasing power would not be eroded by inflation.

gages are inflation-adjusted. It's a necessity. But you don't need the impetus of high inflation to take advantage of this idea.

While the benefits are not as large in a low-inflation economy, they are still quite substantial. Even with 2 percent inflation, an inflation-adjusted mortgage would allow an almost 50 percent bigger loan. Or, you could borrow the same amount and pay one-third less initially, thereby leaving money for furniture and fixing up the house. Inflation-adjusted mortgages can help people at every income level borrow more money to buy the house of their dreams.

We turn now to an example of principled problem solving in our own front yard.

The Silver Scholar Program

The traditional approach to business school is to graduate from college and then go to work for at least two years before returning to pursue an M.B.A. Law schools take a more varied approach. Some students are accepted right out of college, whereas others work for a few years before starting their law degree program. Yale's management school competes with all the other top programs for the best M.B.A. students. In this competition, we at Yale are always on the lookout for ways to achieve a competitive advantage. A sure way to improve the quality of the school is to attract more top students to the program. Yale's undergraduate student body provides an attractive place to look.

The problem is that completing an M.B.A. straight out of college is often a recipe for failure. Few firms are willing to pay M.B.A salaries to students with no work experience. The upside, however, is that students right out of college have a low opportunity cost. They're used to sleeping on a mattress on the floor and won't be giving up very high salaries.

While there are problems with taking kids rights out of college, there are also problems with the status quo (where nearly all M.B.A. candidates have several years of work experience). Cost, for starters. Beyond the not insubstantial tuition cost of an M.B.A. program ($33,000 per year in 2003), the even greater cost is the lost salary for time out of the work force. An M.B.A. could end up costing over $200,000 in tuition and lost salary.

One approach has been to speed up the M.B.A. program and try to fit it into one year. Although a few schools have tried this approach, there's a lot of material to cover even in the traditional two-year program. Speaking from a self-serving perspective, moving to a one-year program would also cut the numbers of courses and hence the required number of faculty in half.

Another tack is to allow students to complete their studies over Fridays and Saturdays and continue working while taking their courses. Not only are these executive M.B.A.'s quite popular, but the schools also charge a healthy premium.

So, here are the ingredients (or principles) that we want to satisfy:

(a) *Preserve the two-year M.B.A. program.*

(b) *Take students right out of college.*

(c) *Make sure they have work experience before they graduate.*

Is there any way to connect all these dots to find a way to reduce the opportunity cost of getting an M.B.A.? Where is the residual freedom of movement?

Why not create a three-year program in which students start their business school right out of college and then, after their first year, take a year (or fifteen months) to work before returning to complete their second year?

Their first year will have a low opportunity cost in terms of forgone salary. While the students may have less work experience, they are better at being students since they haven't been away from school. Work experience is less of an issue for the first-year curriculum, which teaches core subjects such as accounting, economics, finance, game theory, marketing, and organizational behavior. When they come back with some work experience, they will be better prepared for the case-study approach used in the second-year curriculum.

Many firms pay for their employees to get an M.B.A. This program cuts the firms' cost in half (as the firms would only have to pay one year of tuition) and brings their employee back after an absence of only one year.

One potential problem with this approach is that it breaks up the cohesiveness of the class. The college kids take a year off and thus graduate with the following class. Though this is a legitimate concern, the same issue arises for all joint-degree candidates: students combining an M.B.A. with a law degree or environmental science or public health.

It is an interesting idea, and we'll see if it works. Barry's colleagues at Yale, with the support of the dean, have created a three-year M.B.A. pilot program. The first students were enrolled in the fall of 2002. Early indications are very positive. The applicants had more work experience during college than we had expected. Some had started businesses or curated exhibits at major museums. Their grade-point averages and GMAT scores were at the top of their class. Of the eight students admitted, all accepted.

Putting all the constraints together helps shape enough of the answer that you may have just a few degrees of freedom. If you have no options left, that's a problem. That is a time to go back and thoroughly reexamine each of the principles. But, more often, there are too many places to look.

Confidence

It is easier to find a solution to a problem if you know that a solution exists. Of course, this is a bit paradoxical. Unlike a math textbook—where you just have to find the answer to a problem that has already been solved—in the real world, there is no one to tell you in advance whether an answer to your problem exists. If you don't know the solution, how can you be sure that a solution exists?

You can't. But it helps to fool yourself a bit, as Paul Zeitz writes in *The Art and Craft of Problem Solving:* "Most mathematicians are 'Platonists,' believing that the totality of their subject already exists and is it the job of the human investigator to 'discover' it rather than create it. To the Platonist, problem solving is the art of seeing the solution that is already there."[10]

This is a delicate balance. We don't want you to waste all your time looking for a solution that can't be found. Yet, if we can help you believe that a solution does exist, then you are much more likely to find it. You won't give up. You'll try more options.

This is one of the reasons we employ the WWCD approach. For our imaginary Croesus, most problems are solvable. Thus, we start with an answer and work to refine it. Putting ourselves in King Croesus's shoes gives us confidence that a solution exists. If there's no solution for Croesus, then perhaps we should give up.

We expect you to be a bit skeptical. Here's a "three line" problem from Denise Hunter to illustrate the value of confidence.

Can you connect the boxes A, B, and C to their mates without leaving the larger box or having any lines cross?

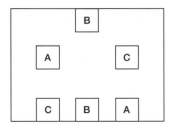

Take a piece of paper and try it out. There is no trick here. It is either possible or impossible, but there's nothing sneaky about this question.

If you are like most people, you realize right away that you can't connect B to B with a straight line, as this would never let you get from A to A or C to C.

So, you start with an A-to-A connection. Then if you swing around A in your B-to-B connection, you'll soon realize that then you can't get from C to C. Congratulations, you've shown that there is no answer. Thus, you haven't wasted too much time looking for an answer that can't be found.

That's where we ended up when we first saw this problem.

But what if we told you that an answer does exist (and we promise that there are no tricks)? Now what would you do? We'll bet that you're quite likely to find it, and without that much trouble. Knowing that a solution exists encourages the right type of boldness. If you need a hint, connecting A to A is a fine start.

What we find often happens is that people look for a reason to give up. They think they've figured it out when they decide it can't be done.

There's often no hard and fast rule for deciding how much you should push to solve something. At some point, it is right to give up. But before you give up, you should attack a problem as if there were an answer and all you have to do is find it. That's one more reason to be an idealist.

Again, principled problem solving can help. Discovering partial answers can boost your confidence, and sometimes the principles that you discover also tell you that you should stop looking because they are mutually incompatible.

How could principled problem solving help solve the three-line problem?

We already figured out one constraint, or principle:

(a) *No solution can involve a straight line between B and B.*

Negative principles can also be powerfully useful in focusing the attention on a smaller set of potential solutions. But let's look first at the A boxes.

How many different ways are there to connect the A boxes? Literally speaking, there are an unlimited number of ways since we are allowing any kind of curved lines, but generically there are only two ways to connect the A boxes—either with a relatively direct path that goes below the upper C box or with a looping path that goes above the upper C box.

So another principle is this:

(b) *The A line must be either direct or looping.*

And because the picture is so symmetric, we can extend this principle:

(c) *The C line must be either direct or looping.*

Now, how can you combine principles b and c? Imagine that you have drawn a direct line between the A boxes. Now think about how you can connect the C boxes.

This experiment leads us to the following principle:

(d) *If the A line is direct, then the C line is looping (and,*
    by symmetry, if the C line is direct, then the A line must
    be looping).

We've almost solved it. We know that between the A and C boxes one of the lines must be direct and one of the lines must be looping. So, why don't we draw these in? (Because the problem is so symmetric, it can't matter which we choose to be straight and which we choose to be looping, but for concreteness we'll make the A line direct.)

Now put your pencil down on the bottom B box and force yourself to get to the top B box without lifting the pencil or crossing the A or the C line. It turns out that principled problem solving has literally created a road map for you to solve the problem.

In one sense, this is an example about literally thinking inside a box, but even here people often apply artificial constraints to the problem. It's much easier to solve this problem by connecting the A and C lines first, but most people draw the lines in alphabetical order, which is a truly artificial constraint and one that should be broken.

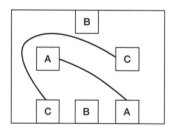

8

The Case
for Honest Tea

This chapter offers the skinny on Honest Tea. We discuss some of the challenges in bringing this why-not idea to market and then consider some other beverage ideas that might be a why-not or an of-course-not.

In 1998, Barry started Honest Tea with a former student, Seth Goldman. For those readers who have not (yet) experienced the joy of Honest Tea, the company sells bottled iced tea.*

As Seth and Barry explained on the back label of their first teas:

We were thirsty. We searched for bottled teas that truly tasted like tea but couldn't find any. So we decided to make our own. Honest Tea is microbrewed in spring water and sweetened—just barely. The result is a subtle flavor and a sixth of the calories of the super-sweet, tea-flavored drinks.

Honestly yours,
Seth & Barry

You'd almost have to be crazy to start a beverage company. With competition from Coke and Pepsi, SoBe and Snapple, Arizona and Gatorade, Glaceau and bottled waters, the idea that the world needs another beverage seems, well, insane.

---

*For readers with a healthy thirst, there's an Honest Tea coupon waiting for you to download at www.whynot.net/coupon.

Perhaps it was crazy. Success is far from assured. Still, considering $5 million in annual sales and sales growing at nearly 50 percent, you might think there was a method to this madness. As we tell this story, pay particular attention to what Seth and Barry didn't do, as well as what they did.

The inspiration for the company came from a class discussion in a course on business strategy at Yale's management school. One of the chestnuts in that course is the Coke-Pepsi case study. In the good old days, Coke had a simple strategy. Its goal was to get a bottle of Coke within arm's reach of every living person. "Coke was it" in more ways than one. Coke offered few options other than your basic Coke. It took a good deal of persuasion for Coke to use its name on Diet Coke, which quickly become the third-best-selling soft drink.

By 1995, when Seth Goldman took the class, the floodgates had opened. There was caffeine-free Coke, caffeine-free Diet Coke, Cherry Coke, caffeine-free Diet Cherry Coke. Coke also had Minute Maid sodas, Fanta, Fresca, Sprite, Mello Yello, Mr. Pibb, Powerade, and TaB. In the coming years, it would add Vanilla Coke, Fruitopia drinks, Dasani water, Mad River, even Planet Java Coffee.

The question asked of the class was, Why do we see so much variation in flavors, but not in sweetness? You can get flavors ranging from colas to uncolas, orange to grape, root beer to ginger ale, Dr. Pepper, even celery. When it comes to sweetness, it's all or nothing. Your choices are (1) liquid candy, (2) diet (which is just as sweet, but without the calories), and (3) water.

For Seth, the class discussion hit home. Seth had developed a reputation among his friends as a high-volume beverage consumer. A Snapple refugee, he had relied on that drink until he could no longer endure another lunch that left a syrupy film on his teeth. After class, Seth and Barry talked about the kinds of beverages that might fill the void between water and supersweet juices and sodas.

A trip to the dining hall showed some people mixing Coke and Diet Coke at the fountain. Others blended their orange juice with club soda. Many drank iced tea at lunch, but put in only one or two cubes of sugar. Left to their own devices, people seemed to favor drinks that weren't as sweet or had fewer calories than the choices offered by the industry.

One of the first lessons we teach in economics is the law of diminishing returns. Your first slice of pizza brings more utility than the second, which is still more valued than the third. Owning one wristwatch is valuable for telling time; having a second wristwatch is still useful as a backup or as a fashion accessory, but is less important. That's why even things that are free (on the margin), such as cable TV, do not end up consuming all our time.

Sugar is no exception. The first teaspoon really helps bring out the flavor. The second teaspoon adds a touch of sweetness. By the time you've gotten to the tenth teaspoon, the incremental value is very little and may even spoil the taste.

Principle 1

As they discussed the seeming void in the beverage industry's offerings, Seth and Barry were engaged in a kind of principled problem solving. Their first principle was simple: Develop a beverage that isn't too sweet.

So why didn't the big guys bring out a soft drink with one-third the sweetness and one-third the calories? We didn't have a good answer, and that was a concern.

As the idea of entering this market was evolving, Barry was stuck on the concept of creating a mixture of orange juice and soda. It would be an all-natural soda with half the calories of OJ and a lighter taste. But there was a fundamental flaw that stopped him from proceeding.

You always have to ask the good-news question: If you succeed, then what? How will you sustain profits? The problem for the OJ-soda product is that Tropicana or Minute Maid could crush you. They have a cost advantage in making juice and an enormous distribution and marketing advantage. They also have better OJ. You'd be spending your money to do their market research. Given their strong brand names, it isn't clear they'd want to buy you to use any brand name that you'd developed. We still think this is a great product, but it isn't a great business unless you're Coke, Pepsi,

Canada Dry, or another well-established player. Thus, the idea of a less-sweet beverage sat on the shelf, in need of a new direction.

Principle 2

The idea for an all-natural, less-sweet beverage seemed promising. But remember that not all good new products are good new businesses. Seth and Barry's second principle: The business must still be viable even if established firms copy the product.

On a balmy fall day in 1997, Seth met a former track teammate for dinner at a diner in New York. The two had just gone for a run in Central Park and were parched. But when it came time to order drinks, they couldn't find anything that satisfied their thirst, had some flavor, but wasn't too sweet. The hole in the market was still there. On the shuttle back to Washington, D.C., Seth recalled the conversation he had with Barry. He e-mailed Barry a note next the day: "Did anything ever happen with your idea of a less sugary juice drink? . . . If you still have any interest, ideas, contacts, let's talk. I'll be in California next month checking out the emerging juice bar scene."

Seth's timing was fortuitous. Barry had just returned from a visit to India to write some case studies with an international perspective. One of the businesses he had looked at was Tata Tea. As part of writing up the case, he had visited a tea auction in Calcutta.

It was—to put it politely—a memorable experience. On long rows of tables sat some five hundred pots of tea to be sampled. In front of each pot was a cup. The dozens of bidders all shared the same cup. Each would slurp the lukewarm tea and then spit it out. Barry was the last one through the line.

Aside from a greater appreciation of Dixie cups, three key lessons were learned: First, there's a huge difference in taste between good and bad tea. Second, Americans drink really bad tea. Third and most important, great tea is one of the world's cheapest luxuries. While it costs fifty times more than the tea-bag-variety stuff, great tea costs only a nickel a cup. In short, there's no reason to drink bad tea.

At the end of his field research, Barry had a chance to meet with Ratan Tata, the head of Tata Group, one of the largest conglomerates in India. (Along with tea, the group sells steel, watches, auto parts, chemicals, hotels, and consulting.) Tata Tea was looking to expand its presence outside India. At the time, the majority of its exports were to Russia and the Middle East, where the tea was sold as a commodity.

Inside India, the Tata name is golden. In a market in which counterfeits are rampant, the Tata brand stands for quality and trust. Few people outside India had heard of Tata. (Had you?) With this in mind, Barry suggested that Tata consider using a different name for its exports. How about what Tata stood for? How about Honest Tea?

Mr. Tata demurred. He quite naturally preferred the Tata name. (But a few years later, he came around and bought Tetley—which has not only a great name but also cutting-edge technology for making drawstring tea bags.)

Upon returning from India, Barry now had an idea and a name for it: Honest Tea bottled iced tea. Honest Tea could do for tea what Starbucks did for coffee. It took a fifty-cent commodity—a regular cup of joe—and turned it into a three-dollar gourmet experience.

Iced tea starts off with some natural advantages. After water, tea is the most popular beverage in the world. (Okay, there are a lot of Chinese and Indians who drink tea.) You don't have to invent new recipes. Dozens of varieties of teas and tisanes are drunk all around the world. Many teas are naturally low in caffeine, and herbal teas are caffeine free.

Tea has remarkable health benefits. There are more antioxidants in tea, especially green tea, than in any other natural food.

What's in a Name?

Actually, Barry's original idea for a name was one word, *Honestea*. But this created an unexpected problem at the trademark office. Nestea objected to Honestea, as it contains "Ho Nestea." That led to Honest Tea, a bit less cute and an even better name.

Varietea

Along with black and green teas, there are oolongs and spiced teas, such as *masala* chai. In Korea, people drink cold barley teas. In Germany, people drink fruit and hibiscus teas. In South America, people drink *yerba mate*. In France they drink *verveine* (lemon verbena). In Thailand, they drink ginger and lemongrass teas.

Research from Harvard University and around the world shows benefits that include a boosted immune system, the prevention of heart attacks, and anticancer properties.[1]

Tea is inexpensive and tastes great. There's a terrific variety, and it's good for you. What more can you ask for?

Everything was looking good and now Seth, quite out of the blue, was calling. Seth was brilliant and charming and had infinite energy. He would be the "TEO" of this new venture.

But there was still the nagging question of why the big guys hadn't done this. The recipe for immersing tea in boiling water was no great secret. The cost economics looked attractive. When it comes to making a bottle of tea, most of the cost is in the packaging. The bottle costs nearly a dime and the label and cap add a few more cents. Filling the bottle and transportation bring the cost up to about twenty-five cents. So if you are going to spend that much to package the product, you can spend a few extras cents on making sure what goes inside is top quality.

Principle 3

If you don't want others to copy you, then don't start by copying what others have done. (Symmetry!) Some players can win head-to-head competition through superior execution or staying power. But with less industry experience (and less capital), Seth and Barry did not want to challenge established players at their own game. Their third principle: The product has to be truly original—no "me-too" offerings.

A little market research gave an indication of what was holding the behemoths back. Tea without any sugar was a tad bitter to many American palates. But if health-conscious customers heard that there was any sugar in the tea, many presumed it would be sweet and were turned off. It was a catch-22. The target customer didn't like the bitter taste of unsweetened tea but was afraid to try tea with even a touch of sugar. Among those who liked sugar, most thought it wasn't sweet enough. Thus market research suggested getting rid of the sugar or adding lots more. As a result, most products were driven to the two extremes.

The trick was getting people to taste Honest Tea. When they did, they got it. For the first time, they understood that something with a tad of sugar (or honey or agave) isn't necessarily sweet. "I'd drink that" was the common reply.

The need to overcome people's misperceptions suggested there would be a communication challenge. The category of all-natural, barely sweetened, and delicious didn't exist. Putting the name *diet* on the drink not only implied something artificial, it also suggested that the taste would be compromised. The point of Honest Tea was that something could taste great without being too sweet.

The only solution would be to get customers to sample the product. They would need to taste it to get it. Eventually, Seth and Barry came up with a picture that helped people get it. (Either that, or it's a cheap excuse to run an Honest Tea ad in the middle of the book.)

Honest Tea is deliberately not for everyone. Instead of going after the sixteen-year-old teenager with a big bladder, the company focuses on the kid's parents. Perhaps this is a smaller market, but 100 percent of an unserved market (say, 20 percent of all customers) is still much better than 1 percent of the market everyone goes after (the 80 percent in the 80/20 rule). The customers who found Honest Tea were passionate about the product:

> *Your tea is fabulous! . . . At last, someone intelligent enough to realize that not all people like that syrupy junk that is on the market, and that Nutrasweet and artificial sweeteners taste like crap. I've grown so tired of "well, it's what the consumers are demanding." Not. The rest of us have spent the last decade or so brewing tea at home and keeping it in our refrigerators since traditional marketing researchers have been incapable of using their research to produce anything innovative. Bravo, bravo, bravo. Nice labels, too.*

> *Your teas are excellent. It is a real pleasure to be able to pick up something that doesn't have high-fructose corn syrup as the first or second ingredient. Of course, I'd smile more if somewhere on your Web site it said, "Honest Tea is the best policy." My mother always told me that.*

> *Help! I need Honest Tea! I love it and must have more. Can you ship it to me? Price is no object (to some degree). If you cannot ship it to me please advise me of any support groups or counseling that I may seek in order to recover from this lack of Honest Tea. I must warn you that I may get desperate, causing me to hijack an Honest Tea truck in the Washington area and bring it back to Pittsburgh. I am becoming a heartless, Honest Tea junkie. I hope that you can help.*

Something seems to be working. Honest Tea has created a new beverage category: mainstream organic. Indeed, it is the first organic beverage to be sold at 7-Eleven. While that's good news for now, at some point the big guys will notice. When they enter the fray, why won't Honest Tea get crushed? Why would this product be in a more defensible position than OJ and club soda?

Perhaps the game will be over. But there are some advantages that favor Honest Tea. The first is a sense of cognitive dissonance. Honest Tea has positioned itself as the anti-Snapple. As a result, it is hard for the majors to play both sides of the fence. Coke drinkers and Snapple drinkers for that matter expect their drinks to be sweet. If a Snapple fancier tries Honest Tea, he or she is likely to be disappointed. It won't be sweet enough for the Snapple drinker. Snapple doesn't want to risk turning off its fans, and it doesn't want to sell against itself. Can you imagine Snapple running the earlier ad?

Never underestimate the value of using dissonance as a way of discouraging others from entering your market. When Compaq saw Dell enter the market with its direct sales channel, Compaq wasn't asleep. It fully understood the advantages of the Dell business model. But Compaq's sales were too dependent on retail stores, which threatened not to carry Compaq if the company went into competition with them by selling direct. It is hard, if not impossible, for large firms to take an action that has a good chance of upsetting their installed customer base, even if it is the right move for the future. Are you ready to give up your existing and very profitable business model even if you know the competitor has a better one?

A second issue for the big guys is that the natural foods stores have a healthy distrust of Coke and Pepsi. Some don't even want a Coke delivery truck in their parking lot. That makes it a bit harder for them to establish a new brand among its target customer group, what is called the "cultural creative" Whole Foods shopper.

Making Honest Tea is also a bit tricky. Most other bottled beverages use syrup and concentrate. They don't mess with boiling water and tea leaves. Until recently, all of Coke's beverages were cold-filled. They used preservatives to achieve shelf stability rather than pasteurization.

The idea of using premium and hence extra costly ingredients also goes against the grain for Coke and Pepsi. Back in the early 1980s, Coke and then Pepsi switched from cane sugar to corn syrup. At the time, it would have been hard to argue that people preferred the taste of corn syrup to sugar. (Now, with teenagers

> ### The Checklist
>
> Honest Tea satisfies the first principle by filling the void in the beverage industry that was selling only cloyingly sweet drinks. Honest Tea satisfies the second principle because there are obstacles that will impede an incumbent's interest in copying the product and thus give Honest Tea a chance to establish a base of loyal customers. The third principle is met as bottled tea that actually tastes like tea is an original product.

weaned on high-fructose corn syrup, perhaps they do.) But the switch saved the companies more than $100 million per year.

For this combination of reasons, the big guys have delayed entry into this market. That has given Honest Tea some time to become established and develop a loyal set of customers (more loyalty than you'd get selling a mixture of OJ and club soda). In the end, the company may still find a home with one of the majors, but that will be because Honest Tea has created something more than just an idea.

As for the future, who knows what other why-nots Honest Tea will bring to the market? It has introduced a new type of tea bag. Does the world need another tea bag? Well, yes, actually. The typical tea bag is filled with tea dust and fannings—not the highest-quality tea. Honest Tea created tea bags filled with whole leaf tea, the same type of tea you would use with a strainer. Perhaps there will be a carbonated tea. Meanwhile, we're still waiting for fizzy orange juice.[2]

Of-Course-Nots?

Having discussed why we think Honest Tea is a why-not idea worth pursuing, let's consider some new beverage ideas that have failed and see if we can find a difference. Could you tell which would be which in advance? Or, are the following of-course-nots really such bad ideas?

Caffeinated OJ

What could be better than putting together the top two morning beverages into one package? People drink coffee for the caffeine and OJ for the sugar, taste, and vitamin C. Put them together, and you've got an unbeatable combination.

> *Lee Strader was juiced up in January about the notion of combining caffeine and orange juice into a new drink. "At the time, caffeinated waters seemed to be catching on," recalled Strader, president of Diehard Beverages in Hailey, Idaho. "I thought, 'If that's working, what better than to have the two No. 1 morning consumption items together?'" Apparently, consumers had a hard time swallowing the concept. Diehard Beverages yanked Juiced OJ + Caffeine after selling 7,000 cases in a few months.*[3]

If you think adding caffeine to OJ is strange, consider that today you can buy OJ with calcium and multivitamins. You can also buy caffeinated waters (Buzz Water and Water Joe), mints, and chewing gums. So what's wrong with caffeinated OJ?

It's not just Lee Strader who hasn't made it work. Others have tried and failed under the names Edge2OJ and Outlandish Orange. Not only have these products failed to wake up the market, Juiced, a caffeinated OJ, even won a coveted spot on the 1997 AcuPoll Precision Research annual list of the worst new products. It edged out a microbrewed beer shampoo that promised to put "a head on your head," frozen tea-sicles treats on a stick, and chocolate-lined edible straws.

So why is the idea of OJ and caffeine so bad?

One problem is that it creates a serious conflict with the wholesome image of orange juice. If you had Juiced lying around your fridge, you might be concerned that your kids would drink it. (For this reason, the product might work better sold in single-serve packages in places where people have lunch, versus in half-gallon containers designed for home consumption.) The same problem would be even worse if the product were caffeinated milk.

Remarkably, coffee ice cream almost never has caffeine. We've seen it with caffeine only when it is sold in gourmet ice cream parlors as an adult flavor. This standard practice suggests that mixing caffeine with products that children might eat is a real no-no. (Somehow, Mountain Dew and Coke are the exception to this rule.) It is fine to put healthy additives, such as vitamins or calcium, into OJ, but adding caffeine is a step in the wrong direction.

Another problem is the temperature. Most people drink their morning caffeine hot—in their tea or coffee. Iced tea and iced coffee are not really a morning drink. Drinking caffeinated OJ would be like drinking iced coffee for breakfast.

That said, we should note that in parts of the South, people pour Coca-Cola over their cereal rather than milk. Now, that's a crowd who could warm up to Juiced!

The product could also work in a culture that did not traditionally drink OJ for breakfast. Thus, in Asia, where soybean milk is the traditional breakfast beverage, caffeinated OJ could be marketed as an adult beverage much like coffee.

Sticking with this theme, where else might caffeine find a home? The next section explores some ideas.

Caffeinated Beer

What do you get if you put together a founder of Starbucks with the founder of Red Hook Ale? You get Gordon Bowker. So it should come as no surprise that he would think of combining two of his favorite foods into one.

Red Hook Ale has a Double Black Stout that brings together dark-roasted barley with dark-roasted coffee. With about one-quarter of the caffeine in a cup of coffee, this beer packs a kick.* But this product is more about the taste than the caffeine, as emphasized by the reviews on AllAboutBeer.com: "Creamy, coffeeish aroma. Big, creamy, firmly textured body. Teasing balance of creamy sweetness and quite dry, burnt roastiness. Like a hard, bitter chocolate with a nut fudge filling."[4]

The taste worked but the caffeine didn't. The product still exists, but it now uses decaffeinated coffee. Just as with milk and OJ, consumers have a compartmentalized view of what they want from a product. Beer is supposed to be a relaxing beverage. Its drinkers don't seem to be looking for a kick.

---

*Those with less sophisticated tastes may remember that Drew Carey promoted the same combination with the fictitious Buzz Beer.

We close this of-course-not discussion with two intriguing ideas for caffeinated products. What about caffeinated soap or toothpaste? If the caffeine could be absorbed through the skin, your shower could be an especially invigorating experience. Indeed, just such a soap exists—Shower Shock.[5] While this is certainly a fun idea, we're not sure that the caffeine molecule is small enough to pass through the skin into the bloodstream. As for caffeinated toothpaste, again we are mixing healthy and unhealthy in a way that leads to dissonance for the consumer.

But here's an idea for caffeine that might work: caffeine packets next to the sugar at lunch tables. There could be packets of sugar, Equal, and Buzz. When you get your coffee or tea, you could mix in your own caffeine.

New Alternative Waters?

The hot new beverage is also the oldest: water. You can get water with vitamins, water with caffeine, water with soy, water from Fiji, water from glaciers, water from Wales in a blue bottle, water with extra oxygen. What will they think of next?

Asking Why and Why Not

The difference between a why-not and an of-course-not idea can be mighty slim. That's one reason why it helps to push hard on the why question: Why hasn't someone done this before? In the case of Honest Tea, market research did provide an understanding of why beverage products were driven to extremes. The reason wasn't a good reason (and that's what you hope for).

Reasons also change over time. It is quite possible that the market wouldn't have been ready for the Honest Tea product five years earlier. Snapple, Nantucket Nectars, and SoBe helped create the acceptance for noncarbonated alternative beverages.

Reasons also depend on geography and accidents of history. Something that is an of-course-not in the United States (caffeinated OJ) might well be a viable why-not somewhere else, especially in a culture where the product has different associations and a different competitive landscape.

Even with a good explanation for why others haven't done it, there is still the question of will you succeed and will your success be long-lasting. This highlights the importance of developing a set of principles to guide your search. Figure out some minimal criteria that your solution must meet. If the answer doesn't meet those principles, consider changing the answer rather than the principles.

Reinventing Regulation

Our primary emphasis so far has been on business why-nots. But the same approach can help stimulate innovation in the public sector. Perhaps the need there is even greater. Voters often complain, "Where are new ideas for better government?" This chapter tries to provide a few answers.

Even some of our business ideas might need a gentle nudge of government action to jump-start private innovation. Massachusetts has given its citizens incentives to use Lojack. And the national don't-call list, by securing households' right to be left alone, could spur private entrepreneurs to create the reverse 900 number.

You'll see our tools put to use as we turn now to an array of problems ranging from strikes to consumer protection to civil rights to patent law.

Virtual Strikes

Labor strikes and lockouts impose huge social costs, not just on labor and management, but on the customers and other people who rely on industry. Think about the children who are heartbroken when a baseball or basketball season is preempted by a work stoppage. Or when a teachers' strike keeps their school from opening in September—especially if there's a baseball strike at the same time.

When the dock workers were locked out in 2002, the disruption costs to the rest of the economy were estimated to be more than $10 billion in the first ten days. (These costs led President George W. Bush to invoke the Taft-Hartley Act and thereby reopen the docks for an eighty-day cooling-off period.) At $10 billion, the third-party costs were fifty to a hundred times larger than the amounts at stake in the contract negotiations between the dock workers and managers. In some cases, the third-party costs can be so catastrophic that the law prohibits strikes. This prohibition arises for "essential industries" during times of war or even during peacetime for police or hospital workers, whose services we cannot afford to do without.

Is there any way to reduce the tragic waste of labor stoppages without altering the relative bargaining power of labor and management? Putting on our translation hats, we might try the well-worn literary idea that a war could be decided by the combat of just two men—so that only one would die. This was the gist of Goliath's challenge to the armies of Israel: "Choose you a man for you, and let him come down to me. If he be able to fight with me, and to kill me, then will we be your servants: but if I prevail against him, and kill him, then shall ye be our servants, and serve us."[1]

Of course, the problem is finding a set of combatants who recreate the same likelihood of winning. In the case of Goliath, no one was willing to fight him. Until David came along, most Israelites preferred taking their chances in a war.

Or we might be inspired by *Star Trek*'s "A Taste of Armageddon," in which Captain Kirk and the *Enterprise* stumble on two planets that have been at war for more than five hundred years. The two planets have agreed to avoid the complete devastation of war by using a computer program that decides who will die. When the program ordains, the people declared "dead" willingly walk into antimatter chambers and are vaporized. This *Star Trek* whynot has the advantage that it is likely to reduce the collateral damage that war causes (although the computer for some reason declares Kirk and Spock "dead"). But there is still the enormous waste of life to the combatants themselves. And how in the world do the parties agree on the program?

It turns out that for well over fifty years there has been a clever idea for how to virtually eliminate all the waste of strikes and lockouts. The basic idea, as in *Star Trek,* is to replicate for both labor and management the pain of a traditional strike.

Normally, the government offers carrots and sticks to change people's incentives, but here we're looking for an intervention that maintains the status quo incentives. We want management and labor to keep feeling the same pain as with traditional strikes. We just want to reduce the pain felt by others. So how do we do it?

Instead of a traditional strike, why not have a *virtual* strike? In a virtual strike, the workers keep working as normal and the firm keeps producing as normal, but they sacrifice to the government an amount of money equal to the pain of the strike.

As a first cut, workers lose their wages and an employer loses its profits during a strike. So during a virtual strike, the workers would work for nothing and the employer would fork over to Uncle Sam (or a charity) all its revenues.[2]

Think of it. During a virtual strike, there is no disruption to the rest of the economy. The UPS consumer is not left stranded without service. And, unlike the *Star Trek* idea, the huge cost to the combatants is transformed into a mere transfer. Management and labor certainly feel the pain (and thus have an incentive to settle), but the government (or charities) gets a windfall.

Instead of banning strikes when they would have catastrophic effects on the public or a wartime effort, why not at least allow workers the right to hold a virtual strike and management the right to hold a virtual lockout?[3]

The virtual strike is not just a wild idea waiting to be tested; it's an idea that has already worked. During World War II, the U.S. Navy used a virtual strike to settle a labor dispute at the Jenkins Company valve plant in Bridgeport, Connecticut. The navy ordered all the company's receipts and all the employees' wages to be paid to a navy comptroller. Harvard Business School professor Daniel Quinn Mills summarized the result: "[T]he government caused production to continue despite the labor dispute, but neither the workers nor the company was able to benefit from the continuation of production."[4]

A virtual strike arrangement was also used by mutual agreement in a 1960 Miami bus strike. After a traditional three-day walkout, labor and management agreed to restart service under the following conditions: (1) The public would receive free bus service; (2) the "striking" drivers would receive no pay and were not to accept any tips; and (3) the employer would pay all the other normal costs of operating the buses.

In his review of this first voluntary virtual strike, economist David McCalmont concluded: "Thus, while the public was to be spared all loss and inconvenience, the parties to the dispute were to remain under heavy pecuniary pressure to compose their differences."[5]

McCalmont goes on to explain that the Miami virtual strike lasted only four days. The company ordered its buses off the streets when it found that some drivers were accepting tips, contrary to the agreement. From then on, the strike resumed its conventional character, and the community was deprived of service for more than thirty-three days.

The Miami experience shows that the company's customers are a natural recipient of the virtual windfall. By just cutting its price, the company can forgo its profits during a strike. But it also shows that sympathetic and grateful consumers can undermine the bargaining-power neutrality in ways that paying the government or a charity may not.

More recently, Italy has become the home of virtual strike innovation. In 1999, Meridiana Airline's pilots and flight attendants staged Italy's first virtual strike. During the four-hour virtual strike, the employees worked as usual but without being paid, while Meridiana donated the receipts from its flights to charities.

The experiment was an outgrowth of Italy's December 1998 Labor Relations Pact for the Transport Industry. It envisaged new forms of collective action, which "although onerous for the enterprises and for the workers who take part in the protest, do not affect provision of the service and do not penalize users."

The virtual strike worked to perfection. The flights that were virtually struck were not disrupted. The cabin crews announced to passengers that their flights would not be affected because the strike was being carried out virtually. Those employees taking part wore a white bow on their sleeves to make their participation apparent.

Other Italian transport strikes have followed the Meridiana lead. In 2000, Italy's Transport Union forfeited 100 million lire from a virtual strike carried out by three hundred of its pilots. The pilots' virtual strike provided a great public relations opportunity, as the strike payments were used to buy medical equipment for a children's hospital. Instead of destroying consumer demand as in the NBA lockout, the virtual strike windfall provides an opportunity to increase the brand's reputation.

But again, somewhat perversely, the public relations benefit of virtual strikes may make them harder to implement. The trickiest part of a virtual strike agreement is to figure out how much the employer should forfeit during the strike. For some employers, the potential loss of customers rather than the immediate loss of revenue is the major reason for averting a work stoppage. Merely asking an employer to forfeit its short-term profits, or even its revenue, may not replicate the true costs of a traditional strike. Unions sometimes derive bargaining power from the pressure that inconvenienced customers and government bring to bear on the employer.

But isn't the whole point of a strike to inconvenience consumers so that they will put pressure on management to settle? Not necessarily. Why must we assume that annoyed consumers will put pressure on management only? If consumers blame the workers for the strike, the pressure will be on them. If the point is to disrupt future business, here again, why does the disruption hit management harder? If there is no future business, workers are out of a job, too. But even if consumers and governments disproportionately pressure management to settle, this only means that management should have to forfeit more money during the virtual strike. The firm might have to sacrifice even more than just its short-term profits. In all four historical examples, management agreed to forfeit its entire gross revenue on all sales during the duration of the strike.

Why would workers ever agree to work for nothing? For the same reason that workers are willing to strike now—to impose pain on management. Indeed, during a virtual strike, we might expect to see labor work *harder* because every additional sale represents additional pain to the manufacturer, who has to forfeit the entire revenue on the sale.

And putting on our symmetry hats, we can apply the virtual strike solution to eliminate the inefficiencies of management-imposed lockouts, such as the West Coast dock worker lockout that arose in 2002. In a virtual lockout, the disputants forfeit money but the work keeps getting done.

The government is in a perfect position to nudge the two sides in the right direction. For example, the feds could offer discounts on the social security obligations of both the employer and the employees if the two sides agree to forgo traditional strikes and lockouts in favor of virtual strikes.

The government subsidy for virtual strikes can be seen as another application of the internalization idea—as it lets labor and management appreciate more of the social benefits of forbearing work stoppages. And since the government could be the recipient of the strike payments when virtual strikes did occur, a tax cut need not blow a hole in the federal deficit. Who knows? The government might even make money.

These few paragraphs are not sufficient to give a full defense of the virtual strike idea.[6] But keep in mind that "thar's gold in them thar hills." Traditional strikes are so massively inefficient to the tune of millions of dollars for the disputants and their customers and suppliers that there are plenty of gains for all parties. Rather than wait until the strike is real, labor and management might agree in advance to employ a virtual strike in the event that their next contract negotiations fail. The potential gains from eliminating the entire inefficiency of traditional strikes justify government efforts to experiment with this new vision for managing labor conflict.

What Does It Really Cost?

In 1992, the U.S. Environmental Protection Agency introduced the Energy Star program (www.energystar.gov), a *voluntary* labeling program designed to help consumers understand the economic benefits of energy-efficient products. At first, the labeling was limited to computers and monitors, but by 1996 the Energy Star program had been extended to cover most home appliances (dish-washers, refrigerators, air conditioners, etc.). Hotels, supermarkets, and even traffic lights now fall under its rating system.

The program is said to save consumers $5 billion annually. How can little yellow stickers do that?

The stickers provide total-cost-of-ownership information. They allow consumers to add in the expected energy costs to the initial purchase price. Without this information, consumers had no good way of figuring out whether the more energy-efficient machine was a good deal. Consequently, people had little motivation to pay a premium price for energy-efficient machines; instead, they mostly chose the low-priced, energy-hog appliances. The result was bad for the environment as well as for consumers, who missed opportunities to save money.

Now, not only do consumers save money, but industry wins, too. The reason is that firms can compete on the energy-efficiency dimension. A firm that finds a way to save $500 in electricity costs can demonstrate this advantage to consumers and either raise the product's price or gain share.

Although firms might like to do this on their own, it isn't so easy to get the program started. Unless most products have the sticker, consumers have a hard time making the comparison. It also helps to have the information standardized and its veracity audited.

Now we have a solution. Let's see how it can be translated to solve other problems.

The problem we'd like to solve is the issue of hidden pricing. Consumers are finding it increasingly difficult to figure out what something really costs.

This problem is almost everywhere—it's even at your video store. Most video rental stores have a midweek two-for-one special. You can get two videos for two nights for the regular rental price. The catch is that this offer does not extend to late fees. If you are late in returning the videos, you have to pay a late fee on *each* video. That second video isn't really free, after all.

These late fees add up. As it turns out, Blockbuster makes about 25 percent of its revenue from late fees.

Of course it's our own fault if we're late.[7] And video store late fees are not the world's most pressing issue. The reason we bring it up at is that it is a telling example of a much bigger problem.

The bigger problem is hidden prices in contracts for items such as cell phones, car rentals, and hotels. What does it really cost to rent a car, taking into account insurance, airport taxes, second-driver surcharges, and refilling or prefilling fees?

This confusion is no accident. In an attempt to make their price offer seem low, some firms employ hidden pricing. Once some firms are pricing this way, others feel they have no choice but to follow suit.

Is Talk Cheap?

Cell phone pricing is a striking example. In the summer of 2002, Sprint PCS offered the following deal: 4,000 minutes for $39.99 per month.[8] At first glance, the cost would seem to be a penny per minute. The rub is that only 350 of those minutes are anytime. The other 3,650 are restricted to evening and weekend usage. If you go over your allotted time, on either segment, you get charged 35 cents per minute. And if you don't use all the minutes, then they are forfeited. So what is the true cost per minute?

Here's a quick guesstimate. Let's say that the off-peak usage is free and that all the cost is based on peak times. It looks like peak minutes cost about a dime. But say that you make 350 minutes of calls a month, on average, with some months at 200 and some at 500. In your low-usage months, you will be paying 20 cents per minute because of the forfeited minutes and in your high-usage months, 18 cents per minute because of the 35-cent charges.

What starts off looking like 1 cent turns into 10 cents and then 20 cents per minute, because of the natural variability in your usage. But the more important point is that no one knows what he or she is paying or which plan makes the most sense.

Well, not quite no one. Sprint knows. And so far, it isn't telling. It could report to you each month and each year the average price of what you've paid for each minute used.

This type of hidden pricing is not only a problem for customers—no surprise there—but also a problem for the firms that practice it. The reason is that hidden pricing induces massive churn; that is, it leads customers to change carriers as frequently as a better deal comes along. Because phone companies know better than the customers do how much money they can make from a person, they go to extraordinary lengths to attract new customers and to steal existing customers from their competitors: "Sign up with Acme Phone, and we'll give you a new antigravity cell phone free!" The churn rate in this industry has topped 40 percent per year.[9] This is a huge cost, in terms of sales, credit loss, and marketing expenses. Churn also changes the nature of the relationship between company and consumer. There is no loyalty. Consumers end up feeling ripped off when their bill again and again is larger than they expected it to be. They respond by chasing after the latest deal.

If clearer pricing reduced the lifetime value of a customer, then firms would pay less money to get new customers or to steal customers from rivals. But they wouldn't necessarily make any less money. In fact, they could make more money because the total cost structure of the industry would be improved. This expansion of the pie could then be shared between customers and vendors.

The translation of the Energy Star program offers us a solution to the problem of hidden pricing. Firms can provide total-cost-of-ownership information. In the case of cell phones, Sprint can provide the per-minute cost you've paid and indicate which plan is best for you.

But what if the terms of the plans are different so that the unit price is misleading? This issue also arises with the unit-pricing information offered at supermarkets. While the quality of one bag of chocolate chip cookies may be better than the competition, it still helps to be able to compare the price per cookie (or per gram).

Imagine that cell phone ads had to state the average price per minute for each plan based on average usage. If people could compare the total user cost of one plan to another, pricing would become more straightforward. In particular, we'd bet that the overdraft fee of 35 cents per minute would disappear.

Does that mean that cell phone companies would make less money? No. There would be less incentive to "buy" new customers. By reducing churn and eliminating up-front subsidies on new

cell phones, Sprint and its rivals could make more money with sim-
plified price schemes.

Fill 'er Up?

Car rental companies are another obvious place to put this
solution to work. Rental companies charge $4, even $5 per gallon
for cars that are not returned with a full tank. Or they sell you a
prefilled tank at a small premium, say $2 per gallon, and you lose
any gas you leave when you return your car. Both systems encourage inefficient behavior. It makes no sense to risk missing a plane to
find a gas station, only to put a couple of gallons of gas in the car.
There is already a pump at the rental agency. That's where the car
should be filled up.

Here too, it is impossible to figure out the real price or which is
the better deal. On average, how many gallons do people leave in
the car when they do the prefill? Or how much does the refueling
surcharge add to the average bill?

We have no problem with letting market competition set the
price. The issue of hidden pricing is a lack of information. The
problem in all these cases is that the seller knows more about
what the customer will do than the customer does. If the prepaid
gas price is really competitive, then the seller shouldn't be reluctant
to disclose that the average customer returns with the tank one-
third full.

Of course, full disclosure of the back-end charges will cause
Hertz (and Verizon and Blockbuster) to charge more on the front
end. Say good-bye to teaser rates. But the result won't be a wash.
There are real efficiencies—perhaps even marriages saved, as
spouses don't battle over the need to fill up before returning the car
and risk missing the flight—that make the pie bigger. Customers
will have a better feeling about their car rental providers.

Given our belief in the market, you might well wonder why
some enterprising company doesn't make this change all on its
own. Sometimes this does happen. Southwest Airlines and Jet Blue
offer transparent pricing in the airline business. Our answer to why
this doesn't happen more regularly is that it is difficult to convince
consumers that simpler pricing actually makes them better off.

Imagine, for example, that Hertz were to give up hidden fees and increase its price by three dollars per day. Hertz would no longer come up first on Expedia and other reservations systems, because it would appear to be undercut by all its competitors. Hertz could advertise: "Attention consumers, we really are the cheapest—everyone else has hidden costs!" But that requires consumers to trust Hertz and be more aware of these costs. Hertz would have to educate the market all by itself. Until it completed this education process, Hertz would be at a disadvantage compared to all its rivals.

Many businesses (even universities) get trapped into hidden cost pricing.[10] They don't make any more money in the end, because the competition for customers forces them to compete away these profits at the front end. If others don't use a hidden-price strategy, but you do, then you can make more because the customer won't appreciate that you've raised the price. If others *do* use hidden pricing (and you don't), then they undercut you in the consumer's eye unless you follow suit.

The solution is, again, the yellow energy sticker. Along with the price, each firm would provide a total purchase cost for the average customer for its product offering.

> *Citibank Visa could disclose the chance that you will pay a late fee on your credit card.*

> *Circuit City or Ford could tell you the odds of actually making a claim against an extended warranty.*

> *Au pair in America could tell prospective families (and au pairs) the chance that they will have to rematch (i.e., that the first au pair will not stay for the full year). By the way, that chance is 30 percent.*

For first-time users, the disclosure might concern the average results for its customers—or for customers like you. But for a repeat customer, the company could go farther and let you know what your own propensity to be hit on the back end has been.

There has been a long tradition of requiring sellers to disclose what they know about themselves and their products. We already require unit pricing in grocery stores to help consumers figure out what things really cost. Sellers have to reveal the amount of fat in a Twinkie. Annual percentage rate (APR) numbers are included in mortgage ads. Why not require sellers to disclose what they know about how much customers really pay for their products?

The Anonymity Tool

Here's a twenty-first-century translation of a nineteenth-century breakthrough—the secret ballot. We think of the secret ballot as an integral part of U.S. democracy. But, in fact, the private voting booth and ballot is less than one hundred years old in the United States. Originally implemented in Australia in the 1880s, the idea spread like wildfire throughout the United States and Western Europe, where it was almost universally adopted within just thirty years.

Why? The voting booth was a response to a specific problem: Prior to the secret ballot, lines of men marching to vote could be seen holding the preprinted, colored ballot of the party that had paid for their votes.[11]

The voting booth changed all this. Anonymous voting made it much harder to buy votes because candidates could never be sure whether a particular voter performed his or her side of the bargain. Anyone can claim to have voted for JFK, but no one can prove it.

Anonymous voting solved one problem. Are there any other problems that the anonymity solution might fix?

Remember that the translation tool asks you to restate both the problem and the solution more generally. So, more generally, the problem is a kind of corrupt deal. And anonymous voting disrupts the deal because one side can't tell whether the other side performs. The translation question now becomes, Are there other types of corrupt deals that the anonymity solution might help?

Anonymity might be usefully applied to other voting contexts. In corporate proxy contests, the concern is not that corporations will *bribe* shareholders to vote in support of management, but that they will *extort* the desired vote from pension fund managers by threatening to shift business away from noncompliant voters. The 1990s showed a shift toward anonymity with regard to proxy contests as a way to protect shareholder/vendors from such retaliation.[12]

But while anonymity might be valuable for deterring other types of voting corruption (e.g., if you don't like logrolling), what about other types of corruption? Can you think of any other types of political corruption? (Okay, this is a an easy one.)

What about influence peddling? In this age of McCain-Feingold campaign finance reform, there is a concern about candidates' selling access or influence to their major campaign contributors. There is a strong consensus that mandating disclosure of donor identity will help deter these antidemocratic deals. The public can punish corrupt candidates who take dirty contributions at the polls, and prosecutors can criminally punish both the contributors and the candidates if they can prove corruption beyond a reasonable doubt.

But instead of mandating *disclosure* of contributor identity, Jeremy Bulow, Saul Levmore, and a handful of other academics have asked what would happen if we took a page from the voting booth and mandated *anonymity?* (By this point, if this last sentence hasn't brought to mind the symmetry tool, you should consider putting down the book and pursuing other interests.)

Just as anonymous voting makes it harder for candidates to *buy* votes, anonymous donations would make it harder for candidates to *sell* influence. (I think that I shall never see an idea without symmetree!*) In both cases, anonymity undermines corrupt politics because the candidate can't tell whether the other side of the deal performed his or her promise.

The translation tool leads us to this new application not only by helping identify the general category of problem that might be solved (political corruption), but also by suggesting *how* the solution might work in the new context.

The anonymity solution will deter corruption only if the candidate remains in the dark about who is actually contributing. What's to stop a contributor from simply telling the candidate that he or she gave money? Nothing. But nothing stops faux contributors from saying the same thing.

*With apologies to Joyce Kilmer.

Talk is cheap. Anyone can make such a claim. Candidates, knowing this, will be hesitant to hand out the influence benefits merely on the word or say-so of an influence seeker. This "talk is cheap" effect is why the secret ballot dried up vote buying—anyone could *claim* to have voted a certain way, but no one could *prove* it.

Of course, corrupt contributors will not sit idly by. We expect that they will try to wave canceled checks and to bombard the candidates' blind trust with donations, telling them to look out for a specific spike in their checking account. But again, translation suggests the appropriate response. The secret ballot makes it possible for people who voted for Gore to pretend that they voted for Bush (or vice versa). The core idea is mimicry. As long as nondonors can mimic the signals of true donors, candidates will not know whom to favor.

In *Voting With Dollars,* Ian Ayres and Bruce Ackerman have detailed how this mimicry principle could be implemented.[13] (They even include a model statute in the book!) By giving all donors a cooling-off period of five days in which to rescind their donation, faux donors could, after sending in a check to the blind trust, receive both a canceled check and a separate refund check. And the blind trust could smooth out the amounts reported as being available so as to prevent spikes that might allow large donors to reveal themselves as the source of the contribution.

At the end of the day, no system of mandated anonymity is likely to work perfectly. Even secret voting can break down when it comes to absentee ballots. (A vote buyer could look over a signed absentee ballot and even mail it in.) But a "donation booth" could work well enough to deter much more influence peddling than the current system does.

You might expect that mandating anonymous political donations would be a political nonstarter. Yet ten states have already applied this idea to judicial elections. These states adopted the 1972 model code of judicial conduct that says "[a judicial] candidate should not be informed of the names of his contributors."[14] The core idea is that elected state judges should be deciding cases based on their merits and not on who gave them money.

The proposal of mandating anonymous donations might be seen as translating the idea from the judicial branch to the other two branches of government. Like the judges, perhaps the legislature and the executive branch could decide issues on the merits instead of on financial obligations.

Paying the Polluter

Here's a legal idea that helps show even more ways to flip things around. We started with the most straightforward flip: If X is a solution, think about "not X." This is how we uncovered the reverse 900 idea and the presumed organ donor consent.

If we go beyond answers with a single dimension, the idea of symmetry opens even more solution possibilities. For example, when there are two dimensions to a solution, X and Y, there are four permutations that might be considered:

(X, Y), (X, not Y), (not X, Y), (not X, not Y)

This process of exploiting two-dimensional symmetry was used to great effect by Guido Calabresi and Douglas Melamed in their classic law review article, "One View of the Cathedral."[15] In studying how judges resolved nuisance disputes, Calabresi and Melamed noticed that there were three traditional legal solutions.

Imagine a classic nuisance dispute between a polluting factory and a nearby complaining resident. Sometimes, courts would find for the resident and simply forbid the pollution. At other times, the court would allow the pollution but force the factory to pay damages to the resident. And still at other times, the court would find for the factory (because the pollution was not sufficiently noxious to be considered a nuisance) and thus allow the factory to continue to pollute without paying any compensation.

Calabresi and Melamed realized that a court in a nuisance dispute was making two basic decisions. First, it decides whether the resident has a basic entitlement to stop pollution. Second, it decides how the resident's entitlement is protected—that is, whether it is backed up by an injunction or whether it is merely an entitlement to be compensated if pollution occurs.

The mixing of the two decisions creates a two-by-two box:

How Entitlement Is Protected	Injunction	Pollution allowed without compensation	Pollution prohibited without compensation
	Damages		Pollution allowed with compensation to resident
		Polluter	Resident

**Who Owns the Initial Entitlement
to Control Whether Pollution Occurs**

The rote process of writing down the box lets us (and let Calabresi and Melamed) see a missing category. Courts had adopted only three of the four possible outcomes. Following the symmetry impulse, Calabresi and Melamed asked, Why shouldn't there be contexts in which courts give a polluter the entitlement, but allow a neighbor to stop the pollution by paying the polluter?

Pay the polluter? This sounds crazy.

But, lo and behold, less than a month after the article was published, an Arizona judge independently decided to use this rule—and with good reason.[16] A developer chose to build a huge retirement home smack dab next to a cattle feedlot that was producing more than "a million pounds of wet manure a day" and that had been operating for more than thirty years. The new retirement home then turned around and sued the feedlot for being, well, smelly. The court ordered the feedlot to move, but ordered the developer to compensate the feedlot for the costs of moving.

Though it initially seems crazy to compensate a polluter, it turns out that when the plaintiff creates the problem by "coming to the nuisance," it can be more equitable to force the Johnny-come-lately to compensate the preexisting polluter for shutting down. This example also shows that moving the symmetry impulse to a second dimension can help identify missing categories of solutions.

Principal Audit

We know that government or employer discrimination on the basis of a person's race is unlawful. But, in practice, it's often difficult to determine whether someone actually discriminated. Here's a simple example of flipping things around to produce a powerful new test of discrimination.

Audit testing is a standard tool of civil rights enforcement.[17] You want to find out if a realtor is discriminating? Send in a white tester and a black tester to see if the realtor refuses to show houses to the black tester. Ian has done just this kind of testing at car dealerships. He found that Chicago dealers quoted systematically higher prices to African-American testers than to white testers who followed the same bargaining script.

Audits can produce powerful evidence of discrimination. But they have two big drawbacks. First, discriminators will always come up with some nonracial explanation. (The landlord might say, "I didn't show the Hispanic tester the apartment because she was poorly dressed or in a hurry.") Second, conducting well-controlled tests is expensive. The researcher has to worry about whether the white testers dress and speak the same as the minority testers.

But in markets that have a middleman, there is a more powerful test for discrimination. We use the example of employment agencies and real estate brokers to show how to flip things around to find this new test.

Consider how to test an employment agency. The traditional approach would be to send in minority and white testers (or male and female testers) pretending to be potential employees and see if they are treated the same.

Now think about how you could use the symmetry tool to flip this around. Instead of sending in *two* testers pretending to be *applicants,* the testing group could send in *one* tester pretending to be an *employer.* If the employment agency offered to discriminate on the tester's behalf, the test produces conclusive evidence of the agent's willingness to violate the statute. We call this a *principal audit* because the single tester pretends to be the principal who hires the services of the employment or real estate agency.

Flipping things around and testing how the real estate or employment agent interacts with his or her principal solves the two big problems with traditional audits. First, the testing is cheaper because you need send in only one tester, and that tester doesn't have to be well matched with an other-race counterpart. And because the test is not based on the comparative treatment of two testers, there is no concern about whether the testers were, in fact, well matched. If the real estate agent agrees to show the house only to white people, then there is direct evidence of the agent's willingness to discriminate.

The idea of testing the other side of the market came to Ian after he encountered a surprisingly blatant example of discrimination. Soon after his first child (Henry) was born, Ian, with bleary eyes, made some calls about hiring a nanny. His first call was to Thank Goodness I've Found, a New Haven nanny agency. The agency representative ignored Ian's questions and launched into what sounded like a canned sales pitch. Without any prompting, she volunteered: "Tell me your prejudices. We'll only send you *pink* polka-dot nannies if that's what you want. If you're not comfortable with an older or a younger girl, we'll make sure that you only have to interview candidates that you like."

The representative expressly offered to discriminate on the basis of age and, in context, we're pretty sure that if Ian had responded by saying, "I'm not really comfortable dealing with Hispanics," the representative would have agreed to send only non-Hispanic applicants.

Ian got off the phone and filed a complaint with Connecticut's Human Rights Commission. The commission is required by statute to investigate allegations of discrimination, but these investigations are usually a waste of time. The commission calls the alleged discriminator and says, in effect, "A complaint has been filed against you. Do you discriminate?" Of course, the answer is always no!

Ian suggested that the commission just replicate his experience as a potential employer. In two minutes, it could have called the agency and obtained the evidence of discrimination.*

To be sure, such principal audits raise important ethical issues. As with traditional audits, there is unavoidable deception. Pretending to be an employer or a real estate seller can also raise concerns of government entrapment.[18] The entrapment concern—that the audit lured an otherwise innocent agent to discriminate—could be reduced if the audits were used only in response to consumers' complaints that they had encountered discrimination.

---

*Sadly, the commission never acted on Ian's complaint.

While these concerns are real, the principal audit has important advantages. Ian's experience suggests that intermediaries may have their guard down when speaking with principals. Testing both sides of markets would let real estate and employment agents know that there's no safe place to propose race discrimination. Just making it more difficult for potential employers and real estate sellers to communicate their discriminatory preferences might drive some discrimination out of the market.[19]

A Safe Harbor for Probationary Hiring

Here's another way to use symmetrical thinking to help prevent discrimination. The insight relies on the fact that people need to be hired before they can be fired.

The vast majority of employment discrimination suits today are filed after an employee has been fired. While much of the rhetoric concerning Title VII is about giving a fair opportunity to be *hired*, in practice there are six suits claiming discriminatory firing for every one suit claiming discriminatory hiring.

This shouldn't be surprising. Existing workers have more information about discrimination (Why did you fire me when you let Jack stay on?) and are more invested in the job than applicants who are passed over in the first place because of their race or sex.

The greater scrutiny given to firing decisions can, however, perversely impact employers' hiring decisions. Employers who worry about firing suits may be less willing to engage in probationary hiring of minorities or women. Employers may think it is better not to hire a minority applicant—explicitly discriminating against the person in hiring—because they know that they're less likely to be sued at that point. When they hire someone on a probationary basis, they may face a lawsuit if they later decide (on a nondiscriminatory basis!) that the employee isn't up to snuff.

The fear of suit by short-term employees is not hypothetical. An American Bar Foundation sample of employment discrimination firing suits found that more than one-quarter were brought by employees who had worked for the defendant less than a year.

Were these employees fired because of their race? As Stanford and Fordham Law School professors John Donohue and Peter

Siegelman have pointed out, "It hardly makes sense to hire workers from a group one dislikes . . . only to fire them once they are on the job."[20] In the end, we worry that our attempts to ferret out firing discrimination with probationary lawsuits may end up inducing hiring discrimination against the very classes of people that the law was intended to protect.

So, what's to be done? With some trepidation, we suggest that firms and their employees be allowed to contract out of Title VII *for a short period.* Suggesting a rollback of our most important civil rights statute seems wrongheaded. But a three-month opt-out provision would give firms the freedom to take chances with probationary employment of minorities without exposing themselves to the risk of civil rights liability for subsequent discharge.

Patents

Let's shift gears from a moral to an economic imperative. What can our tools say about intellectual property rights?

Patenting Questions

Current patent law protects good solutions. Why not flip things around and allow people to patent good questions?

This is just being symmetric about the creative process. Sometimes identifying and clearly framing the question is more important to the creative process than finding the right answer. But we force inventors to both ask the good question and answer it before they are granted a patent.

It is fairly straightforward to apply the limitations to question-type patents that we apply to the more traditional solution-type patents. To be patentable, the question must be a nonobvious improvement over the prior art. You shouldn't get a patent today for asking how to end world hunger or how to generate cold fusion, because these questions are already well known.

The reason to offer question patents is to give innovators the incentive to publicize their questions. Without any protection, companies keep their questions secret. They don't want to give away what they are working on, because they don't want to get beaten to the punch.

In mathematics, there is a reward to those who share their great questions. Hilbert helped set the agenda for the next century of mathematics with his twenty-three questions asked in a 1900 Paris lecture. Fermat was perhaps best known for his unproven Last Theorem and all the false attempts to prove or disprove it. (It was finally solved by Princeton mathematician Andrew Wiles in 1993.[21]) The Riemann Hypothesis is the most famous outstanding problem. There is even a million-dollar prize to the person who can resolve it.[22]

Before going all the way toward patenting questions, we could take the intermediate position of allowing a patent on a conjecture. There is one arena in which conjectures are, in effect, patentable. Biotech firms are awarded patents for targeting how a drug will react with a particular site. What they have established is what the drug does on a molecular level. In that sense, they have demonstrated its utility. But they have not shown that this mechanism will have the desired effect on health. They conjecture that this mechanism will lead to a treatment for diabetes or migraines, but they have no proof at the time of the patent.

When a big pharmaceutical company decides to investigate this lead, it is aware that if the drug works, it will have to share the rewards with the patent holder at the molecular level. This often leads to complicated negotiations. Most biotech companies realize that even a good mechanism of action is still only 5 percent of the game, and so they tend not to get too greedy.[23]

Of course, the person who discovers the answer deserves a patent. We could prevent the bargaining problem with a statute that allots to the question holder some share—say, 10 percent—of the profit and licensing fees.

Splitting the profits will diminish the incentives that any individual will have to find an answer. But we expect that this will be more than offset by the increased number of people who will be aware of the question. Publishing questions would catalyze translation solutions. For example, it would be much easier for a physicist to learn what problems chemists were trying to solve, and vice versa. In short, patenting questions would allow questioners to share their problems and allow answerers to find out what questions people want to have solved.

Patenting "Law"

As a lawyer, Ian feels a bit left out of the patent game. GE can patent a better light bulb. Jay Walker can patent a better business process. But Ian can't patent a better law. Is that something we should correct? Does it make sense to translate the idea of patent protection to law?

Ian's Yale Law colleague Roberta Romano wrote a classic article with the provocative title "Law as Product."[24] She saw that states with useful corporate law are supplying an important input for effective business. Romano went on to show that states in fact compete for corporate business, especially by being responsive in amending their business corporations' statutes.

But there's a problem with this market for corporate law. Unlike other markets, we don't give any of the states intellectual property protection if they come up with a truly innovative legal solution.

Individual states have a reduced incentive to solve problems of corporate governance because successful statutory solutions may be quickly copied by rival jurisdictions. Thus, even if state legislatures are racing to the top in their competition to supply corporate law, the lack of protection for intellectual property is a strong reason to predict that the race will not proceed at an efficient pace.

A vivid example of the absence of patent protection can be seen in the state competition for antitakeover statutes. In the 1980s, many corporations were looking for protection from hostile takeovers. But any state that went to the trouble of crafting a statute that passed constitutional muster would find that other states could immediately copy the sum and substance of its statute.

Indeed, this imitation occurred with lightning speed. Within a year and a half of the Supreme Court decision upholding the constitutionality of the Indiana antitakeover statute, twenty-six other states had passed similar statutes. Indiana and a few other innovating states bore substantial costs in creating legal certainty, but gained virtually no advantage in attempting to compete for corporate charters. Even though Indiana's incentive to protect its incumbent corporations was sufficient in this case, there's no reason to believe that Indiana or any other state will have enough incentives to experiment with other legal innovations.

Is there really any such thing as a true legal innovation? Think about Marty Lipton's creation of the "poison pill." The poison pill is a contingent security designed to pay huge dividends to preexisting shareholders if anyone acquires a controlling share of the stock without approval of the board of directors. Taking over a corporation that has a poison pill is no longer attractive, because doing so would give away a large portion of the firm's value to other shareholders. Who needs an antitakeover statute if individual corporations can protect themselves from attack by private contract? But Lipton's pill was easily and often copied.

Most people balk at the idea of patenting statutes or contracts. But if you believe that intellectual property rights are necessary to motivate innovation, then it follows that the incentives to improve the law are inadequate.

It's Patently Obvious

Here's a translation that's inspired by penguins. Really.

Adelie penguins have a problem. As they congregate on an ice floe, they all want to dive into the water to feed on the fish. But no one wants to be the first to dive in, just in case a leopard seal or an orca is looking for some lunch.

Each penguin stands at the edge of the ice acting like it's going to jump, but really waiting for the others to jump in first. This behavior is described with great flourish in the Antarctic journal of Peter Brueggman:

> So what does it take for them to jump in? They watch the water and when a large group of penguins comes swimming into their immediate area, the Adelie penguins start getting very vocal. They start jostling, jockeying for position, squabbles break out, beaks peck back and forth, some flipper bashing back and forth, lots more loud discussion, more jostling, more pecking, and finally the braver ones will jump in followed by an immediate chain reaction of everyone rushing to jump in the pool all at the same time, no waiting,

*every person for themselves. . . . Watching the penguins go
through their behaviors of marching up and down the
shoreline en masse and then waiting for incredibly long
periods of time to jump in starts to make sense if you are the
chicken of the sea.*[25]

The problem is that there is no great reward for being first. As soon
as it becomes clear that the first mover isn't going to be eaten, the
other penguins jump in.* The first mover takes all the risk and gets
no special reward, as it has to compete with its fast followers for
the fish. This sounds like just the case where a patent-type reward
would be called for so that the first mover receives more of the benefits of taking the big risk.

The U.S. patent system doesn't help solve these first-mover
problems. To be patentable, the system requires that the innovation
be "nonobvious" to a person well versed in the subject matter. The
idea is that the law doesn't need to give protection to obvious innovations, because they will be brought to market—even without
patent protection.

But the penguin story suggests that even obvious ideas might
not be brought to market. Although jumping into the water is an
obvious idea to the penguins, they nonetheless hesitate. When the
free market produces a first-mover *disadvantage,* we might need
patent law to prevent second movers from copying.[26]

Such a law already exists for pharmaceuticals. Under the Hatch-
Waxman Act, a generic manufacturer that successfully challenges
the patent of an incumbent gets a 180-day period of exclusivity
before any other generic firm is allowed to enter the market. The
challenger that made the effort to open up the market gets a six-
month head start on the competition.

Following this penguin logic, Aaron Edlin suggests another
obvious idea worthy of protection: price-cutting. When prices are
uncompetitive, the first firm to cut price does consumers a big
favor. But that "innovation" might not get a big payoff if rivals
match it right away. If the price-cutter doesn't gain market share, it

---

*Even if the first mover is going to be eaten, it may still be safe for the others to
jump in as the leopard seal will have been fed.

ends up worse off. For that reason, price-cutters should get a kind of intellectual property protection to prevent imitators.[27]

Edlin looks at airlines with a monopoly on a particular route. For example, US Airways is the only carrier flying out of New Haven. For the privilege of taking its one-hour flight to Philadelphia, the fare is a whopping $334 (each way).

US Airways can get away with the high price because it knows that if another carrier starts offering a low-price service, US Airways can match the price and remain competitive. The other airlines know it, too, and realize that there's no percentage in trying to enter the market. Like the penguins, other airlines know that if they jump first and cut prices, US Airways will follow their lead.

Edlin's solution? Give the initial price-cutter a temporary patent that prevents US Airways from cutting its own price for a period of six months in response to a new entrant in the market.

Price-cutting is pretty obvious. It would never satisfy the traditional test that innovations must be nonobvious. But translating what we have learned from penguins suggests that even obvious ideas may be too risky to bring to the market.

Best of all, giving price-cutters a temporary patent will lead US Airways and others with route monopolies to drop their price before any entry occurs. The monopolists know that they'll be clobbered if someone enters and the law prevents them from cutting their price in response.

Preventing US Airways from cutting its price in response to the entry of a rival induces it to cut its price before an actual entrant ever arrives. Edlin has ingeniously found a way to get the benefits

Advance Warning

A version of Edlin's solution was used in the early 1990s. The Federal Communications Commission required then-dominant carrier AT&T to wait up to 120 days before it could cut (or raise) its price. In contrast, Sprint and MCI could change price with one day's notice. This regulation was used to great advantage by the entrants to gain share.[28]

of more competitors without the need of actually producing more competitors.

Price-cutting might be obvious, but it's risky all the same. Edlin's proposal rewards the risk taker.

Publish or Perish

A couple of years ago, University of Pennsylvania law professor Gideon Parchomovsky asked whether there might not be times when innovators would be better off publicly disclosing their innovations instead of trying to patent them. Such a question seems confused. Publication would just give away your ideas to your competitors so that you could never patent the innovation.

While most firms are trying to avoid inadvertent disclosure of their ideas, Parchomovsky wondered whether more disclosure might be beneficial. We see the application of the symmetry tool, but to what purpose?

Publishing ideas not only stops you from being able to patent the idea, it also stops your competitors from patenting it. The U.S. Patent and Trademark Office will only grant patents on ideas that are nonobvious improvements on the prior art. Publishing one of your unpatented ideas changes the prior art and thus makes it harder for your competitors to steal the market from you.

Imagine that an innovation has to be ten steps ahead of the prior art to be patentable. Let's say that Motorola and Nokia are racing to get a patent on some new technology. If Nokia realizes that it has only discovered five steps whereas Motorola has already achieved nine steps, it might make sense for Nokia to publish the five steps that it has discovered. Publishing will change the prior art and mean that Motorola is now just four steps ahead of the prior art. It might be a lot easier for Nokia to catch up when it is down 4 to 0 in a ten-step race than when it is down 9 to 5.

Nifty idea. But when we first heard it, we still couldn't believe that businesspeople would ever willingly disclose their unpatented ideas.

It turns out, however, that there is an increasing trend to do just that. The *Financial Times* reports that "companies are increasingly adopting 'defensive publishing' strategies. That is, by publishing information about their invention they create 'prior art' to disqualify anyone else from patenting it."[29]

Specialist journals and Web sites, such as *Research Disclosure* and ip.com, publish about four hundred disclosures each month. The mere threat of publishing might lead to some new motives for joint-venturing. Imagine that you're Motorola and are poised to file a patent, when Nokia calls suggesting that it may publish its partial results unless you invite them to join your research team.

Suggestion Box

We told you there were tons of low-hanging fruit. Here are a few short but sweet confections.

Buycotts

What is the opposite of a boycott? No, it's not a girlcott! It's a buycott.

Under a boycott, the protesters agree not to buy some product until the company changes its behavior in some way. Under a buycott, the protesters would promise to buy the company's product if it changes its behavior in some way.

While boycotts are common, buycotts might be an even more powerful tool. Take the case of the students against sweatshops. Many students are opposed to the sweatshop conditions under which licensed apparel is made. Thus, they have called for a boycott of all Champion (and other) sweatshop sweatshirts.

Turn the protest around. Instead of saying that they won't buy a sweatshirt made by sweatshop labor, imagine that a large number of students committed to buying a sweatshirt made under approved labor conditions. If a manufacturer could count on such demand, we think it would be quick to enter the market. Then, the loss of share to this entrant would lead the incumbents to follow suit.

The reason a buycott is potentially so much more effective than a boycott is that most people don't buy most products. Thus, if a thousand people say that they won't buy Absolut vodka, it isn't really clear how many of them would have bought the product otherwise. Perhaps the company would be losing only ten sales. In contrast, if a substantial group of consumers all agreed to buy the product, this would have a large impact on the company. In fact, rather than suffer a boycott, Absolut generated huge customer loyalty when it became the first national account to advertise in *Out* magazine.

The best example of a buycott is the stunning rise of the FUBU clothing line. FUBU stands for For Us By Us, where the "Us" is black-owned business. The positive affirmation of supporting FUBU businesses has proven to be a great success.

Pre-IPO Trading

New companies often give away money when their stock first goes public. Why? Because the stock is sold at a fraction of what the public is willing to pay. Whenever the stock price triples on the first day of trading, the company that issued it has got to be kicking itself because it could have received a lot more money for creating the business. Even if the stock only goes up 20 percent, that's a good deal of money left on the table.

Why not reduce the discount of IPOs by allowing a limited amount of pre-IPO trading? If Queequeg Coffee is planning to issue its shares a week from today, there is no reason that speculators should not be able to sell futures in Queequeg stock today—promising to deliver shares of Queequeg in a week's time. The price of these future contracts would let the market determine the value of the stock so that the issuing company could issue the actual stock at a much more accurate price. Voilà! No price spikes on issuing day.

Of course, established investment banks would be opposed to this idea, as it would deprive them of the profits—aka bribes—that can be given to favored clients and executives whose business they are courting. But the upstart WR Hambrecht + Co developed the

Q. Who's Queequeg?

A. A harpoonist who worked alongside Starbuck in *Moby Dick*. Although Queequeg's Coffee doesn't yet exist, Peet's Coffee and Tea was one of the firms to use the Hambrecht OpenIPO. In 2001, Peet's IPO raised $26.4 million.

OpenIPO in 1999, an online auction system that allows the market to set the IPO price.

Licensing Microsoft's Old Windows

Some people have suggested that the appropriate remedy for Microsoft's antitrust violations is to break it up—to force Microsoft to compete against itself. But as Humpty Dumpty learned, breakups can be expensive in and of themselves. There's a way, however, to get Microsoft to compete against itself without incurring the costs of required divestiture. Jeremy Bulow and Hal Varian have suggested that a court could force Microsoft to compete against its *past* self.

One option is to require any site license to be both perpetual and resalable. That would lead to large numbers of Windows 2000 and NT licenses on the used market from people who've upgraded. Another option is to order Microsoft to license its last version of Windows at a discount price, say, $25 per copy.

A court licensing order would create an immediate competitor, as some people would prefer to simply buy Windows 2000 instead of Windows XP. If the old source code were also made available, new entrants could improve Windows 2000 and even sell it just as long as they continued to give Gates and company a $25 license fee for every unit sold.

It is no surprise that Microsoft is moving in just the opposite direction. Microsoft isn't selling prior versions (or licensing the source code). It doesn't even want to sell you the current version. Instead, the company wants to rent you the software and have you pay an annual license fee. That way, Microsoft doesn't have to worry about competing with its former product or even its current one. If you don't continue the license, you have nothing.

Campaign Finance Vouchers

Instead of basing public financing on which parties garnered votes in the *last* election, follow Bruce Ackerman's suggestion, and give each citizen "Patriot dollars." These Patriot dollars are vouchers that can be given to the candidate of your choice. Think of this as food stamps for politicians. Citizens are given money that can only be used to support political candidates.

Scheduled Jury Duty

Why not allow people to schedule jury duty? Many people think of going to jury duty as akin to a trip to the dentist—painful but necessary. But with dentists, at least you can schedule your appointments.

Give Palestinians Stock in Israel

Here's a pure internalization idea from Gideon Parchomovsky and Peter Siegelman. The idea is to give individual Palestinians a tangible, financial stake in peace. The United States and Israel would buy $9 billion of shares from the Israeli stock market. The stock would be put in escrow and dispersed to Palestinians ten years after an effective peace plan was in place and certified by the World Court as being honored. At today's stock prices, $9 billion is more than $3,000 per Palestinian—and after a peace agreement might easily grow to double that amount.

Why not bribe the masses to make peace?[30]

Standardized Calendar

Why not have a more standardized calendar? For example, have thirteen four-week months plus a New Year's Day. Each month would begin on a Monday. That would mean the fourteenth of the month would always be a Sunday. While the logic is compelling, there are a few problems. Many people would lose their birthdays. And what should we name that thirteenth month? We suggest Berbube, to honor the proposer.

Ask Not Why; Ask Why Not?

It's no surprise to find that parts of government don't work well. But this chapter has shown that our core questions can be used to improve legal regulation as well as business. Asking government decision makers to "flip things around" or to "feel your pain" can produce great public policy ideas. There's plenty of low hanging fruit just waiting to be picked.

10

Implementing
Why-Not

There is real joy in problem solving for its own sake. That's why many love tackling the Sunday *New York Times* crossword puzzle. Others find plenty of puzzles in everyday life. Why are things done one way rather than some other way? Could they be done differently and better? Even if it never happens, we take satisfaction in imagining how we'd run the company, the country, or even the world better.

Ultimately, we aspire to something more. Karl Marx got one thing right. We shouldn't be satisfied with just analyzing or interpreting the world: "[T]he point is to change it."[1]

Coming up with a great idea is only the beginning of the battle. If you really want to change your company or the world, you need to sell the idea and you need others to buy in. The art of persuasion is particularly important because, as we've repeatedly emphasized, many ideas for great new products or services are *not* great ideas to start new businesses. Sometimes—usually, in fact—the best entity to put the idea into practice will be an existing firm.

Even if your idea is, objectively speaking, brilliant, you won't necessarily have an easy time selling others on it. Be prepared to encounter remarkable levels of resistance and prejudice along the way. Take right turn on red, for example. Although this is one of the most obvious why-not ideas, it still doesn't exist in Germany. It's not that the Germans are unfamiliar with the concept. Prior to unification, right turn on red did exist in the East, but not in the West. When East and West unified, the Germans lost right turn on red on the presumption that everything from East Germany was wrong. There is a lot of prejudice to overcome in this case.

Good ideas are often ignored because of what the prison warden in *Cool Hand Luke* called a failure to communicate. Being right is not enough. This chapter is about how to get others to buy in—even when they aren't in the market for new ideas.

The Art of Persuasion

How do you go about persuading people with power to support your idea? Ever since Aristotle's *Rhetoric,* scholars have been thinking about how you convince others to support your cause. The many recent articles on this topic contain good advice on how to design organizations to make them more receptive to new ideas.[2] Our focus is on what you, the *individual,* can do to be heard.

For most of us and for most ideas, the key to implementation is not going out and making the idea happen yourself. Although Barry did go out and make Honest Tea a reality, most of the ideas in this book are not the kind that could or should prompt you to start up a new business. Sure, if you happen to be the CEO of Citicorp, you have the power to implement the auto-refinancing mortgage, but most of us do not wield that kind of power. The best we can do is frame a pitch so that it is most likely to be heard. And then deliver that pitch to the right batter.

In Praise of Sound Bites

We start with the art of the pitch—often referred to as the *elevator pitch*. What can you say during a brief elevator ride you happen to share with the right batter when luck puts you two together?

We are fans of extreme brevity. Despite the growing disdain for sound-bite journalism, we still think that an effective sound bite is a good way to pitch a good idea. In fact, we've put that approach into practice throughout this book to get you hooked on ideas:

> *If IKEA can provide baby-sitting, why can't movie theaters?*

> *If treasury bonds can be indexed to inflation, why not mortgages?*

Of course, not all good ideas can be easily described in a single sentence. For example, it's not easy to convince people of the potential virtues of a virtual strike in even a paragraph. But we are leery of those who claim that *their* ideas just can't be expressed in fewer than two thousand words.

When preparing your pitch, you definitely need the two-hundred-word description (and probably a two-thousand-word description as well). But you should also struggle to have a one-line version of the idea at the ready.

Progressive Insurance made the case for pay-per-mile insurance in ten words:

You drive, you pay; you don't drive, you don't pay.

Now it's our turn. In ten words, we can summarize what this book is about:

How to solve problems big and small using everyday ingenuity.

These sound bites may not do the ideas justice, but they at least start the dialogue.

In the end, nothing beats clear reasoning. What's the nub of the idea, and why is it likely to work? Straightforward reasoning need not be packaged in an exhaustive treatise. Even the shortest of sound bites can contain powerful rationales for action. Sometimes these are explicit, but sometimes a powerful hook naturally leads the listener to do the work. We've found that merely asking a question (e.g., Why not have an adjustable-rate mortgage whose term adjusts instead of the monthly payment?) is sufficient to lead most audiences to see for themselves the core argument (e.g., that borrowers can better handle the risk of having a longer mortgage than the risk of having their monthly payment go up).

KISS: Keep It *Similar,* Stupid

In pitching an idea, try to make it *familiar*. Think of the injunction KISS. Normally, this stands for Keep It Simple, Stupid. We use it to mean Keep It *Similar,* Stupid. It's hard enough for listeners to absorb a radically new idea. Don't make them also have to absorb a new context. The idea of keeping the idea similar or familiar

means trying to translate the idea so that the product or service is as similar as possible to the status quo.

Colgate has done this brilliantly with its new Simply White tooth-whitening gel. The home-use tooth whitener is an unfamiliar product. Yet the Colgate product evokes a strong déjà vu—it seems like Wite-Out for teeth.

Colgate's tooth-whitening gel helps you correct the mistake of less-than-perfect teeth. You dab it on, just as you would apply Liquid Paper or Wite-Out to fix a typo. Even the packaging looks familiar. The company has done such a good job that we'd bet you'd be surprised that its product isn't a paper-white liquid—it's a clear gel.

Thus, KISS is our call for a final type of translation: translating the great idea you've come up with so that the listener can more easily understand it.

CASE STUDY

Who Took My Cookie Jar?

The more complicated the product, the more important it is to keep it similar to a known product. For example, the Virgin One account was conceptualized as a way of consolidating your savings and mortgage into one net debt position. While the single-account idea appeals to us as economists, it is it harder for consumers to absorb the idea.

Virgin had to educate consumers. The virtue of a single net debt position is also a vice. It can be depressing to look at your bank balance and always see a negative number.

Gordon McCallum heads up marketing at Virgin. He knew that the product would be a difficult sell: "In the U.K., people don't see mortgages as a debt but rather as something that pays for the house. They are not keen to mix up their home ownership with their retirement savings and their credit card account."

We find it's much easier to describe the Virgin One account by saying:

> *Wouldn't it be great if you could earn your mortgage rate of interest on your checking account?*

Woolwich Bank took the cookie-jar approach to go one up on Virgin. Under the Woolwich Openplan, customers are allowed to have up to twelve different "cookie jar" savings accounts. Money in any of these accounts is used to offset the mortgage. It is just as if the customer gets the mortgage interest rate on each of the savings accounts. But instead of paying the interest on the mortgage and getting it back on the savings account, the interest is neither paid nor received.

Cookie Jars

A new field called *behavioral decision theory* incorporates elements of psychology into decision making.[3] Behavioral decision theory tells us that people employ what might be called a *cookie-jar* approach to savings. In one jar, they put aside money for a kitchen upgrade. In another jar, they set aside money for the kids' college. The IRA and 401(k) plans are jars set aside for retirement savings. Christmas clubs are jars set aside for holiday presents.

Although money is fungible and so all that really matters is the combined amount across all jars, it is hard to keep track of progress that way. Smaller goals tend to get lost in the bigger picture. It becomes all too easy to borrow from the kitchen fund for the holiday season and from the college fund for the kitchen. Why not let people have their cookie jars?

To our eye, it is remarkable how much easier it is to understand this way of doing things. If you want to create an account to save £16,000 to buy a Mini Cooper, it's much more satisfying to watch your savings balance increase from zero to £16,000, rather than seeing your mortgage gradually fall from £198,000 to £182,000.

The evolution from the Virgin One to the Openplan account helps us understand how to bring a new idea to the market. When you are doing something very different, try to make it seem similar to the status quo to the customer. Look for a way in which the customer can get the benefit without having to change his or her behavior.

Openplan-type accounts have become the standard mortgage product in the U.K. Now that we know how to pitch the product, it's time for someone to bring this innovation to the United States.

CASE STUDY

Adjusting the Frame

In chapter 3, we implicitly used the KISS principle when we proposed this why-not:

> *Why not have a fixed-rate mortgage that automatically refinances if interest rates fall?*

This way of framing the product suggests that it is a simple twist to the traditional fixed-rate product. Perhaps the surprise is that we could just as well frame this innovation from the perspective of an adjustable-rate mortgage:

> *Why not have an adjustable mortgage that only adjusts one way, namely, down?*

In both cases, we keep the description similar to a familiar product. Which perspective works might depend on the customer. For customers predisposed to an adjustable-rate mortgage, we think the one-way adjustable framing makes for an easier sell.

It isn't just consumers who have to be sold. Lenders need to see the advantages, too. The stumbling block is to convince lenders that this is not just a plan to give away their profits. The customer has to pay something to offset the loss to the lender from refinancing or adjusting the rate. The KISS approach can help sell the lender on the product, too.

If we start from the perspective of a fixed-rate mortgage, we'd propose that the customer pay a fee (which could be rolled into the new mortgage) when the rate is adjusted. This is just like paying points on a new mortgage.

If we start from the perspective of a one-way adjustable mortgage, then paying points every time the rate drops would be a foreign concept. But we have to do something to compensate the adjustable-rate lender for adjusting only one way. We could charge a premium rate up front, but that might make the two mortgages hard to compare and it would also increase the initial payment, something to be avoided. A better way would be to modify the adjustment. For example, the mortgage might adjust only halfway down—by 0.5 percent when rates fall by 1 percent, or by 0.25 percent when rates fall by 0.5 percent.

The traditional adjustable mortgage adjusts up or down on a one-to-one basis. The revised mortgage only adjusts downward, but the adjustment is halfway. We'd bet that many customers would be willing to give up half of the downward adjustment to avoid all the risk of an increase in rates. The lender still makes money because it keeps half the downward adjustment.

The innovation can be sold equally well to fixed-rate customers. The revised fixed-rate mortgage still automatically refinances, but the new rate only goes halfway down. And there's no extra charge for this. You could get a standard fixed-rate mortgage. Or for the same price, you could get a fixed-rate mortgage that automatically gives you half of any decrease in the market interest rate. Which would you choose? The lender still makes money, because it only gives away half of the rate drop and keeps half for itself. It holds on to that half gain longer by slowing down the customer's incentive to refinance.[4]

Economists have known for a long time the power of the KISS principle. We tend to throw around the Latin phrase *ceteris paribus,* which means "all other things equal." That's what you should strive for in constructing your pitch: keeping all other things equal so that the listener can focus on the single change that makes this idea work.

Implementing KISS is hard work. Crafting a compelling, easily digestible pitch takes a lot of thought. Part of the KISS principle is tailoring the idea to make it easier for the listener to understand. That means that you have to take on more of the work of communication yourself. Believe us, as academics, we know lots of brilliant eggheads who aren't at all willing to work at communicating. They'd much rather leave it up to the listener to decipher their cryptic musings, and—no surprise—their impact on the world suffers accordingly.

To Whom Should You Pitch?

Who is best placed to move forward with your idea? If you want to have coffee served at your public library, you need to decide whether you are better off approaching someone at the library or someone at Starbucks.

The former chair of the Federal Communications Commission, Reed Hundt, was particularly helpful on this "who" question when we explained our sound bite about reverse 900 numbers: *You should get paid for listening to telemarketing calls.* He suggested that we first pitch this idea to telemarketers as a way to facilitate direct marketing to faxes and cell phones.[5] Federal law prohibits essentially all telemarketing to faxes or cell phones. But if a household, in return for compensation, authorizes Verizon to pass along fax or cell phone advertisements, there is no reason why the law should block the transaction. Hundt understood that telemarketers, who are likely to fight tooth and nail any regulation that forces them to pay for ordinary calls, might be amenable to a system that opens up a new avenue for solicitation.

Or let's go back to a sound bite concerning home-equity insurance: *For a one-time cost of 1.5 percent, homeowners can be protected against a decline in their local real estate market.* Who besides home buyers are potential purchasers of this insurance? Consider who else has a financial stake in the value of your home. Mortgage lenders have a stake, perhaps, but they're already pretty well protected by an equity cushion, the 10 or 20 percent down payment that they require (or by private mortgage insurance in those other cases).

Think about cities. They get most of their revenue from taxes based on property values. If housing prices fall by 10 percent, then the city will collect 10 percent less in property taxes. A general decline in a city's property values wreaks havoc with city finances. To cover the shortfall, a city could raise its tax rate, but this would hurt the local economy (and further depresses property prices) at the worst possible time.

For a cost of $1.5 million, a town like New Haven could insure $100 million of its property tax revenue. But it's a tough sell. Even if the purchase of insurance is prudent, the city might take a pass. Where would a city find $1.5 million in its current budget to protect itself from future shortfalls?

Just as we asked who besides you has an interest in the value of your property, we can go a step further and ask who has an interest in the city's financial well-being. This leads us to the city's bondholders.

By insuring itself against declines in property values, a city should be able to cut the interest rate it has to pay to bondholders. The city's purchase of home equity insurance would be a credit enhancement that reduces the risk of default. If New Haven could drop the interest that it pays on its bonds even by one-quarter of a percent, this would go a long way toward covering the cost of the insurance.

Our point here is that paying close attention to each group's interests helps identify different audiences to pitch. Instead of just convincing home owners, you may have good reasons to think of cities and their bondholders as potential customers when going out to pitch the product.

Knowing your audience is part of applying the familiarity principle. As the English say, different horses for different courses.

And don't limit yourself to one course. Even if your pitch doesn't initially convince the person with power to make it happen, pass along the idea to others. There is, at times, a certain momentum of innovation, and a decision maker who is initially reluctant often becomes less reluctant in the presence of a building consensus.

Ian remembers with horror learning about the extent to which students were surfing the Internet and playing games (Solitaire, Minesweeper, etc.) on their laptops during law school classes at Yale. For the first time in his life, Ian sent a memo to his colleagues warning them that "we've got trouble here in River City." Ian proposed that the dean announce that laptops should be used in class only for note taking unless the professor explicitly authorized other uses. Alas, the memo to his colleagues produced almost no response.

But then a funny thing happened. Ian reworked the memo and published it as an op-ed in the *New York Times*. Suddenly students were receiving e-mails (*not* during class) from their friends and family all around the country asking them if what Ayres was saying about classroom surfing was true. And other professors started addressing the issue in their classes. It was easier for Ian to influence his colleagues by communicating to third parties than by sending the identical message directly. Sometimes it's easier to pitch decision makers by passing along the idea to others.

Pathos: Instilling the Coventurer Perspective

In chapter 7, we underscored the value of confidence in getting people to be creative. You're more likely to solve a problem if you can trick yourself into thinking that an answer exists. An optimistic attitude can become a kind of self-fulfilling prophecy. As Henry Ford once intoned, "Whether you think you can or you can't, you're right."

We're not quite as dogmatic in our thinking as Ford—after all, confident alchemists wasted a lot of time trying to turn lead into gold. But, within limits, social science suggests that confidence spurs innovative success.[6]

The literature on confidence and optimism is about changing your mind-set. Turning this around (as is our wont), here we emphasize how to go about changing the mind-set (what Aristotle called the *disposition*) of the listener.

Aristotle understood that there are many ways to be persuasive. What he called pathos is the effect of "creating a certain disposition in the audience." A good pitch invites the listener to join and collaborate in the enterprise. "Let us go then, you and I."[7]

A cynical reason for inviting your audience to participate in your enterprise is merely to co-opt a potential adversary. A reporter asked Lyndon B. Johnson, early in his presidency, why he chose to reappoint the irascible J. Edgar Hoover as FBI director. LBJ answered, "It's probably better to have him inside the tent pissing out, than outside the tent pissing in."[8]

But we suggest inviting the listener to be a joint venturer for a less cynical reason: It will lead to more constructive criticism. As a young professor, Ian was in a seminar in which an Israeli scholar was using an economic model of the kibbutz to explain the behavior of U.S. law firms. For the better part of an hour, Ian and other participants tore apart the scholar's presentation. At the end of the hour, the presenter said, "It's too bad you don't like my model because I was hoping to find a co-author who could help rewrite it for a U.S. audience."

Ian still remembers how this single sentence changed his outlook. Instead of seeing all the flaws in the model, he started to see its benefits and to think about how the flaws could be overcome.

The same holds true for why-not ideas. When test-marketing some of the proposals in this book, we've occasionally encountered the person who devotes all of his or her intellectual energy to finding flaws in the idea, but doesn't try at all to find good responses to the objections.

Let's be clear. It's not that you want your listener to be uncritical. Even when we—idea junkies that we are—hear a new idea, our first impulse is still to try to poke holes in it. A critical listener is probably also a listener who is truly paying attention to what you've been saying. But a genuine *coventurer* tries both to identify an idea's problems *and* to figure out how to overcome them. It's a cliché to favor constructive criticism, but we're still amazed, when looking at our *Why Not* Web site, at how easy it is to divide the commentators into the constructive criticizers, who seem genuinely engaged in the creative process, and the trashers, who are never satisfied with anybody else's ideas.

How do you change the mind-set of your audience so that people are more disposed to engage constructively with your ideas? Here,

Are You Listening?

Another value of sound bites is that they act as a barometer of your listener's disposition. Any fifty-word pitch must leave out the details of implementation. So, if a listener responds by rattling off *easily answered* objections, it's a strong indication he or she has not adopted a coventuring attitude.

we suggest employing Robert Cialdini's psychological theory of influence. His most important principle of "ethical influence" is reciprocity. If you start by giving your listener partial ownership of the idea, you are much more likely to receive in return. Cialdini emphasizes that reciprocal altruism is deeply ingrained in the human psyche; that is, when someone is nice to us, it's difficult not to respond in kind. Think of this as giving someone "half your kingdom."

Gratuitously giving up your rights tends to trigger an altruistic inclination in the recipient. It is also a great way of improving the listener's incentive to help develop the idea.

Open Source and Egoboo

Don't get carried away with secrecy. If you can't make money on an idea by yourself, instead of taking your ball and going home, share your idea. While some people jealously guard every new idea (and even some not-so-new ideas), there is a strikingly different model for innovation.

The open-source movement in software development shows that a dispersed community of code writers can succeed in developing interlocking products that are free to the world. The evolution of the Linux operating system is an extreme example of an egoboo economy.[9]

Why not create an open-source movement for everyday ingenuity? Why not accept egoboo as a reward for sharing your low-tech

A Definition for Innovators

egoboo (EE.goh.boo) *n.* Recognition and praise for a task well done, particularly a task that is performed for free. Also: ego-boo.[10]

Example citation: "In science-fiction-fan-speak there's a phenomenon called 'egoboo.' . . . It means a boost in reputation. Hackers operate in a gift economy in which giant-size egos compete with one another for attention and reputation on the Net. If you do something cool, like reduce the length of a subroutine by 50 percent, you score major egoboo." (Mark Frauenfelder, "Man Against the FUD," *LA Weekly,* 21 May 1999.)

Come Join the Revolution

Come join us in cyberspace at **www.whynot.net.** Come add your ideas to the *Why Not* Web site. Come for inspiration and come to react to other people's ideas. The site is literally an idea free-for-all where contributors can help improve each other's ideas. When you visit the Web site, please vote on the ideas. What do you like, and why? How could the idea be improved? How could it be pitched?

We'll periodically announce readers' choice and editors' choice awards to publicize and recognize your innovations. We'll write about the best submissions in our *Forbes* column and talk about them on *Marketplace*. We'll also challenge industry leaders to respond to your ideas: Why haven't they already put these ideas into practice, or why won't they? We'll work to spur industry reaction, not to scapegoat industry, but to start a dialogue to help identify the really good ideas and make them happen. In short, we'll do our best to give you a maximum shot of egoboo and give your idea a national audience and a jump-start at becoming real.

Saying good-bye is hard to do, and so we'd rather not do it. We'd like to keep in touch through an e-mail update that shares why-not ideas and reports the progress on these ideas. If you'd like to continue this why-not connection, sign up on the Web site.

ideas? We've put this sharing principle to work in this very book by sharing with you scores of ideas for new products and services. The "just share it" principle is also at the heart of our *Forbes* column and our why-not commentaries on public radio's *Marketplace*.

Our open-source seeding of ideas has met with some fertile ground. After sharing the idea about the one-way mortgage and the reverse 900 number in *Forbes*, literally giving away the ideas, we were contacted by incumbents in the industry who wanted us to help them make the ideas happen.

One lesson here is that if you generate valuable ideas, even ones that seem to speak for themselves, you are likely to be in demand to help put them into practice. Being known as an idea person tends to pay big rewards in our society. Instead of hoarding ideas in hopes of a killer payoff, just put the ideas out there and see what happens.

Tests of Success

Has this book been a success? We'll leave that up to you and to history.

First, we'll let history be the judge. Instead of just looking backward, we have highlighted dozens of ideas that are just waiting to happen. And we think that these ideas are on the cusp of happening. One way to judge whether we've been successful is to come back five or ten years from now and see whether any of our ideas have caught on. We don't think that all of them will; after all, we've already gone for decades without adjustable-term mortgages. But we won't say that we've done a good job if we don't have more success stories to add to our list over the next few years.

The ultimate test of this book's success is whether it helps you see things that you couldn't see before—new solutions to problems and new problems for solutions. And, so, this is the final test, the final question that we leave you with: What is your best why-not?

Commencement

You've made it this far—you are now an official why-notter. Ingenuity is not just for the very few. This book has shown that there are plenty of great ideas just waiting to be done—ideas that you might have dreamed up yourself. We bet that in the course of reading this book, you independently came up with some of the ideas discussed, even improved upon them, and developed some more why-not ideas of your own.

It is your job now to go forth, share these ideas and give feedback to others. We'll do our part, helping to publicize them and create a billboard for the world to see. (See "Come Join the Revolution.") With some luck and your help, together we can start an open-source movement for ideas.

It is our hope that *Why Not* will help revitalize an attitude of pragmatic optimism. Why not dream of things that never were and work to make them real? As Mahatma Gandhi wrote, "You must be the change you wish to see in the world."

Why not, indeed.

The first steps in the text allowed us to plant seven seeds in two lines. At this point, the problem is small enough that we can begin to experiment with trial and error.

Except for seed number 1, which is used in both the vertical and horizontal rows, all the other seeds have been used only once. So we need to think about how we are going to reuse these six seeds as we plant the remaining three.

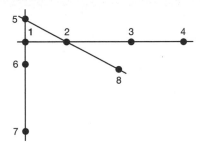

As seen above, the new seed—number 8—allows us to get double duty from the upper left two seeds (5 and 2), but this seed is not well positioned to be reused in another row. If we shift 8 up to the left on the line a bit, seed 8 can also align with seeds 7 and 3.

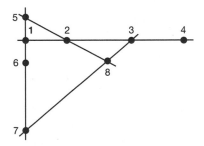

Now we really are close. We have used everything but 4 and 6 twice. If we draw the line connecting them, that tells us where to plant our last two seeds, 9 and 10.

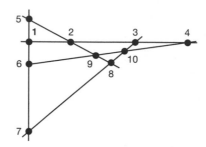

There are five rows, each with four seeds. Along with our original 1-2-3-4 and 5-1-6-7 rows, we have 5-2-9-8, 3-10-8-7, and 6-9-10-4.

Trying to solve this problem from scratch is quite difficult. But by figuring out parts of the solution, we narrowed our search considerably. Then, using our first principle—that seeds must, on average, serve double duty—we were able to place the last three.

Now we return to look at the solution from the opposite perspective. The way we first tried to answer the puzzle was via planting seeds and then finding the rows. Think symmetrically. We could have first drawn five rows and then figured out where the ten seeds must lie.

We started with five parallel lines, and that didn't work. Let's try another way of drawing five rows.

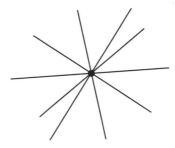

This is also a failure. The one seed in the middle gets used five times, but each of the five rows still needs another three seeds. So we need a total of sixteen seeds—better, but still well over our limit of ten.

We need the lines to cross more often. Perhaps we've been trying too hard to guess the answer. Just draw five random lines, one for each row.

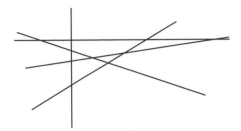

There is nothing special about these lines other than the fact that three lines don't meet in a single point. If we then plant a seed where the lines intersect, we've stumbled on the answer. There are ten seeds and each of the five lines has four seeds.

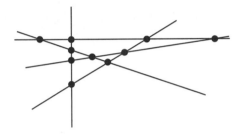

In this case, starting with the lines and looking for the seed would have been a much easier approach. This is not something that one could have predicted before we started, however. In fact, our experience suggests that almost everyone first tries locating the seeds and not the rows. We hope that this example will help you see the value of using symmetry at the outset to find different ways of approaching a problem. Before you get stuck on one path, you can try different approaches to see what works best.

As you've made it this far, allow us to share an "aha" solution to this problem.

The five-pointed star offers a much prettier way of planting the ten seeds into five rows of four. But coming up with the star from scratch is rather hard to do.[1]

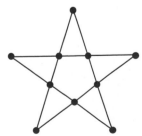

Note: All Web sites were current as of May 2003.

Preface

1. Calum Fisher is one of the contributors to <www.halfbakery.com>.

Chapter 1

1. Panasonic offers this feature with its hybrid phone system, but it costs several hundred dollars.

2. For more details, see Allyn Freeman and Bob Golden, *Why Didn't I Think of That?* (New York: John Wiley, 1997), 36–40, and Mary Bellis, "Liquid Paper: Bette Nesmith Graham (1922–1980)," About Inventors Web page, <http://inventors.about.com/library/inventors/blliquid_paper.htm>.

3. Those who swam this way kept winning breaststroke events until the rules were changed, specifying a below-water recovery. In the process, a new event, the butterfly, was born. As early as the 1950s, Japanese swimmers would swim breaststroke events underwater, but this wasn't a compelling advantage. In the 1970s, swimmers began doing the backstroke and butterfly (using the same kick) underwater. Swimming the first 33 meters underwater, Dave Berkoff (U.S.) set a world record in the 100-meter backstroke in 1988; Misty Hyman (U.S.) and Denis Pankratov (Russia) did the same for butterfly in the mid-1990s. The rules were changed in 1998, limiting the underwater portion of the race to 15 meters.

4. Maimonides, Sanhedrin 9:I. See *Maimonides' Commentary on the Mishnah Tractate Sanhedrin,* trans. Fred Rosner (New York: Sepher Hermon, 1981).

5. Aaron Schreiber, *Jewish Law and Decision-Making: A Decision through Time* (Philadelphia: Temple University Press, 1979).

6. Benedict XIV, *De Beat. et Canon. Sanctorum* (On the Beatification and Canonization of Saints) 1:xviii, <http://www.newadvent.org/cathen/01168b.htm>.

Chapter 2

1. Robert W. Weisberg, *Creativity: Genius and Other Myths* (New York: Freeman, 1986).

2. As of 11 June 2003, Priceline closed at $3.99, leading to a market cap of $900 million.

3. We first heard this idea from Steve Lubet of Northwestern University.

4. "Holidays of a Lifetime," YourMortgage information page, <www.yourmortgage.co.uk/07_flex/holiday.htm>.

5. Ian Ayres and Steven D. Levitt, "Measuring Positive Externalities from Unobservable Victim Precaution: An Empirical Analysis of Lojack," *Quarterly Journal of Economics* 112 (1998): 43–77.

6. There is one important caveat. This ripple effect of Lojack goes away if too many people have one. My having Lojack doesn't prevent your car from being stolen if Lojack is already protecting your car. The insurance companies, therefore, would want to subsidize Lojack to get adoption rates up to, say, 10 percent, not 100 percent.

7. The Blockbuster "Guaranteed to Be There" promise is that if a guaranteed feature is not available to rent at a participating store, you get a rain check to come back and rent that title for free. See <www.blockbuster.com>.

8. Martin Peers, "After Living on Rented Time, Blockbuster Plunges Into Sales," *Wall Street Journal,* 13 February 2003, A1.

9. Numerous lawsuits were filed after Blockbuster reached this agreement with the studios, but the first to make it to court was dismissed in 2002. Blockbuster wasn't engaging in any exclusive practices; it just had the ability to track sales well enough to make the revenue sharing work. Some local chains tried this, but their volume was so small that they could only bargain for the wrong side of a 40/60 split, and the numbers didn't add up.

10. Austrian Eduard Haas invented Pez candy in 1927, but the dispenser came much later. Next time you fly into San Francisco, you can visit the Pez Museum in nearby Burlingame.

11. Patent issued 11 May 1993 to Thomas J. Coleman and William K. Schlotter IV. For more details on the history of the Spin Pop, see "Spin Pop Collector" at <www.spinpopcollector.com/History.htm> and Mark Frauenfelder, "Gross National Product," *Wired Magazine,* 7.06 (June 1999), available at <www.wired.com/wired/archive/7.06/candy_pr.html>.

12. Robert Berner, "Why P&G's Smile Is So Bright," *Business Week,* 1 August 2002.

13. Or perhaps it does. One of us has a respectable video and DVD collection. Many of the movies are kept to share with our kids. But in the meantime, they mostly collect dust or are lent to friends and neighbors. If the video store were to offer us a small compensation for allowing it to rent out the movie, say, twenty times, we would offload much of our inventory to the store. This arrangement would be especially helpful to the store in managing the peak load demand for new movies.

14. Most states allow left turn on red from a one-way to a one-way street. Five states (Alaska, Idaho, Michigan, Oregon, and Washington) permit left turn on red from a two-way onto a one-way road, but it must be done with extra caution; see Justin Jih, "Right Turn on Red Light and Left Turn on Red Light," available at <www.geocities.com/jusjih/transport/turn-red.html#us>.

Chapter 3

1. See <www.diynet.com/DIY/article/0,2058,1886,00.html>. Spraying cooking oil on snow shovels is another good idea, as it prevents the snow from sticking.

2. One executive proposed that our unconstrained consumer could place an ad in the *New York Times* to let people know not to call after 10 P.M. While this suggestion is folly, the basic idea is sensible. The right place to put this ad is on the voice mail message.

3. We first heard this idea from Jeremy Bulow, an economist at Stanford University's Graduate School of Business.

4. Cingular is the exception to the rule; it allows rollover minutes in some contracts.

5. *Report of the Yale/Neighborhood Reinvestment Home Equity Project,* 14 December 2001, p. 10. Available from Tom Skinner at Realliquidity.com. See also Matthew Spiegel and William Goetzmann, "The Policy Implications of Portfolio Choice in Underserved Mortgage Markets," Harvard Joint Center on Housing Working Paper, 2000.

6. In several European countries, people can borrow up to 105 percent of the purchase price.

7. In some states, the PMI companies can still come after you for any payments they make. PMI coverage is often capped at 30 percent of the house value.

8. The concept of home equity insurance was first proposed by our Yale colleague Robert Shiller in 1994; see Robert Shiller and Allan N. Weiss, "Home Equity Insurance," Cowles Foundation discussion paper 1074 (1994), available at <http://cowles.econ.yale.edu/P/ab/a10/a1074.htm>.

9. For more information on home equity protection, see <www.equityhq.org>.

10. As with any new program, implementation is a learning process. We discovered that customers want current house price indices before purchasing the policy. But some lags are inevitable as each quarter's index level only becomes reliable once there are a sufficient number of transactions to include in calculating that index. Recognizing and resolving these types of issues early on is one of the advantages of running a pilot program. For more details on the Syracuse implementation, see the report "Home Equity Insurance: A Pilot Project," available from andrew.caplin@nyu.edu.

11. Motorola introduced this feature on one of its high-end cell phones in 2003.

12. One service, based out of Wales, uses the phone as the input device for voice recognition. The problem with this company's implementation is that it insists on using human proofreaders, both slowing turnaround down to twenty-four hours and raising the cost to two dollars per page. Many of us would prefer an imperfect but cheap and fast voice-to-text option.

13. Callwave built its customer base with an advertising-supported model. It moved to a fee model and charges $36 per year, while Pagoo collects $60 per year. Consulting company IDC forecasted these businesses to have 22 million subscribers and $400 million in revenues by the end of 2003. These fees, along with the proliferation of the digital subscriber line (DSL) and cable modems, would lead us to a more conservative projection.

Chapter 4

1. See <www.bts.gov/oai/ontime.annual/otannual.html>. The on-time statistics are now available in the DOT's monthly Air Travel Consumer Report, <airconsumer.ost.dot.gov/airconsumer/reports/delay.htm>.

2. Implementing that solution may be hard. In the case of poor incentives, you may not have the power to change the incentive system by yourself, either as an individual or even as a company. The examples that follow of Patrick Butler (pay-per-mile insurance) and Indiana University (grade inflation) show how it can be done.

3. Most insurance policies do offer a low-mileage discount, typically for cars driven less than 7,500 miles. But this discount is on the order of 15 to 20 percent, much less than the reduced accident risk that the low mileage would call for.

4. Aaron Edlin, "Per-Mile Premiums for Auto Insurance," working paper NBER 6934, University of California at Berkeley, 2002.

5. See <www.insure.com/auto/progressive700.html>. Initially, the savings came from a selection effect, as it was the low-mileage drivers who signed up. The incentive effect will kick in when enough low-mileage drivers migrate over to the companies offering per-mile coverage. Then, the insurance companies will no longer be able to subsidize the high-mileage drivers, since the customers who have paid those subsidies will be gone.

6. Andrew Tobias, *Auto Insurance Alert! Why the System Stinks, How to Fix It, and What to Do in the Meantime* (New York: Simon and Schuster, 1993).

7. Progressive's pilot was actually based on pay-per-minute rather than pay-per-mile insurance. The rate depended on time of day and location, not on speed or distance. See <www.insure.com/auto/progressive700.html>.

8. Patrick Butler has drafted a model insurance bill; see <www.now.org/issues/economic/insurance/bill.html>.

9. The savings are not as large as you might first guess. This is because people who drive fewer miles are often worse drivers. Although the causality may run the other way, the per-mile charge to low-mileage drivers would, on average, be higher than for high-mileage drivers.

10. Only a few companies sell transmitters for monitoring vehicles on the road. AirIQ, which sold Acme its equipment, markets primarily to rental car companies. So far, the major rental companies use the GPS system to find cars reported stolen, not to track speeding. A Budget licensee in Tucson made headlines for using AirIQ's GPS tracking to impose fines for violating the contract's prohibition on driving out of state.

11. The result is not quite the same, as Acme would be limited to collecting just one speeding violation per day. Even one ticket at $150 seems plenty high to deter speeding.

12. For GM cars with OnStar, this location service could be provided today.

13. While forcing people to retire at a particular age is illegal, it is permissible for an employer to stop making contributions to a retirement plan after the employee has worked for some number of years. Similarly, a defined benefit pension plan that does not adjust in accordance with life spans can also create strong incentives to retire.

14. Patrick Healy, "Harvard Looks to Raise Bar for Graduating with Honors," *Boston Globe*, 31 January 2002.

15. Michael Cohen, James March, and Johan Olsen, "A Garbage Can Model of Organizational Choice," *Administrative Science Quarterly* 17, no. 1 (March 1972): 1–25.

Chapter 5

1. See <www.airlinesafety.com/letters/toddlers2.htm>.

2. See <www.cami.jccbi.gov/AAM-600/630/9419.html>.

3. See <www.cato.org/pubs/briefs/bp-011.html>.

4. Although many people think that the change to satellite detection of speeding would be an invasion of our privacy, the current system is also ripe for abuse. Because just about everyone speeds, the police now have the right to stop just about any car. The real impact of satellite speeding tickets would be to change the speed limit.

5. See <www.mmmutants.com/files/documents/singnote/singnot3.html>.

6. See <www.santacruzsentinel.com/archive/2002/May/26/biz/stories/01biz.htm>.

7. Christine Whitehouse, "Just the Ticket," *Time Europe* 156, no. 8 (21 August 2000).

8. This idea from David Aiken was posted on <www.forbes.com/whynot>.

9. See <www.2.auspost.com.au/stamps/pstamps2/home.html> and <www.canadapost.ca/personal/collecting/default-e.asp?stamp=postage>.

10. An early proponent of this idea was Edward de Bono; see <www.edwdebono.com>.

11. David Pogue, "Wish List: Nine Innovations in Search of Inventors," *New York Times,* 28 March 2002.

12. Lawrence Lessig, "Fidelity in Translation," *Texas Law Review* 71 (1993): 1165.

13. This idea comes from A. Park, posted to our *Forbes* Web site <www.forbes.com/whynot>.

14. After presenting this idea in a *New York Times* op-ed, we learned that Eugene Steuerle had proposed this idea a decade earlier; see Steuerle, Gene, "A Gift for the New Year: Allow Charitable Deductions Until April 15," *Tax Notes,* 6 January 1992, 93–94, and "Increasing Charitable Giving: The April 15 Solution," *Tax Notes,* 9 July 1990, 221–222. We have found broad bipartisan support for this idea. Mr. Steuerle reports that when he presented this idea to the Clinton administration, their one concern was that this would increase the opportunity to engage in tax fraud by double-counting a charitable contribution in two tax years. For gifts above $250, that could be resolved by requiring the donor to specify that tax year and the required confirmation would indicate this selection. For smaller donations, the default could be the previous tax year.

15. Even if parents don't want their kids to know how much they earn, they can still disclose the percentage.

16. Mark Frauenfelder, "Social-Norms Marketing," *New York Times Sunday Magazine,* 9 December 2001, 100.

17. Sweden has the lowest motor-vehicle death rate in the world at 5.7 per 100,000 people; it also has the lowest death rate per miles driven, 1.2 per 100 million miles, 30 percent below the U.S. number of 1.7 per 100 million miles. See <www.benbest.com/lifeext/causes.html> and page 13 of <www-nrd.nhtsa.dot.gov/pdf/nrd-30/NCSA/Rpts/2003/2002EARelease.pdf>. The U.S. fatality rate has declined substantially from 3.5 per 100 million miles in 1975, but has leveled off at the end of the 1990s; <www.nap.edu/issues/17.2/realnumbers.htm>.

18. This result is reported in *Event Data Recorders: Summary of Findings by the NHTSA EDR Working Group,* August 2001, Section 10.8: 66.

19. NHTSA, *Event Data Recorders: Summary of Findings.*

20. Event data recorders are a first step. There are a couple of systems that go one step further. Drivecam provides a minicamcorder that goes in front on the rear-view mirror and records what the driver sees, along with speed and g-forces.

21. Robert Davis, "Teen at Wheel Makes Driving Doubly Deadly," *USA Today*, 5 July 2002.

22. Ron Thackery, quoted in Rebecca Fairley Raney, "A Parental Black Box for Young Drivers" *New York Times*, 22 August 2002, G5.

23. Davis, "Teen at Wheel."

24. See <www.nada.org/template.cfm?section=MediaCenter>.

25. The seven states are California, Massachusetts, New Jersey, North Carolina, Tennessee, Vermont, and Wisconsin (Davis, "Teen at Wheel").

26. Susan Dominus, "The Year in Ideas: A to Z; Nonromantic Dating," *New York Times Sunday Magazine*, 9 December 2001, 84.

27. See Marianne Bertrand and Sendhil Mullainathan, "Are Emily and Brendan More Employable Than Lakisha and Jamal? A Field Experiment on Labor Market Discrimination," working paper, Department of Economics, Massachusetts Institute of Technology, Cambridge, MA, 2002. The authors demonstrate that prospective employers are much less likely to respond to résumés with African-American names.

28. For more on Studio Realty, see Clayton Christensen, "Studio Realty," Case 9-697-036 (Boston: Harvard Business School, 1996).

Chapter 6

1. See <http://slate.msn.com/id/2067407>.

2. See <www.curtisbatts.com>.

3. See <www.post-gazette.com/businessnews/20020523upside0523bnp4. asp>.

4. Symmetry leads to another flip: Why not have all the seats face the back of the plane? That way, a sudden stop would throw you into the back of your seat. This change would be an almost free safety improvement. Rear-facing seats are the norm in military planes, where safety counts for more than comfort. Some think that passengers prefer facing forward. Would they continue this preference if they understood the safety implications?

5. See <www.thirteen.org/bucky/gif/header.map?306,24>.

6. See <www.caranddriver.com/xp/Caranddriver/roadtests/2002/january/200201_shorttake_gmcdenali.xml>.

7. Edward de Bono, *Lateral Thinking* (London: Penguin, 1977).

8. Adam M. Brandenburger and Barry J. Nalebuff, *Co-opetition* (New York: Currency/Doubleday, 1996).

9. Andrew Grove, *Only the Paranoid Survive: How to Achieve a Success That's Just a Disaster Away* (New York: Doubleday, 1998), and Preston McAfee, *Competitive Solutions: A Strategist's Toolkit* (Princeton: Princeton University Press, 2002).

10. In 1999, Chet Danzel of the Direct Marketing Association told *CBS This Morning* that more than 209 billion calls were made in 1998— on average, that amounts to 550 million calls per day. See <http://www.proactiveprivacy.com/tele_industry.htm>.

11. Ian Ayres and Matthew Funk, "Marketing Privacy," *Yale Journal on Regulation* 20, no. 1 (Winter 2003): 77–137.

12. Ron Shachar and Bharat Anand, "The Effectiveness and Targeting of Television Advertising," *Journal of Economics and Management Strategy* 7, no. 3 (1988): 363–396, show that commercials are informative just by the very fact that you have seen them. Because advertisers are targeting their audience, you can infer that, having seen a commercial, you were one of the target customers for whom the product was designed.

13. The idea of e-mail postage or bonded e-mail has many inventors. We first read about it in Esther Dyson, *Release 2.0: A Design for Living in the Digital Age* (New York: Broadway Books, 1997).

14. If the caller is making a local call, then the caller pays nothing. If the calling party is making a long-distance call to reach the cell phone, then the caller will pay long-distance charges and the recipient will be charged for the minutes used.

15. These high prices seem immune to competition. Although British Telecom charges a high price for a call to a T Mobile cell phone, it has to pass along most of this amount to T Mobile as a terminating charge. Thus, T Mobile is the one that makes the money. T Mobile has little incentive to lower the terminating fees, as its customers aren't footing the bill. You might expect that T Mobile (and even its rivals) would make lots of money from this system. They don't. That's because each player, realizing that having a phone out there will lead to a bonanza of terminating fees (read *kickbacks*), competes like crazy to get people on its network with offers of hugely discounted phones.

16. This proposal can be found in Nicholas Albery, ed., *The World's Greatest Ideas: An Encyclopedia of Social Inventions* (Gabriola Island, British Columbia: New Society Publishers, 2001).

17. See <www.txorgansharing.org/Vital_statistics.htm>.

18. James Choi et al., "For Better or for Worse: Default Effects and 401(k) Savings Behavior," <www.economics.harvard.edu/~jchoi/papers.html>. Economists Richard Thaler and Shlomo Benartzi have developed a novel way to increase retirement savings through their SMarT (Save More Tomorrow) plan (see <http://institutional.vanguard.com/pdf/SmarT_112002.pdf>).

19. One might penalize people who opt out by giving them lower priority if they ever need an organ themselves. In the event of a shortage, priority would be given to those who have not opted out. The longer you've opted out, the lower your priority. If religious beliefs prevent people from donating organs (but not from receiving them), their beliefs are respected but the opt-outers wouldn't have the same priority as those who've agreed to be a part of the social pact.

20. The networks are being paid 32 cents for you to watch twelve minutes of ads per hour—which translates to $1.60 for watching an hour of ads. That's well below minimum wage.

21. Mary Currie at the Golden Gate Bridge Authority attributes the idea to Dale Luehring, the former general manager; see <www.goldengatebridge.org/research/faqs.html#OneWayToll>. For the George Washington Bridge, see <www.fortleeonline.com/gwb/trivia.html>.

Chapter 7

1. The two approaches have been applied to computer chess programs. One school's approach works on making the machine faster and faster so that it looks further ahead in the game and evaluates a greater number of moves. The second approach looks at far fewer moves and instead concentrates its efforts on doing a better job evaluating the strength of any position. In this way, the computer conducts a much more targeted search. This idea is explored by John Geanakoplos and Larry Gray, "When Seeing Further Is Not Seeing Better," *Bulletin of the Santa Fe Institute* 6, no. 2 (1991).

2. We first saw this problem in Edward de Bono, *Lateral Thinking* (London: Penguin, 1977).

3. This problem comes from Henry Dudeney's great book, *539 Puzzles and Curious Problems* (New York: Scribner's Sons, 1967), problems 439–440.

4. Whether there would be demand for adjustable-term mortgages in the United States is harder to predict. The U.S. consumer market favors fixed-rate mortgages, while in the U.K., the fixed-rate market is less developed, so there is a greater need for innovative adjustable-rate products.

5. A second way to attack the affordability problem is by changing what the person ends up buying. Buying a house is a combination of two separate activities: obtaining a place to live and making a large investment in real estate. Investors would be willing to pay for part of your house if you agree to share some of the upside (and downside) potential with them. The Royal Bank of Scotland has done this to an extent with its SAM (shared appreciation mortgage) product. The bank offers a reduced interest rate in return for part of the profits when the house is sold. A version of direct equity sharing is gaining traction in Australia. More information on these approaches can be found in Andrew Caplin et al., *Housing Partnerships* (Cambridge: MIT Press, 1997).

6. These numbers are based on the industry standard rule of a 28/36 ratio. No more than 28 percent of pretax monthly income can go toward housing expenses (mortgage payments, taxes, and insurance), and no more than 36 percent of gross monthly income can go toward total monthly debt expenses (including housing).

7. Inflation-indexed bonds come in two forms. With Treasury Inflation-Indexed Securities (TIPS), the principal adjusts to maintain a constant real interest rate. The other option is series I bonds, for which the interest rate adjusts. Both are available online; see <www.treasurydirect.gov> and <www.publicdebt.treas.gov/ols/olshome.htm>.

8. Inflation-adjusted bonds also reduce the government's incentive to print money, and they thus make inflation fighting more credible.

9. We first heard this idea from Stanford economist John Shoven.

10. Paul Zeitz, *The Art and Craft of Problem Solving* (New York: John Wiley, 1999).

Chapter 8

1. Black tea contains L-theanine, a substance that boosts T-cell production and thereby strengthens the immune system; see Jack F. Bukowski et al., "Nonpeptide bacterial antigens contained in tea-beverage prime human V-gamma-2V-delta-2 T cells *in vitro* and *in vivo* for memory and nonmemory

antibacterial cytokine responses," *Proceedings of the National Academy of Sciences,* 28 April 2003. A Harvard study published in the American Heart Association's journal, *Circulation,* reported that people who drank two or more cups of tea per day had a 44 percent lower death rate after a heart attack than non-tea-drinkers. See Kenneth J. Mukamal, Malcolm Maclure, James E. Muller, Jane B. Sherwood, and Murray A. Mittleman, "Tea Consumption and Mortality After Acute Myocardial Infarction," *Circulation* 105 (May 2002): 2476–2481. Even more moderate consumption was associated with a 28 percent reduction in death rates. In a six-year study of nearly five thousand healthy individuals, Dutch researchers found that green and black tea may help prevent heart disease; see Johanna M. Geleijnse, Lenore J. Launer, Deirdre A. M. van der Kuip, Albert Hofman, and Jacqueline C. M. Witteman, "Inverse association of tea and flavonoid intakes with incident myocardial infarction: The Rotterdam Study," *American Journal of Clinical Nutrition* 75, no. 5 (2002): 880–886. Subjects who drank more than three cups of tea per day were 43 percent less likely to have a heart attack and 70 percent less likely to die from one than non-tea-drinkers. At Case Western Reserve University, Hasan Mukhtar found that EGCG, a powerful antioxidant ingredient in green tea, kills human cancer cells in laboratory experiments; see Hasan Mukhtar, "Consumption of Black Tea and Cancer Risk: A Prospective Cohort Study," *Journal of the National Cancer Institute* 88 (5 June 1996).

2. Orangina is a juice-based soda containing bits of pulp, but it is only 12 percent juice. Fizzy Lizzy, Hansons, the Switch, and Wild Fruitz have all introduced carbonated fruit juice beverages (though they are sweeter than the original, because of the addition of concentrated apple juice and the like). Some of these products are even doing okay. But we're concerned about their future if Minute Maid or Tropicana brings out carbonated OJ.

3. *Cincinnati Enquirer,* 27 December 1997.

4. See <www.allaboutbeer.com/beertalk/taste/dblstout.html>.

5. See <www.thinkgeek.com/caffeine/accessories/5a65>.

Chapter 9

1. Samuel 17: 8–10.

2. You might argue that the firm should only have to give up its profits rather than its revenue. In theory, this is right, but in practice, it would be hard to enforce. There would be a dispute about what costs are avoidable and what costs are not. Since the firm is not paying any labor costs, a much higher fraction of its revenue would be profits. Finally, for symmetry, workers should only have to give up their "profits" from working—that is, their net gain from working compared to being out on strike. For simplicity, workers give up all their wages and the firm gives up all its revenue.

3. Harvard negotiation gurus Howard Raiffa and David Lax proposed using a virtual strike to resolve the 1982 NFL strike; see "Touchdowns in the Football Impasse," *Los Angeles Times,* 9 November 1982, 7. In their twist, the salaries and revenues are put into a temporary escrow that can be given back to the parties when the strike settles. This would give them a greater "bonus" to settle. Each week, more of that escrow would be given to charity. We have to avoid being too greedy and not try to produce a system that elim-

inates the pain of the strike to the disputants themselves. If the parties will get back all of their strike costs (plus interest), the disputants also have less reason to ever settle.

4. Daniel Quinn Mills, *Labor-Management Relations* (New York: McGraw-Hill, 1978), 195. It is unclear whether the money was held in escrow and ultimately returned or whether it remained with the navy's comptroller.

5. David B. McCalmont, "The Semi Strike," *Industrial and Labor Relations Review* 15, no. 2 (1962): 191.

6. There are difficult implementation issues. For example, unions that have promised to strike only virtually may subsequently decide that it is better to stage an informal slowdown and be paid, rather than formally strike and receive nothing. It may not be a coincidence that Italy's virtual strikes began with commercial airline flights, which might be more difficult to slow down. And the slowdown problem is no more problematic under a virtual strike agreement than it is under the statutes that prohibit strikes for certain essential industries. Management can always retaliate against a nonstrike slowdown with a virtual lockout.

7. When you take advantage of the two-for-one offer, you're more likely to be late than if you rented only one film. If you don't have time to finish the second movie, you may decide to delay returning the movies for an extra day.

8. This offer was advertised in the *New York Times,* 1 July 2002. If you want to read the fine print, Sprint's statement of terms and conditions is more than 15,000 words long, almost a quarter as long as this book.

9. *New York Times,* 3 September 2001, C7 (for the churn rate, not the antigravity phone). The churn rate in Chicago topped 4.5 percent monthly, or 68 percent annually. Customers listed pricing as the primary switching cause in two of the top five markets.

10. In an attempt to keep tuition increases low, universities started adding health care fees, social fees, athletic fees, copying fees, and more.

11. The early versions of the secret ballot were far from perfect. People would make extra marks on their ballots to defeat the anonymity; as a result, ballots with even irrelevant stray marks were disqualified. (One hundred years later, these strict rules on disqualified ballots would lead to George W. Bush's election.) See also Pam S. Karlan, "Elections and Change under 'Voting with Dollars,'" *California Law Review* (forthcoming 2003).

12. Roberta Romano, "Does Confidential Proxy Voting Matter?" <www. ssrn.com>, however, has shown that, to date, anonymous voting procedures have not increased the success rate of proxy proposals.

13. Ian Ayres and Bruce Ackerman, *Voting With Dollars: A New Paradigm for Campaign Finance* (New Haven: Yale University Press, 2002).

14. E. Wayne Thode, *Reporter's Notes to Code of Judicial Conduct* (Chicago: American Bar Association, 1973). Contributor anonymity, however, was not required if the candidate was separately "required by law to file a list" of contributor names.

15. Guido Calabresi and A. Douglas Melamed, "Property Rules, Liability Rules and Inalienability: One View of the Cathedral," *Harvard Law Review* 85 (1972): 1089.

16. *Spur Industries, Inc. v. Del E. Webb Development Co.,* 494 P.2d 701 (Ariz. 1972).

17. Employers also secretly audit the quality of their employees' performance to assure everything from airport security to "service with a smile."

18. While as a legal matter the entrapment defense immunizes only criminal defendants, a civil suit analog might arise, especially if a government official went farther and directly asked if the real estate or employment agent would be willing to discriminate against minorities.

19. As part of their licensing, realtors might have a duty to report discrimination requests. Under such an honor code, an agent who hears a solicitation for discrimination would either have to report it or fear being disciplined for failure to report.

20. John Donohue and Peter Siegelman, "The Changing Nature of Employment Discrimination Litigation," *Stanford Law Review* 43 (1991). Of course, probationary discrimination is possible. The person who fires may be different from the person who hires.

21. There was a glitch in the proof, which took another year to work out with the help of Cambridge University mathematician Richard Taylor.

22. See <www.claymath.org/prizeproblems/index.htm> for details, assuming the problem hasn't been solved by the time you read this.

23. We thank Professor Wesley M. Cohen, Fuqua School of Business, for this example.

24. Roberta Romano, "Law as Product: Some Pieces of the Incorporation Puzzle," *Journal of Law, Economics, and Organization* 1, no. 2 (1985): 225–283.

25. See <http://scilib.ucsd.edu/sio/nsf/journals/peter97.html#nov25>.

26. Michael Abramowicz has noted that the test should be whether the invention would have been created in the absence of patent protection. See, for example, *Roberts v. Sears, Roebuck & Co.*, 697 F.2d 796 (7th Cir. 1983) (Posner, J.), and A. Samuel Oddi, "Beyond Obviousness: Invention Protection in the Twenty-First Century," *American University Law Review* 38 (1989): 1101.

27. Aaron Edlin, "Stopping Above-Cost Predatory Pricing," *Yale Law Journal* 111 (2002): 941–991.

28. Paul W. MacAvoy, *The Failure of Anti-Trust and Regulation to Establish Competition in Long-Distance Telephone Markets* (Cambridge, MA: AEI Press and MIT Press, 1996).

29. Richard Poynder, "Inside Track," *Financial Times*, 25 September 2001.

30. Of course, bribes can work both ways. The Saudis might use their OPEC revenues to give Palestinians a short position on the stock market.

Chapter 10

1. Karl Marx, *Theses on Feuerbach* (1845), ch. 11. Institute of Marxism-Leninism in Marx-Engels Archives, Book I, Moscow, 1924.

2. See, for example, Teresa Amabile, Dorothy Leonard, and Jeffrey F. Rayport, *Harvard Business Review on Breakthrough Thinking* (Boston: Harvard Business School Press, 1999).

3. There are some interesting books that show how these ideas connect to management and policy; see, for example, Max Bazerman, *"You Can't Enlarge the Pie": Six Barriers to Effective Government* (New York: Basic Books, 2002).

4. The half-adjustable mortgage doesn't eliminate the refinancing risk when market rates drop, but it substantially reduces it. If it normally takes a 1 percent drop to induce refinancing, with this product it will take a 2 percent drop in the market rate. Thus, except in the rare case of a 2 percent drop, the customer will most likely never refinance.

5. Telemarketing calls that are manually dialed may be made to cell phones. The 1991 law prohibits the use of autodialers in making telemarketing calls to cell phones, which, in practice, means a prohibition of almost all telemarketing to cell phones.

6. See, for example, Jennifer Gerarda Brown, "The Role of Hope in Negotiation," *University of California at Los Angeles Law Review* 44 (1997): 1661–1682.

7. T. S. Eliot, "The Love Song of J. Alfred Prufrock," in *Prufrock and Other Observations* (London: The Egoist, 1917); see also <www.bartleby.com/198/1.html>).

8. See <www.bartleby.com>.

9. Yochai Benkler, "Intellectual Property and the Organization of Information Production," *International Review of Law and Economics* 22 (2002): 81. More than 60 percent of Web servers use the open-source Apache software, and more than 75 percent of Internet mail servers use the open-source Sendmail relay program.

10. Definition, pronunciation, and citation example all from Paul Mc-Fedries, "egoboo," Word Spy definition page, <http://www.wordspy.com/words/egoboo.asp>.

Appendix

1. One way to come up with the five-pointed star is to build up to it. For example, you can plant three seeds into three rows of two using a triangle formation. Think about the formation required to plant seeds into four rows, each with three seeds. Hint: It takes six seeds, each of which is used twice. Solving the problem in this incremental fashion helps reveal the star or pentagon pattern for the five-rows-of-four-seeds problem.

Some fifty years ago, J. P. Guilford wrote that there were embarrassingly few studies of creativity. His review of *Psychological Abstracts* turned up 186 articles bearing on creativity—out of a total of 121,000 articles. That state of affairs is no longer the case. The following list of books, articles, and Web sites provides some of the resources we found most helpful.

Edward de Bono is the pioneer of this field. He is perhaps best known for the concept of lateral thinking. Among de Bono's twenty-plus books, a good place to start is *Lateral Thinking: Creativity Step by Step* (New York: HarperCollins, 1990). His *Six Thinking Hats* (New York: Little Brown, 1999) introduces a multiperspective approach to problem solving.

Those who like puzzles will especially enjoy Edward de Bono, *The 5-Day Course in Thinking* (New York: Basic, 1967). Math puzzlers should also seek out Henry Dudeney, *539 Puzzles and Curious Problems* (New York: Scribner's Sons, 1967), and Paul Zeitz, *The Art and Craft of Problem Solving* (New York: John Wiley, 1999).

Along with de Bono's books, no one should miss James L. Adams, *Conceptual Blockbusting: A Guide to Better Ideas* (Cambridge: Perseus, 2001). This short paperback is a brilliant and inspiring book. People who are skeptical that creativity is an integral part of legal problem solving might want to check out Carrie Menkel-Meadow's excellent article, "Aha? Is Creativity Possible in Legal Problem Solving and Teachable in Legal Education," *Harvard Negotiation Law Review* 6 (Spring 2001): 97–114.

Our imagination is always stimulated by the ideas posted on Halfbakery .com. This Web site, founded by Jutta Degener, specializes in inspired ideas that are slightly off center. You can read about bubble wrap filled with helium (to lower postage costs), cream cheese slices with precut holes to put on bagels, and custard-filled speed bumps (soft at slow speeds, but hard when crossed too fast). There is also an extensive set of links to other idea-generation Web sites at www.halfbakery.com/editorial/links.html.

The Global Ideas Bank offers an annual award for the best new social innovation. Many of the best hits are collected in Nicholas Albery, ed., *The World's Greatest Ideas: An Encyclopedia of Social Inventions* (Gabriola Island, British Columbia: New Society Publishers, 2001). One of our favorites: To ensure that suitors bring their dates home on time, they should leave a twenty-dollar deposit, which would be forfeited in the event of a late return, similar to late fees at Blockbuster. More ideas can be found on the group's Web site, www.globalideasbank.org.

We thank George Dyson for leading us to I. J. Good, ed., *The Scientist Speculates: An Anthology of Partly-Baked Ideas* (New York: Basic Books, 1963) for a wonderful collection of scientific why-nots. For example, you can find speculative ideas for how ocean water can be desalinated and transported to the desert. It is quite informative to see leading scientists discuss ideas that are not yet fully worked out. Robert W. Weisberg, *Creativity: Beyond the Myth of Genius* (New York: W. H. Freeman, 1993), is a page-turner. Taking the reader through a series of famous historical inventions, Weisberg masterfully debunks the perceived wisdom that creativity requires "aha" moments of genius.

On the business frontier, we recommend Gary Hamel, *Leading the Revolution* (Boston: Harvard Business School Press, 2000); Michael Michalko, *Thinkertoys* (A Handbook of Business Creativity) (Berkeley: Ten Speed Press, 1991); and Robert Sutton, *Weird Ideas That Work: 11½ Practices for Promoting, Managing, and Sustaining Innovation* (New York: Free Press, 2002). Robert Shiller, *The New Financial Order: Risk in the 21st Century* (Princeton: Princeton University Press, 2003), offers six important why-not ideas for financial innovation.

Design is another good place to look for innovative thinking. Tom Kelley and Jonathan Littman, *The Art of Innovation: Lessons in Creativity from Ideo, America's Leading Design Firm* (New York: Currency/Doubleday, 2001), provides an inside look at product design. Their case study of the redesign of the shopping cart is a brilliant example of taking a fresh look at an old problem.

There is also a large literature on creativity from the perspective of organizational behavior. Our emphasis has been on what you do inside your head, how to increase your individual creativity. The literature in organization behavior emphasizes how to manage groups or organizations to make them more creative and open to change. Some good starting points here are found in Teresa Amabile, Dorothy Leonard, and Jeffrey F. Rayport, *Harvard Business Review on Breakthrough Thinking* (Boston: Harvard Business School Press, 1999). A classic in this field is Michael Cohen, James March, and Johan Olsen, "A Garbage Can Model of Organizational Choice," *Administrative Science Quarterly* 17, no. 1 (March 1972): 1–25.

Two idiosyncratic titles that we recommend are Mihaly Csikszentmihalyi, *Creativity: Flow and the Psychology of Discovery and Invention* (New York: HarperCollins, 1996)., and Jonathan S. Feinstein, *The Nature of Creative Development* (Palo Alto: Stanford University Press, forthcoming).

Of course, this is just a jumping-off point. Links to these books and an updated list can be found at www.whynot.net.

ACKNOWLEDGMENTS

Our why-not approach is inspired by the work of Edward de Bono. (Several of his books are in our Further Reading list.)

We are very fortunate to have a wonderful collection of friends, family, and colleagues who not only put up with our why-not ideas but read this manuscript and provided feedback and a host of ideas.

An especially big thanks goes to Jeff Kehoe, our editor at Harvard Business School Publishing. His enthusiasm, levelheadedness, and willingness to be a guinea pig are all appreciated. The HBSP review process was an unexpected bonus. The constructive critiques of the four anonymous reviewers helped focus our book. Our agent is Barbara Rifkind. Her guidance, support, charm, smarts, and willingness to call it as she sees it make her a great partner in this endeavor.

Thanks to readers Michael Abramowicz, Bill Barnett, Adam Brandenburger, Shannon Deegan, Jutta Degener, John Lapides, George Michas, David Gerber, Michael Iannazzi, Russell Korobkin, Alvin Lim, Eric Mankin, Chris Meyer, Diane Ruben, Peter Siegelman, Jeffrey Sonnenfeld, Andrew Tobias, Max Ventilla, and Nasser Zakariya. Will Whitehorn and Gordon McCallum at Virgin Group were generous with their insights. We thank Rafe Sagalyn for his early encouragement.

Many of our colleagues were roped into contributing ideas. Meghan Busse, Andrew Caplin, Aaron Edlin, Nat Keohane, John MacBain, Ben Polak, Tom Skinner, Joseph Stiglitz, and John Shoven rose to the occasion. David Gerber helped us see how these ideas could apply to manufacturing. Reed Hundt graciously helped us develop innovations for telecom. Jeremy Bulow at Stanford is a special source of inspiration and a fountain of ideas on everything from refinancing mortgages to licensing windows. (In Bulow's why-not list, he would limit the amount of commercials on any sporting event televised from a publicly subsidized venue to four minutes per hour.)

We owe a special debt to Bill Baldwin at *Forbes* and Liza Tucker at *Marketplace;* both have helped push us and our ideas. And to our deans, Jeffrey Garten and Tony Kronmen, who have generously supported us in the endeavor.

Thanks to research assistants Jonathan Busky, Michael Edelschick, and Daniel Gottlieb. Patrick Butler helped us understand pay-per-mile insurance. Michael Gibbert is a great sounding board and source of ideas on knowledge management. Natalie Jeremijenko provided the world with her beautiful tree sculpture and directed us to Kevin Kennefick's stunning photograph.

In the best *Why Not* spirit, Eric Hangen and Beth Prentice at Neighborhood Reinvestment and Tom Skinner at RealLiquidity.com were instrumental in making home equity insurance a reality.

Ann Olivarius is a friend and commentator without peer. Freelance editor Rena Henderson has helped us now for the third time. Her charm and style are everywhere. (You can contact her at renahen@telocity.com.) Marcia Nalebuff went beyond the call of duty and motherhood as a proofreader and fact checker. Project editor Sarah Weaver and copy editor Patty Boyd at HBSP were good humored and patient as they gently corrected our why-not approach to style conventions and other illogical aspects of English. Their red pen was both a mighty sword and an artist's brush.

The cartoons in the book come from the slightly disturbed mind of Kiva Sutton. We truly appreciate the effort Kiva made to illustrate why-not ideas with his stinging pen. You can find him at www.smartfunusa.com.

We end our acknowledgments with an apology. We know that somewhere someone is implementing an idea we discussed and we were not aware of it. We ask that you accept our apologies. We'd like to give credit where credit is due; please e-mail us to let us know (whynot@yale.edu) and look to our Web site (www.whynot.net) for updates.

EXPANDED TABLE OF CONTENTS

Problems in Search of Solutions

Solutions in Search of Problems

ABOUT THE AUTHORS

BARRY NALEBUFF is the Milton Steinbach Professor of Economics and Management at Yale School of Management. An expert on game theory, he has written extensively on its application to business strategy. He is the coauthor of *Thinking Strategically: The Competitive Edge in Business, Politics, and Everyday Life* (with Avinash Dixit) and *Co-opetition* (with Adam Brandenburger). Professor Nalebuff is on the boards of Trader Classified Media and Bear Stearns Financial Products, and is the chairman and cofounder of Honest Tea. A Rhodes Scholar and Junior Fellow at the Harvard Society of Fellows, Nalebuff earned his doctorate at Oxford University.

IAN AYRES is an economist and a lawyer. He is the Townsend Professor at Yale Law School. Professor Ayres has been ranked as one of the most prolific and most cited law professors of his generation. His more than one hundred articles cover a wide variety of topics, including patents, bankruptcy, corporations, contracts, and civil rights law. His research has been featured on *PrimeTime Live* and *Good Morning America* and in *Time* and *Vogue* magazines. His most recent books are *Voting with Dollars: A New Paradigm for Campaign Finance* (with Bruce Ackerman) and *Pervasive Prejudice: Unconventional Evidence of Race and Gender Discrimination*. Professor Ayres has a J.D. from Yale Law School and a Ph.D. in economics from M.I.T.

Ayres and Nalebuff are bimonthly columnists for *Forbes* magazine and regular commentators on Minnesota Public Radio's *Marketplace*. They can be reached at whynot@yale.edu and at www.whynot.net.